O9-BUC-800

QUIET TIMES
FOR COUPLES

H. NORMAN WRIGHT

HARVEST HOUSE PUBLISHERS

EUGENE, OREGON

Cover photos © Image Source / Getty; Ingmarsan / Fotolia

Cover by Dugan Design Group, Bloomington, Minnesota

Author photo copyright © 2010 by Lifetouch, Eden Prairie, Minnesota. Used by permission.

QUIET TIMES FOR COUPLES
Copyright © 1990 by Harvest House Publishers
Published 2010 by Harvest House Publishers
Eugene, Oregon 97402
www.harvesthousepublishers.com

ISBN 978-0-7369-2994-3

Library of Congress Cataloging-in-Publication Data
  Wright, H. Norman.
  Quiet times for couples: a daily devotional / H. Norman Wright.
    p. cm.
  ISBN: 0-89081-816-9
  1. Married people—Prayer-books and devotions—English. 2. Devotional calendars.
  I. Title.
  BV4596.M3W75 1990   90-35981
  242'.dc20   CIP

Printed in the United States of America

11 12 13 14 15 16 / VP-SK / 10 9 8 7 6 5 4 3 2

A Deeper, More
Resilient Marriage

❧

Twenty years have come and gone since this book was just an idea in my mind. I'm amazed and delighted at what's taken place. Over a half a million couples have used this resource to enhance the spiritual intimacy in their marriage! And with the various translations available in other countries, who knows how many others have been guided by this book. And now I pray that even more marriages will be strengthened and enriched.

I almost didn't write *Quiet Times for Couples*. I was scheduled to begin the project in March of 1990. But before I could start, my 22-year-old retarded son, Matthew, was released from his limited human condition and went into the presence of Jesus Christ. A few days after the memorial service I called Harvest House Publishers and told them I wasn't sure I was emotionally prepared to start writing the book. I wondered whether it would be better to postpone the project. They were very supportive and left the decision up to me.

As I thought about it, I realized that the involvement with the Word of God required for writing this book was just what I needed during my time of grieving. Three days later I called Harvest House to say I would begin working immediately. It was a wise decision. God's Word brings comfort, support, insight, and clarity to the meaning of life and its events. In the process of creating a book that I trusted would help others, I was ministered to. My experience reinforced the importance of reading and meditating on God's Word during traumatic transitions as well as in everyday life.

My wife, Joyce, and I read this book aloud to one another after it was published. That's one of the many cherished memories from our almost 50 years together. I wish I could read these selections aloud to her again and hear her quiet voice read to me, but that will have to be in a different time and place, for she too is now in the presence of our Lord. I'm so thankful for every moment we shared reading God's Word and praying.

When Joyce and I began reading aloud to each other we discovered a dynamic that is often missing when a book is read silently. We found that we remembered the selection longer, and the truths we shared together penetrated our lives more deeply. Maybe it was more significant because we were simultaneously aware of what was being read. Maybe it was because whoever read felt responsible for communicating the selection clearly to the listener. Perhaps the dynamic was simply the result of a new expression of two becoming one. Whatever the reason, the result was tremendous. We drew closer to each other and to God. So I encourage you to try it! When you read aloud to each other, you'll progress spiritually at a similar rate. Hearing the same information also assists in having deeper discussions on spiritual issues.

After three years of adjusting to life without Joyce, God has blessed me by bringing a new love into my life. Tess and I are now married, and we read *Quiet Times for Couples* aloud every night to help us solidify our togetherness in the Lord. And I know the questions contained in some of the meditations will guide you in applying God's Word to your life and your marriage. I hope that as a result of your daily discussions, your marriage will reflect a new expression of the presence of Jesus Christ and the reality of God's Word. That's why this book was written.

Norm Wright

JANUARY

*Gentleness is an attitude of thoughtfulness
and servanthood. It means being willing to see
God's pattern for marriage as the healthiest way
to develop personal security and to reflect the
presence of Jesus Christ in your marriage.*

JANUARY 1

Be still, and know that I am God (Psalm 46:10).

Stillness.
Quiet.
Silence.

Do you ever hear the sounds of silence? They are there. In their own way they speak loudly. Quietness for some is a way of life. Quietness for others is uncomfortable. It can be a time to reflect, a time to create, a time to recover, a time to grieve, a time to rejoice, or a time to listen to God.

Quiet time for a married couple can create a deep bond of love and closeness. It is a time to share the deepest kind of intimacy possible in our humanity: spiritual intimacy.

No one said that it would be easy or comfortable to be quiet together. Barriers to this time will have to be confronted. Time schedules will have to be juggled. Outside interruptions and intrusions will need to be blocked so they don't control you.

Reflect for a moment. Don't share your answer with your spouse immediately, but sit and think about each question.

What are the times of quiet you value most?

What do you think about when you are quiet?

What feelings do you experience when you are quiet?

How does God speak to you when you are quiet?

The psalmist tells us to be quiet for a very specific reason. When we fill our lives with activities and busyness, it's easy to forget our Creator. There are times in the midst of the most hectic day when we need to close the door, unplug the phone, sit down in a chair, lean back, and close our eyes. The busiest day of your life is the best day to do it; it is the time you need it the most. Take time each day to come together as a couple expecting God to speak to you. Even 60-90 seconds of silence as you sit together can be a time for God to speak to you. Share with each other what He is doing in your life. And share together your answers to the four questions you considered above.

JANUARY 2

*For this cause a man shall leave his father and
his mother, and shall cleave to his wife; and they
shall become one flesh* (Genesis 2:24, NASB).

L*eave* and *cleave*—different words, significant words.
When you exchanged your wedding vows, these two words became part of your life. But do you understand them? To leave means sever one relationship before establishing another. This does not mean you disregard your parents. Rather it requires that you break your tie to them and assume responsibility for your spouse.

To cleave means to weld together. When a man cleaves to his wife they become one flesh. This term is a beautiful capsule description of the oneness, completeness, and permanence God intended in the marriage relationship. It suggests a unique oneness—a total commitment to intimacy in all of life together, symbolized by the sexual union.

Years ago I heard a choice description of the coming together that is involved in cleaving. If you hold a lump of dark green clay in one hand and a lump of light green clay in the other hand, you can clearly identify the two different shades of color. However, when you mold the two lumps together, you see just one lump of green clay—at first glance. When you inspect the lump closely you see the distinct and separate lines of dark and light green clay.

This is a picture of your marriage relationship. The two of you are blended together so you appear as one, yet you each retain your own distinct identity and personality. But now you have a marriage personality which exists in the two of you.

A Christian marriage, however, involves more than the blending of two people. It also includes a third person—Jesus Christ—who gives meaning, guidance, and direction to the relationship. When He presides in a marriage, then and only then is it a Christian marriage.

Since your wedding, how have you handled leaving your parents? How have you become one flesh, coming together and yet retaining who you are as individuals? Why not talk about it?

January 3

The Lord God said, "It is not good for the man to be alone.
I will make a helper suitable for him" (Genesis 2:18).

God created marriage for companionship. As John Milton observed, "Loneliness was the first thing God's eye named not good." Loneliness and isolation are contradictions to the purpose of God's creative act. God made man to live with others, and the first "other" was woman.

God also created marriage for completeness. The woman was to be "a helper suitable for him." The woman was created to be a complement or counterpart for the man. Woman assists man in making his life (and hers, too) complete. She fills up the empty places. She shares his life with him, draws him out of himself and into a wider area of contact through the involvement they have with one another. The partners in a marriage relationship are actually fulfilling God's purpose of completeness or wholeness in life. They belong together.

Dr. Dwight Small describes the relationship in this way:

> When a man and a woman unite in marriage, humanity experiences a restoration to wholeness.
>
> ...The glory of the man is the acknowledgment that woman was created for him; the glory of the woman is the acknowledgment that man is incomplete without her. The humility of the woman is the acknowledgment that she was made for man; the humility of the man is the acknowledgment that he is incomplete without her.[1]

Marriage brings with it the opportunity for either competition or completion. Completion is God's plan. Have you made the rich discovery of completeness as man and wife?

It takes humility to say to your partner, "Let me share with you the ways in which my life has been made more complete and full by being married to you." Try it. You might just like it!

JANUARY 4

*But the fruit of the Spirit is love, joy, peace, patience,
kindness, goodness, faithfulness, gentleness, and self-control.
Against such things there is no law (Galatians 5:22).*

Is it possible to cultivate some fruits of the Spirit in our lives without the others? Frankly, I don't think so. I believe the fruits of the Spirit tend to increase and decrease together. When you mature in self-control, you also grow in patience and gentleness. You can't choose to emphasize only one or two, because they all come in the same package.

Furthermore, manifesting these fruits in our lives is not an option. Jesus wasn't just offering a suggestion; He was very clear as to the place of these attributes in our lives. He said, "I am the vine; you are the branches. If a man remains in me and I in him, he will bear much fruit....You did not choose me, but I chose you...to go and bear fruit—fruit that will last" (John 15:5,16).

Have you ever thought about the fact that the spiritual gifts can be faked, but the fruits of the Spirit cannot? They have to be genuine. One writer suggests that some people tend to be spiritual-fruit impostors. But Jesus said, "By their fruit you will recognize them....Every good tree bears good fruit, but a bad tree bears bad fruit" (Matthew 7:16,17). When the fruits of the Spirit are expressed in your life you actually become a delivery system of Christ's love to those around you, most notably your spouse. But when you fail to nurture the growth of love, joy, peace, patience, kindness, goodness, faithfulness, gentleness, and self-control, your spouse and your marriage will suffer as a result.

In what ways are the fruits of the Spirit reflected in your life and marriage relationship?

JANUARY 5

For I know the plans I have for you, says the Lord,
plans for welfare and not for evil, to give you a
future and a hope (Jeremiah 29:11, RSVB).

One of the joys and delights of the Christian life is being able to believe more in the future than the past. The Bible tells us that God is a loving God who intends good for His people. Sometimes married couples become discouraged because their marriage isn't turning out the way they intended it to, and their anticipated dream has turned into a nightmare. Marriage definitely comes with its own unique problems, but even within the unexpected surprises, new dreams and delights can be fashioned.

The best way to handle the challenges of marriage is by following God's plans: the teachings of His Word. This sounds simplistic, but it's not. It takes commitment and a willingness to allow God to sand off those rough edges. It means seeing your mate through the eyes of God and realizing the high value He places on each one of us. It means treating one another with the same regard that God has for each person. It means willingly obeying God's commands in our response to each other in marriage. In fact, this is how we move toward the hope and the future that the prophet Jeremiah writes about. In Romans 7:12, Paul states that God's commandment is "holy, righteous and good." He certainly doesn't ask us to do anything that is not good. And in your marriage, God requests only good things as well. According to God's Word, are the guidelines and commands for women and wives good? Are they practical and possible in this day and age? Are they realistic? The answer is yes. Are the guidelines in the Bible for men and husbands good, practical, realistic, and possible? Yes, they are.

Let God work in your heart and mind. Let Him give you the courage, strength, and power you will need to follow His good plans in your marriage. They work—they really do!

JANUARY 6

Be subject one to another out of reverence
for Christ (Ephesians 5:21, AMP).

How much are you worth compared to your partner? Go ahead—make a guess. Is one of you worth more than the other? How would you even measure such a thing?

When you go shopping for clothes, you will definitely find a variation in cost, whether it be women's or men's clothing. Because they are produced by different companies, the clothes we buy are widely varied and have different brand names. Yet in our culture, many people are hung up on designer clothes; the jeans, dress, or suit must have the label of the "in" designer or they are considered inferior in quality. Actually, they may be no better in quality than those without that special label. Perhaps we are the ones who place the value on those labels.

Many of us make the same kinds of superficial judgments about people when we ascribe a certain value to them using unscriptural criteria. Some men look down on women, seeing them as second-class citizens. It was that way in the time of Jesus. Women had very few rights and were treated accordingly. Men lorded over them and saw women as their possessions. Sometimes we become conditioned to think a certain way toward the opposite sex, a way that is not correct nor in keeping with God's Word.

God has a design for both men and women. Neither is superior to the other; neither is inferior to the other. They were created equally in God's image. They both bear the stamp of God's image on their lives. Ephesians 5:21 implies the equality of male and female. Yes, there are other specific guidelines for each to carry out in their daily lives, but that has nothing to do with superiority or inferiority. The value of a woman and a man to God is taught in the story of creation.

If we were designed for equality, how should a husband and wife view and treat one another? Perhaps equality means mutual respect, affirmation, and seeing your partner as being created in the image of God. Not a bad idea!

JANUARY 7

Wives, submit to your husbands as to the
Lord. For the husband is the head of the wife
as Christ is the head of the church, his body, of
which he is the Savior (Ephesians 5:22,23).

You have just read the guidelines God designed for wives. Please remember that these verses were directed toward wives, and were never meant for husbands to quote to their wives! This is a wife's blueprint for married life.

As we consider these words, it helps to remember that men and women are recognized equally before God, and both receive spiritual gifts from the Lord. A man and woman are equally "one in Christ Jesus" (Galatians 3:28). They are both "heirs...of the gracious gift of life" (1 Peter 3:7). And there is mutual submission (Ephesians 5:21).

There are a number of things that submission does not require of a wife. It does not mean that she is a slave or a nonperson without a thought, wish, or desire of her own. She does not have to put on blinders and ignore the faults or behaviors in her husband which may contradict God's Word. It does not mean denying her giftedness and talents. In fact, there will be many occasions in which a wife has greater wisdom, insight, or ability than her husband. When this is the case, the partner with the most to give should have the opportunity to do so.

The scriptural pattern of authority and responsibility contained in the passages concerning headship and submission are sometimes difficult to live out. Because of the results of the Fall, we tend to live in fear of domination. It is so easy for power struggles to emerge.

Submission simply means arranging oneself under the authority of another. Because of abilities and giftedness, this can shift back and forth between partners. This attitude is vital in the marital relationship. Resistance, resentment, and rebellion allow no place for love and intimacy to grow. Biblical submission calls for the wife to trust, respect, and honor her husband from her heart. Submitting to a husband is also an act of submission to the Lord. This is not man's plan but God's. And it works!

JANUARY 8

*Husbands, love your wives, just as Christ
loved the church and gave himself up for her
to make her holy* (Ephesians 5:25,26).

I f you could enter a time machine and emerge back in the first century
when Paul's letters hit the culture of the day, you would be in for
some real excitement. His instruction to husbands in Ephesians 5:25-27
must have caused a riot! They went contrary to the way men treated
women at that time. Paul's writings called the husband to a ministry
of loving servanthood to his wife in a culture which treated women as
little better than household furnishings!

A husband is to love his wife with the same sacrificial self-abandon-
ment that Christ adopted toward each of us. When a man considers
headship in marriage, he needs to look at the life of Jesus. Jesus said,
"The Son of Man came not to be served, but to serve" (Matthew 20:28).
Jesus is presented in Scripture as both Head and Servant. He is the
"head over everything for the church" (Ephesians 1:22) who took "the
very nature of a servant" (Philippians 2:7). And Jesus instructed us,
"The greatest among you will be your servant" (Matthew 23:11).

As believers, we are all called to servanthood as an expression of our
new life in Christ. However, when it comes to marriage, modeling this
attribute of God's Son is a calling extended to husbands. A husband
expresses love to his wife by regarding her as a completely equal partner
in everything that concerns their life together. He asserts his headship to see that this equal partnership works. Loving headship affirms
and defers; it encourages and stimulates. Loving headship delights to
delegate without demanding. But a husband must remember that he
bears the responsibility before God for the maintenance of a healthy
marriage.

JANUARY 9

Finally, brothers, whatever is true, whatever is
honorable, whatever is right,...let your mind
dwell on these things (Philippians 4:8, NASB).

The direction of your thought life can determine the course of your marriage. You can choose to emphasize and concentrate on faults or on positive qualities.

There is a big difference in the feeding habits of buzzards and bees. Buzzards fly overhead searching for dead animals. When they spy a decaying animal, they swoop down to gorge themselves on the carrion. Honey bees, however, look only for sweet nectar. They are very discriminating as they search through the flowers in a garden.

Just as the bees and buzzards always find what they are seeking, so you will always find what you look for in your marriage relationship. If you focus on your partner's faults or mistakes, you will always find them, and your relationship will be colored by that negative attitude. However, if your daily quest in your marriage is to find and affirm the positive qualities in your spouse, you'll be surprised at how many you find and how those discoveries will enhance your relationship.

We tend to choose either a negative or positive path for our marriage by the way we think about it. Our choices and experiences result in the building of memories, feelings, and attitudes which couples carry through to their later years. You may be just starting your marital journey or you may be enjoying your fiftieth wedding anniversary. But the memories you are gathering for the future will be influenced by the way you think today. Perhaps you could share a special memory with your partner right now.

No matter what your age or length of marriage, there is still time to make a choice. You can still choose to concentrate on the positive in your marriage, to make it even more fulfilling. There is still time to practice and apply the suggestions found in these pages. Your commitment and plans for the remaining years of your marriage remain your choice!

JANUARY 10

Above all else, guard your heart, for it is the
wellspring of life (Proverbs 4:23).

What is it that really makes a marriage alive and vital? Is it following the Scriptures or a strict adherence to a plan for the marriage? Living according to God's Word is important, but of equal importance is the couple's attitude of heart as they comply with Scripture. Sometimes attitudes of defiance or hostility underlie the outward behavior of following God's Word. This does not develop a healthy marital relationship. A proper attitude of heart is the basis for living out God's plan for husbands and wives.

Many couples live today as though they were card-carrying magicians. They are very adept at creating illusions. Some couples create the illusion of intimacy in their marriage; others portray an illusion of spiritual closeness. Others give lip service and appear to be living out God's Word in their marriage, but their actions do not spring from a right attitude of the heart. Some husbands and wives are deeply devoted to following God's scriptural roles for them. Others respond grudgingly or discard or misinterpret the clear teaching of Scripture.

It is important for each of us to periodically take our own temperature concerning the attitude of our heart. Is your spirit open to God's leading? Do you have a deep desire to allow God's Word to be reflected in your marriage? Do you perceive God's guidelines for your marriage to be personally limiting or liberating?

You know your heart.

God knows your heart.

You can't change your heart.

But God can change your heart. If you need Him to work in the spirit of your heart, let Him do so. He knows what He's doing, and He wants the best for you.

JANUARY 11

I can do all things through Christ
who strengthens me (Philippians 4:13, NKJV).

Sometimes couples find it scary to look at their marriage, evaluate its strengths and weaknesses, and then take action. "What if it doesn't work?" they fear. Many people are not inclined to be risk-takers because of the fear of failure. This is why many dreams remain dreams. The fear of failure keeps us from experiencing even greater joy and delight in life. Risk-taking in marriage may be threatening, but it's better than the alternative of shriveling up and dying as a couple.

Spend some time talking through the following lines about risk-taking from an anonymous writer as they apply to your marriage. What implications does Philippians 4:13 hold for risk-taking in your marriage?

> To laugh is to appear the fool.
> To weep is to risk appearing sentimental.
> To reach out for another is to risk involvement.
> To expose feelings is to risk exposing your true self.
> To place your ideas, your dreams, before the crowd is to risk
>   their loss.
> To love is to risk not being loved in return.
> To live is to risk dying.
> To hope is to risk despair.
> To try is to risk failure.
> But risks must be taken, because the greatest hazard in life is
>   to risk nothing.
> The person who risks nothing, does nothing, has nothing, and
>   is nothing.
> He may avoid suffering and sorrow.
> But he simply cannot learn, feel, change, grow, love, and live.
> Chained by his certitudes, he is a slave.
> He has forfeited freedom.
> Only a person who risks is free!

January 12

*Husbands, love your wives, just as Christ
loved the church and gave Himself up for her
to make her holy* (Ephesians 5:25,26).

By being the spiritual leader in the home, a husband indicates his concern for his wife's spiritual welfare and continual growth. Once again the pattern of Jesus must be considered. He died to take away the sin of each person in the world. He loved the church and gave Himself for it. This model of Christ's love for the church reaches down into the life of every husband. A husband and father doesn't save his family. Only Christ does that. But God holds every husband accountable for the spiritual welfare and atmosphere of the home. The many ingredients and responsibilities of the husband include

- a personal prayer life;
- interaction, reading, and understanding of the Scriptures;
- participation in the local church worship service;
- modeling the proper use of time for his family;
- encouraging his wife to grow in the Scriptures and become involved with other women, taking time out for Bible study groups or weekend conferences that may help her develop spiritual leadership. This also entails providing the funds for this to occur, along with a willing attitude to care for the kids for an entire weekend while she attends the meetings! This is real sacrifice!
- developing spiritual intimacy with his wife. This is a major responsibility, and it means reading the Word together, sharing meaningful spiritual thoughts and experiences, praying together, and letting his wife know that he is praying for her.

This is spiritual leadership. And the blessings benefit both of you. No one said it was easy, but it is worth your time and effort. Let God guide you in this.

January 13

Don't store up treasures here on earth (Matthew
6:19, TLB); *Stop loving this evil world and
all that it offers you* (1 John 2:15, TLB).

What gives you personal value? What is your own self-worth tied to? Reflect on these questions for a minute and then share your thoughts with your partner.

When it comes to building our self-worth and personal value, we all face a conflict. We hear two messages: what society tells us and what the Word of God tells us. One is changeable and shaky, and the other is permanent and stable. Many men and women look at their possessions and the amount of money they have as the source of their self-worth. If they don't possess, they don't feel worthwhile. Consider some thoughts from God's Word:

> Don't store up treasures here on earth where they can erode away or may be stolen. Store them in heaven where they will never lose their value, and are safe from thieves. If your profits are in heaven your heart will be there too (Matthew 6:19-21, TLB).

> Stop loving this evil world and all that it offers you, for when you love these things you show that you do not really love God; for all these worldly things, these evil desires—the craze for sex, the ambition to buy everything that appeals to you, and the pride that comes from wealth and importance—these are not from God. They are from this evil world itself (1 John 2:15-17, TLB).

Do these words seem strong? confronting? convicting? Yes, they are. But they are words designed to help us put our lives, values, and marriages in perspective, words designed to help us really understand and experience security in our life, words which stem from God's love for each one of us.

How do you, as a married couple, need to respond to these admonitions from Scripture?

JANUARY 14

God, after He spoke long ago to the fathers...in these last days has spoken to us in His Son (Hebrews 1:1,2, NASB).

Who are you, and what do you do?"
Have you ever been asked that question? Most of us have, and our answers vary greatly. Some respond with the first thought that comes to mind. Others respond with an answer that reflects their occupation. But some people say, "Well, I'm not really that significant, and I really don't do all that much." How sad for someone to feel this way about himself or herself. Unfortunately, many people do.

There is a person who not only has great significance, but gives us significance as well. His name is Jesus. Those who follow Him soon discover that God highly values and affirms them. Why? Because He has created them and provided for their lives here on earth through His Son.

Let's consider the significance of Jesus Christ. As we do, remember: He loves you, cares for you, and died on the cross for your sins.

Who is He? Look at the first chapter of the book of Hebrews.

He is greater than any human prophet (vv. 1,2).

He is God's Son; He is eternal God Himself (vv. 2,3,8,9).

He is heir of all things (v. 2).

He created the world and He upholds all things (vv. 2,3).

He cleanses us from sin (v. 3).

He sits at the right hand of the Father (v. 3).

He is greater than angels; angels worship Him (vv. 4,6).

He has the name of God (v. 5).

His throne is forever (v. 8).

He is the ruler of the coming age (vv. 10-12).

What about it? Is He significant? If He is part of your life, you too have an even greater significance than you imagine. Just think about that!

JANUARY 15

Those who wait for the Lord will gain
new strength (Isaiah 40:31, NASB).

Hikers and backpackers soon learn one of the most important lessons of survival. Even when it seems to take longer to reach the destination, always stick to the trail. Novice hikers are prone to look for shortcuts, and often they are the ones who have to be rescued. What seems to be a shortcut often turns out to be either dangerous or a dead end.

We look for shortcuts in many areas of life because they appear to save us time and a lot of hard work and effort. Even in marriage we look for quick and easy answers to fix problems or stabilize the relationship.

In many ways, we are a "hurry up and get there" society. Waiting is not welcomed. It's resisted; it's resented. Even in our Christian life and walk, we want results now. That's our plan. But is it God's plan? Why does Scripture say so much about waiting? There must be a reason.

> In repentance and rest you shall be saved, in quietness and trust is your strength (Isaiah 30:15, NASB).

> Yet those who wait for the Lord will gain new strength; they will mount up with wings like eagles, they will run and not get tired, they will walk and not become weary (Isaiah 40:31, NASB).

> I am the vine, you are the branches; he who abides in Me, and I in him, he bears much fruit; for apart from Me you can do nothing (John 15:5, NASB).

Resting, quietness, waiting, abiding, dependence on God—these are foreign terms in today's society. Couples must make many decisions in their marital journey. There are times when it is best to say to one another, "Let's pray about this and wait upon God for the answer." Have you tried that recently? It can add a new dimension to your life as a couple.

JANUARY 16

You were justified in the name of the Lord
Jesus Christ (1 Corinthians 6:11).

Dread and anxiety! There is no other way to describe the feelings of sitting in a courtroom waiting for the verdict from the judge or the jury.

Have you ever been on trial? Yes, you have. Everyone has. It may not have been in an actual courtroom, but at some time in your life, you've been on trial. It could have been before your parents, friends, employer, teacher, spouse, or even yourself! Some people feel as though they are on trial every day of their lives. They have someone who criticizes, accuses, or condemns them each day. That's not very pleasant, but it happens. When it does, it seems that others have control over our lives. It's painful. How do you handle the pain of unwarranted and unjustified criticism?

When criticism continues throughout our lives from other people, that's bad news. The good news is that God has brought down the gavel and pronounced us justified! This is a legal term which means we have been acquitted, vindicated, and declared righteous. We were guilty, but God stepped down from behind the bench, took out His wallet, and paid the fine. He provided the payment through the sacrifice of His Son Jesus Christ. His death brought us life.

Justification isn't the same as a pardon. When you are pardoned from the penalty for a crime, you are excused from the penalty. Your crime is still on the books. Justification means total acquittal, not only for the penalty, but for the accusation as well! The charges are wiped out. God looks at you and says, "Acquitted! Vindicated! Justified!"

How do you react to your partner when he or she offends you? Do you hold your spouse accountable in the recesses of your memory for days, weeks, months, or years? God can help you wipe clean your memory of hurt and anger, and you then can wipe clean the accusation. Justification makes marriage and life so much better than the alternatives of dread, anxiety, and guilt.

JANUARY 17

*I will have mercy on whom I will
have mercy* (Exodus 33:19).

Have mercy on me! Please!"
If we've heard that expression once, we've heard it dozens of times on television and in films. Mercy is probably easier to receive than to give. Do you know what mercy is? Literally, it is the outward manifestation of pity. That sounds like some vague emotional reaction. However, mercy is more than emotions. It is really active compassion which meets a need.

Do any of us have a right to mercy? Not really. Mercy is given because of the heart and compassion of the merciful person. Mercy is not giving a person what he deserves. You can't buy it. You can't earn it. You don't deserve it. That's what makes it mercy.

Jesus extended mercy to the woman who had been caught in the act of adultery (John 8:3-11). Her accusers reminded Jesus that the law required the adulteress to be stoned, then asked Him, "What do you say?" (v. 5). His reply indicated that He was more concerned about her soul and her salvation than her sin. After the convicted accusers left, He asked, "Has no one condemned you?…Then neither do I condemn you.…Go now and leave your life of sin" (vv. 10,11).

Do you realize what Jesus did? He looked past her fault. He also does that for you and your partner. He saw her need; He sees you and your partner's need. He forgave her sin; He forgives you and your partner's sins. He set her free; He sets you and your partner free. He gives you mercy. We receive His mercy because of His compassion.

What a model for the way we are to respond to one another in marriage, with compassion and mercy. The next time you feel offended, remember mercy. It is probably not your first thought, nor is it a natural human response. But that's why Jesus Christ makes a difference in our lives. Because of Him, there is a new and better way of life available to us—even in our marriage.[2]

JANUARY 18

*If you abide in My word, you are My disciples
indeed. And you shall know the truth, and the
truth shall make you free* (John 8:31,32, NKJV).

During World War II, there were occasions when U.S. troops penetrated a country held by enemy troops. After months of fierce battle, the enemy was driven back and the people were liberated. They were set free from the oppression and tyranny of their captors.

Well, whether you realize it or not, you also used to be a captive. You were held in bondage by sin, and when you invited Jesus Christ into your life, you too were liberated. The basis of your freedom is stated in John 8:31-36. Jesus said, "The truth shall make you free" (v. 32). This verse is a statement of your emancipation.

But many people say, "I don't feel free." They still feel imprisoned and trapped, often within the citadels of their own minds and feelings. Our thoughts can imprison us; our feelings often victimize us. And there is a direct correlation between the two. Your negative thoughts produce the negative feelings that plague you.

How does a person break loose from the bind of negative thoughts and the ensuing feelings they create? Jesus said, "Abide in My word" (v. 31). You are called to abide in Christ's word and allow His teaching to dwell in you. His words are to be the basis of how you think about life, yourself, your partner, the future, God, etc. What Jesus Christ did and said needs to become the standard for your beliefs, convictions, attitudes, and reactions. As Lloyd Ogilvie says, "Bringing all thought captive to Him who is sublime truth is the source of liberated emotions. All that we feel that makes us unfree is tied to some thought inconsistent with Christ's truth."[3]

Do you feel imprisoned in any way? Talk about it with your partner today.

JANUARY 19

Have mercy on me, O God, according to your
unfailing love; according to your great compassion
blot out my transgressions (Psalm 51:1).

Have you experienced the delight of reading the 150 psalms aloud? Some people feel a sense of discomfort when they read the Book of Psalms. Why? As you read it, you are confronted with cries for help, complaints, confessions of sin, depression, times of celebration, expressions of love for God, commitments being made to God as well as expressions of hope. These prayers are not just expressions of thoughts, but deep emotions. This is the way prayers are to be expressed—with our whole beings. What are your prayers like? How would your partner describe the way you pray? Do you pray with thoughts *and* emotions?

The psalms give us patterns of prayers. Psalm 51 is a pattern of prayer for any person who has been made aware of his sin and need for forgiveness. It is a plea for mercy based upon God's love for each person. Verses 1 and 2 express David's cry for mercy. This psalm was written by David after Nathan the prophet had confronted him for his sin with Bathsheba (2 Samuel 11,12).

In Psalm 51:3-6 David admits that his sin was against God. David then asks God in very graphic terms to make him clean. He wants the stain of his sin cleansed from his life (vv. 7-9). He prays for restoration and cleansing inside his heart and mind.

Verses 10-12 are a prayer which most of us could offer each day. It reflects the fact that we need the strength of God for moral purity within us and in our behavior. In verses 13-17 David said that he was going to teach others what he had learned and tell everyone about the Lord.

What portions of this prayer speak to you at this time? Was there a time in your life when a prayer like this was a spiritual step for you? Why not close today's meditation by reading this psalm aloud, alternately verse by verse. Then share what the experience meant to you.

JANUARY 20

The fruit of the Spirit is love (Galatians 5:22);
We love because he first loved us (1 John 4:19).

The kind of love mentioned in Galatians 5:22 and 1 John 4:19—*agape*—is the ultimate expression of love. Agape love is not based upon feelings; it is an act of the will. It doesn't come from within us, but from God. We can only experience and express agape love by relinquishing our will to the will of Christ.

Agape love is costly. It is unconditional. It is not based upon your partner's performance. The other person does not have to earn it. Nor does he or she have to live down the past in order to be loved in this way.

Agape love is also transparent. Transparency involves openness, honesty, truth, and sharing positive and negative feelings. It is strong enough to allow your partner not only to get close to you, but to see inside you. It is a love which has a deep reservoir from which to draw. This is the love which gives strength and stability to marriage during the times of stress, distance, and conflict.

Agape love is based upon unconditional commitment to an imperfect person. It is a love which allows your partner to become all that he or she can be even if you are threatened by his or her progress. Love which is willful, deliberate, and committed provides stability when feelings of love weaken or waver. Booth Tarkington described this kind of love beautifully:

> It is love in old age, no longer blind, that is true love. For love's highest intensity doesn't necessarily mean its highest quality. Glamour and jealousy are gone; and the ardent caress, no longer needed, is valueless compared to the reassuring touch of a trembling hand. Passersby commonly see little beauty in the embrace of young lovers on a park bench, but the understanding smile of an old wife to her husband is one of the loveliest things in the world.[4]

JANUARY 21

The fruit of the spirit is…joy (Galatians 5:22); *These things I have spoken to you, that My joy may remain in you, and that your joy may be full* (John 15:11, NKJV).

What has brought you the greatest joy in life? Think about it for a minute. Share it with your partner. What has brought your partner the greatest joy in your marriage? You probably didn't expect that question, did you? But it's just as important as what has brought you the greatest joy.

Many people equate joy with fun, like going to Disneyland or taking a cruise to the Caribbean. To other people joy is a good feeling or what we call happiness. "Happiness" comes from the same root as the word "happening," and may be equated with something happening to us, something circumstantial. Happiness and laughter are good, but they come and go with circumstances. Joy, however, defies circumstances. It can be present even when times are tough.

Joy is an attitude. It is not based upon outside situations and happenings; it is purely an inside job. Tim Hansel puts it so well: "Pain is inevitable, but misery is optional. We cannot avoid pain, but we can avoid joy. Joy is simple. At any moment in life we have at least two options, and one of them is to choose an attitude of gratitude, a posture of grace, a commitment to joy."[5]

Joy in your life is an option, a choice. Think about this statement:

> In the biblical sense, joy then becomes a spiritual balance between expectations and achievements—the ability to approach problems objectively by accepting things as they are and working toward solution and adjustment. Assuming this stance, joy is a sense of imperturbable gladness that sings when rejected, praises when persecuted, and stands when attacked.[6]

Do you have this kind of joy?

JANUARY 22

The fruit of the Spirit is...peace (Galatians 5:22);
*And the peace of God...will guard your hearts and
your minds in Christ Jesus* (Philippians 4:7).

Here is a slightly different way to look at peace. Perhaps you can relate to it.

J.L. Glass has written a humorous article, titled "Five Ways to Have a Nervous Breakdown." He lists the ways as follows:

1. Try to figure out the answer before the problem arises. "Most of the bridges we cross are never built, because they are unnecessary." We carry tomorrow's load along with today's. Matthew 6:34 says: "Do not worry about tomorrow, for tomorrow will worry about itself."

2. Try to relive the past. As we trust him [God] for the future, we must trust him with the past. And he can use the most checkered past imaginable for his good. See Romans 8:28.

3. Try to avoid making decisions. Doing this is like deciding whether to allow weeds to grow in our gardens. While we're deciding, they're growing. Decisions will be made in our delay....Choice "is man's most godlike characteristic."

4. Demand more of yourself than you can produce. Unrealistic demands result in "beating our heads against stone walls. We don't change the walls. We just damage ourselves." Romans 12:3 says, "Do not think of yourself more highly than you ought, but rather think of yourself with sober judgment."

5. Believe everything Satan tells you....Jesus described Satan as the "father of lies" (John 8:44). He's a master of disguise, masquerading as an angel of light. But our Lord declared that his sheep follow him because they "know His voice" (John 10:4). They have listened to it in his Word.[7]

JANUARY 23

The fruit of the Spirit is…patience (Galatians 5:22).

Have you ever felt that inner twinge of wanting a person, an event, or even yourself to hurry? It's called impatience. You feel like a cattle driver at round-up time saying, "Move 'em out. Get 'em going. Push 'em along. We don't have all day!" Some individuals and some couples live their lives this way. Most of us want patience, but we want it right now!

In a marriage, when one spouse is a hyper, alert, wide-eyed, energetic, early-morning person, you can pretty well guess who he or she is married to. Right—a partner whose metabolism is a bit slower, who needs more sleep, and who doesn't function well before 9:00 a.m! This difference is often the breeding ground for impatience and frustration. Usually the early-morning individual wants to talk at the break of dawn but is fast asleep when the night person is ready to converse. Proverbs 27:14 captures the contrast: "If you shout a pleasant greeting to a friend too early in the morning, he will count it as a curse!" (TLB).

What is patience as mentioned in Galatians 5:22? The old English word long-suffering means not being quickly or easily provoked by the unsatisfactory conduct of others. Oh, how that quality is needed in marriage and parenting!

When you are patient you have the ability to persevere. Have you ever seen fishermen sit by the lake or wade through streams hour after hour? That's patience. It doesn't seem to bother them that they may not catch a fish all day long. Patience means you can handle things not going your way. You can put up with situations which are not to your liking.

Talk about patience together. Where do you see patience working well in your life? Where is it working in your marriage? Where do you need more patience as a husband or wife?

JANUARY 24

The fruit of the Spirit is...kindness (Galatians 5:22).

I t's a lost art."

"It's an invitation to others to take advantage of you."

"It's something only a naive person would do in this day and age."

These responses were given regarding the character quality of kindness. Is this shocking? Perhaps. But we live in a society where we have been taught to protect ourselves and grab what belongs to us. And yet words and deeds of kindness often mean more to people than money or status.

When we look at the biblical concept of kindness, we find that it means a gentle or tender action springing from a spirit of compassion or concern. Kindness is manifested in speaking and acting nonoffensively to others. A kind person goes out of his or her way to help and encourage others. Kindness is also an attitude of the heart, not just an outward, momentary display. This teaching goes contrary to the content of popular self-centered books such as *Looking Out for Number One.*

When you consider God's character you discover the attribute of kindness: "And God raised us up with Christ and seated us with him in the heavenly realms in Christ Jesus, in order that in the coming ages he might show the incomparable riches of his grace, expressed in his kindness to us in Christ Jesus" (Ephesians 2:6,7). Kindness is tied into the grace of Jesus. In Titus, we read, "But when the kindness and love of God our Savior appeared, he saved us, not because of righteous things we had done, but because of his mercy" (3:4,5).

Kindness as expressed in Colossians 3:12 is the opposite of malice or badness. As God's chosen people we are asked to reflect His attribute of kindness in our lives. Look at Luke 10:25-37 and discover how you could perform an act of kindness toward another person at this time, perhaps, even your partner.

JANUARY 25

The fruit of the Spirit is…goodness (Galatians
5:22); *He [Christ] poured God's goodness
into us!* (2 Corinthians 5:21, TLB).

Most of us distinctly remember the words of our father and mother
when we were growing up: "Be a good boy" or "Be a good girl."
Similarly, in sports such as basketball or tennis we hear "Good shot!"
or "Good serve!"

There are many definitions for the word *good*. Webster's *New World
Dictionary* lists 17 categories of definitions for *good*—and each category has three or four meanings! The Greek word for good appears
102 times in the New Testament. The meanings of the word vary,
including such words as genuine, uncontaminated, honorable, healthy,
generous, dependable, and honest. Goodness involves habitual actions
which reflect an inward disposition. It includes the concept of helping;
but, interestingly enough, it can also include rebuking, correcting, and
disciplining.

One of the characteristics of God is goodness. Scripture is filled
with references to His goodness. Moses heard God say, "I Myself will
make all My goodness pass before you" (Exodus 33:19, NASB). Again
and again the psalmist talks about God's goodness in providing for
physical and spiritual needs. When was the last time you thought about
God's goodness? When did you last say, "God really is good!"? We have
hope because God is good. He is the source of every good and perfect
gift (James 1:17). That is a promise to you. Even when you are destitute
and wonder where your next meal will come from, God is still good.
His goodness is seen in His ultimate gift, Jesus Christ.

Sometimes men and women fear being seen as good. There could
be ridicule and misunderstanding. Sometimes it's difficult to stand out
as being different. In what way do you see your partner as being good?
In what way does your partner see you as being good? Talk about God's
goodness and your partner's goodness.

JANUARY 26

The fruit of the Spirit is...faithfulness (Galatians 5:22).

I s there someone in your life that you can always depend on, someone who will always come through regardless of the circumstances? If so, rejoice! One of the defects in our society today is the lack of people who are faithful. Employers, voters, spouses, and government officials look for others who reflect reliability, trustworthiness, and fidelity in their lives.

Faithfulness in God's Word has many synonyms: reliability, loyalty, dependability, assurance, and trustworthiness. Try to replace faithfulness with something else. It's impossible! It just won't work! Nothing takes the place of faithfulness: "Talent will not—nothing is more common than unsuccessful people with talent. Genius will not—unrewarded genius is almost a proverb. Education will not—the world is full of educated derelicts."[8]

Can others count on you? Does anyone ever raise the concern that you won't come through? That doesn't need to be a problem when you walk in the Spirit. Here again we have a beautiful model. God is faithful. Because of His faithfulness, we too are now able to see this character quality develop in our own lives. "The one who calls you is faithful" is the promise of Scripture (1 Thessalonians 5:24). God is always available, dependable, and always means what He says.

Jesus Christ is called "Faithful and True" (Revelation 19:11), and He expects each believer to be faithful as well. This is the calling extended to us from Scripture: "Let a man so consider us, as servants of Christ and stewards of the mysteries of God. Moreover it is required in stewards that one be found faithful" (1 Corinthians 4:1,2).

Hopefully, God will be able to say to each of us, "You have been faithful!" Hopefully, you can say to each other as husband and wife, "You have been faithful!"

JANUARY 27

The fruit of the Spirit is...gentleness (Galatians 5:22,23).

What comes to mind when you hear the word gentle? Certainly it involves sensitivity, a soft touch, or a very light caress. Gentleness is carrying a fragile egg with great delicacy. Gentleness is a mother cat carrying her kitten in her mouth. Gentleness is someone rubbing your back so softly and smoothly that you drop off to sleep.

But what does gentleness mean as one of the fruits of the Spirit? In the New Testament gentleness means being submissive to the will of God, as reflected in the words of Jesus: "Take my yoke upon you, and learn of Me; for I am gentle (meek) and humble (lowly) in heart, and you will find rest" (Matthew 11:29, AMP). Gentleness also means being considerate of other people. Paul wrote: "By the meekness and gentleness of Christ, I appeal to you—I, Paul, who am 'timid' when face to face with you, but 'bold' when away!" (2 Corinthians 10:1).

Gentleness has been used for hundreds of years as the goal for taming wild animals. Taming is definitely a part of the marriage relationship. That doesn't mean a husband's task is to tame his wife, nor should a wife attempt to tame her husband. For one thing, it will never work! But it does mean that both partners need to be tamed by the Holy Spirit. Our tempers need to be tamed. Negative or critical attitudes need to be tamed. A very difficult task is the taming of our tongues (James 3:6-8). Impulsive behaviors need to be tamed. Desires which are contrary to the Christian life need to be tamed.

What about you? Is there an untamed animal roaming through your life? through your marriage? Share your thoughts with your partner about areas that need to be tamed. Then ask the Holy Spirit to do the taming.

JANUARY 28

The fruit of the Spirit is...self-control (Galatians 5:22,23).

Self-control—what does it mean to you? Does it mean pushing yourself away from the table to avoid that second piece of pie? Does it mean resisting the enticement of the television commercial which tempts you to consider buying a new set of golf clubs? Does self-control mean resisting a second look at an attractive person of the opposite sex?

Self-control means different things to different people. It is the last-mentioned fruit of the Spirit in Paul's list, but it is not the least important. Rather it is one of the fruits we have the most difficulty cultivating in our lives. We all struggle with self-control. We all seem to have our weaknesses in disciplining our appetites. What is your greatest weakness? What is your partner's greatest weakness? Do your weaknesses affect your marriage in some way?

Let's face it: None of us is totally consistent in self-control. The only way this quality can flourish is through the presence of the Holy Spirit in your life. When you are exercising self-control, it means that you are subject to the sovereignty of God in your life at that time. You have relinquished the control of your life to God's Spirit.

There are several areas in which we need the Spirit's control. Our thoughts need to be controlled by the Spirit because our minds are continually influenced by the sinful culture in which we live. Our emotions are in need of the Spirit's control because we often tend to live by our feelings instead of our thoughts. And our behavior, which is so closely tied to our thoughts and feelings, needs to be Spirit-controlled.

The key to realizing the Holy Spirit's control is our will. If we are determined to do things our own way, we will continually struggle with God. We have a choice. We can live under the tyranny of our own thoughts, feelings, choices, and behaviors, or we can live under the control of the Holy Spirit. Think about it. Your choice will change your life!

January 29

If you love someone...you will always believe in him,
always expect the best from him (1 Corinthians 13:7, TLB).

Did anyone tell you before you were married that one of your roles as a spouse was being a cheerleader for your partner? That's right, a cheerleader. You know what a cheerleader is; perhaps in your school days you were one for your school. Now your team is made up of one person—your partner. And that person needs you to cheer him or her on in life! We all need someone to believe in us and cheer for us, especially when things aren't going well.

Anne Morrow Lindbergh was a woman who experienced a deep personal tragedy. Her husband, famous aviator Charles Lindbergh, was always in the limelight. As a result of the kidnapping and death of their son, Mrs. Lindbergh also became a public figure. Here are her thoughts about being loved and believed in:

> To be deeply in love, of course, is a great liberating force and the most common experience that frees....Ideally, both members of a couple in love free each other to new and different worlds. I was no exception to the general rule. The sheer fact of finding myself loved was unbelievable and changed my world, my feelings about life and myself. I was given confidence, strength, and almost a new character.[9]

Do you release your partner to discover his or her hidden potential which has yet to emerge? Your partner belongs to the Lord, and He wants the best for both of you.

Perhaps your partner needs a little more cheering on from you. Perhaps he or she needs a phone call or a personal note from you which says, "Go for it; you can do it. I'm here for you; I believe in you. Give it a try; I'm praying for you." These are the kinds of words that cheer a person on. Make cheerleading a consistent pattern in your marriage relationship.

JANUARY 30

For thus the Lord God, the Holy One of
Israel, has said, "…In quietness and trust
is your strength" (Isaiah 30:15, NASB).

Pollution—the curse of our century! One of the worst offenders is noise pollution: blaring stereos and televisions, roaring freeways which can be heard from a mile away. What happened to quietness? Where did it go? Some people are noise addicts. The louder their environment is, the better. They don't know what quietness is.

You may be uncomfortable with silence and inactivity. Some people stay in the fast lane of life to avoid slowing down to contemplate their lives. Many of these people received a message during childhood which urged them, "Always be busy and productive. You can't accomplish anything if you're just sitting around."

Chuck Swindoll comments about the quietness we need today:

> You know something? That still, small voice will never shout. God's methods don't change because we are so noisy and busy. He is longing for your attention, your undivided and full attention. He wants to talk with you in times of quietness (with the TV off) about your need for understanding, love, compassion, patience, self-control, a calm spirit, genuine humility…and wisdom. But He won't run to catch up. He will wait and wait until you finally sit in silence and listen.[10]

Perhaps you could begin today by taking 5 to 15 minutes to sit in a quiet room together and reflect on what God is doing in your lives. Sometimes turning on a fan to drown out other noises helps. Our best refreshment comes when we are quiet in the presence of the Lord. Take a few minutes to sit quietly with your partner holding hands and thinking about God's love, power, and peace. Quietness is rare in today's society. But God is saying, "Be quiet, and know who I Am." Try it; it's worth it.

January 31

May the God of peace...equip you with everything good
for doing his will, and may he work in us what is pleasing
to him, through Jesus Christ (Hebrews 13:20,21).

Scripturally based blessings can be a powerful element in a marriage. The following blessing is often read at the conclusion of wedding ceremonies. Read this blessing aloud and reflect upon its message for your marriage.

Blessing for a Marriage
by James D. Freeman

May your marriage bring you all the exquisite excitements a marriage should bring, and may life grant you also patience, tolerance, and understanding. May you always need one another—not so much to fill your emptiness as to help you to know your fullness. A mountain needs a valley to be complete; the valley does not make the mountain less, but more; and the valley is more a valley because it has a mountain towering over it. So let it be with each of you. May you need one another, but not out of weakness. May you want one another, but not out of lack. May you entice one another, but not compel one another. May you embrace one another, but not encircle one another. May you succeed in all important ways with one another, and not fail in the little graces. May you look for things to praise, often say, "I love you!" and take no notice of small faults. If you have quarrels that push you apart, may both of you hope to have good sense enough to take the first step back. May you enter into the mystery which is the awareness of one another's presence—no more physical than spiritual, warm and near when you are side by side, and warm and near when you are in separate rooms or even distant cities. May you have happiness, and may you find it making one another happy. May you have love, and may you find it loving one another![11]

FEBRUARY

What makes the difference in our marriages in the face of life's many surprises? Worship. Coming face to face with God and focusing on Him helps us handle life's surprises.

FEBRUARY 1

It is not good for the man to be alone (Genesis 2:18).

Do you realize that the very first thing that God declared to be "not good" was for a human to be alone? There is pain in being by oneself. God designed us to live in relationship with others. He did not create us to be hermits! Unfortunately, some men and women choose to live in emotional seclusion even when they are married. One of the greatest types of pain in life is being married while feeling alone and isolated.

We were created for intimacy. Adam and Eve were created with a need for one another. This need was not just a physical one, but a healthy, emotional need also. Have you ever shared with your partner your idea or definition of intimacy? Take a minute to do so right now.

Many couples think they have intimacy in their relationship and are fulfilling God's design. But are they? Intimacy suggests a very strong personal relationship, a special emotional closeness which includes understanding and being understood by someone who is very special. Intimacy is an affectionate bond which includes mutual caring, mutual responsibility, mutual trust, and open communication of feelings and thoughts.

Intimacy requires vulnerability, but it also provides security. Intimacy can be scary, but the acceptance which occurs in the midst of it can bring a wonderful sense of safety and assurance. Intimacy means becoming fully exposed—naked but unashamed (Genesis 2:25). But it also brings the promise of being fully accepted as well.

Intimacy in marriage begins with each of us being alone and intimate with God. When you allow God to have a close relationship with you, He can then free you to touch your partner's life with the gifts of your emotions and trust. This is what God wants for you. He made you with the need and ability to have an intimate relationship as a married couple. Let intimacy develop in your marriage and rejoice in the results.

February 2

Christ redeemed us (Galatians 3:13).

You were once a hostage! Surprised? It's true. You were led into bondage by an act many years ago. The kidnapping was carried out in a beautiful, tranquil garden that was provided by God. The kidnapper very cleverly enticed Adam and Eve into sin and, through that abduction, made hostages of everyone to follow them. They were alienated from their home and sentenced to separation and death. Their only hope was to be released on receipt of ransom.

In 1932 the son of aviator Charles Lindbergh was kidnapped and held for ransom. The Lindberghs paid the ransom in full and yet ended up being victimized. The kidnapper killed the 20-month-old child. The Lindberghs tried to save their son but could not. Even the ransom wasn't enough.

You can rejoice that the payment God paid to redeem you was successful and complete. The two Greek verbs for redeemed mean "to release on receipt of a ransom" or "to buy out." Dr. Lawrence Richards says that the word redeemed is "cast against the background of helplessness…human beings captured, held captive by the power of forces they cannot overcome. Only by the intervention of a third party can bondage be broken and the person freed."

We were victims and didn't have the power to free ourselves. But a child of God has power and is free. Satan still tries to work on us, but his power is broken. Jesus said, "If the Son sets you free, you will be free indeed" (John 8:36).

Sometimes we hold our partner captive. We discourage him or her from growing and developing. We don't let our spouse forget a mistake or a violation. But we are to forgive as we have been forgiven. Marriage was never meant to be a captive situation. Just the opposite; we are to set one another free. And we can. Redeemed people want to see others set free.

FEBRUARY 3

Husbands ought to love their wives as their own bodies....
No one ever hated his own body, but he feeds and cares
for it, just as Christ does the church (Ephesians 5:28,29).

The idea of feeding and caring for one's own body is a very practical illustration of how a husband can express Christ's love for his wife. Many husbands are quite proficient in providing for the material needs of their wives and children. In fact, making money and paying bills may be the easiest way for a man to provide for his family. It's actually less painful sometimes than having to provide for the other areas within the family. This doesn't mean that a wife cannot be employed outside of the home as well. Often both need to work or are called to work by virtue of their talents and abilities.

The King James Version translates the verb *feeds* as *nourisheth*. This word broadens our understanding of a husband's responsibility. He must nourish his wife mentally, physically, emotionally, and spiritually. As one author puts it:

> When a man makes provision for his wife to be the best-educated, most well-adjusted, and most spiritually mature woman she can possibly be, he is fulfilling his mandate to nourish her as he would his own body. To do less (especially if his motive is selfish or self-protective) is to ignore the example of Christ, who has selflessly provided for and encouraged the development and exercise of each believer's giftedness. A husband should want his wife to be all that she can be. It is part of loving her sacrificially.[1]

Perhaps you can think of some other ways this passage can be expressed in your marriage at the present time. It usually takes some talking together to discover the best way to apply the Scriptures in a marriage relationship. However, it's a discussion which can make a big difference in your life together.

FEBRUARY 4

*I have summoned you by name; you
are mine* (Isaiah 43:1).

There are times when being called by name can be one of the most
comforting experiences of the entire day. We look forward to
hearing someone call our name when we step off a plane after a long
trip or when we arrive home at the end of a hectic day. It's encouraging
to be known and recognized by another person by name. Each of us
has a need to feel that we are personally known, cared about, and called
by name. Of course, the tone of voice that accompanies the use of your
name can certainly make a difference. There were probably times when,
as a child, your parents' tone of voice when they called your name told
you trouble was on the way!

It's difficult for some of us to comprehend that God in all His
majesty, power, and might would know us by name. How could He
be so personally aware of each one of us and love us? And yet He does.
One of the great preachers of years ago, Charles Haddon Spurgeon,
wrote of this fact: "He who counts the stars, and calls them by their
names, is in no danger of forgetting His own children. He knows [you]
as thoroughly as if you were the only creature He ever made, or the
only saint He ever loved."[2]

Even when you come home and no one is there to greet you, God is
always calling you by your name. He wants you to grasp the message
that you don't belong to anyone else, nor do you belong to yourself.
You are His. You do belong, and that's one of the reasons why you are
special. There is great comfort in knowing that we belong.

How frequently do you and your spouse call each other by name
in a way or tone which conveys the depth of the love and regard you
have for each other? Each time you address your partner, remember
that you are talking to someone that God has claimed and told, "You
are very special." That thought may help you to respond in a more
positive manner.

FEBRUARY 5

He has made us accepted in the Beloved
(Ephesians 1:6, NKJV).

Your loan application has been accepted and approved."
"Your application for school has been received, and you have been accepted to attend."

"I asked her to marry me and she accepted! I'm so excited!"

Acceptance—such a simple word. But we put so much emphasis upon it. And who wouldn't, considering the alternative: rejection? Remember the rejections you experienced as you were growing up? We have all been on the receiving end of rejection. Many adults are still seeking the acceptance of their parents. They say, "Oh, if only Dad or Mom would approve of me."

There are husbands and wives today who are still seeking the acceptance of their partner, and thus they live in a continual atmosphere of rejection. Rejection in marriage happens in small, subtle ways as well as the blatant visible responses. Ask your partner these questions: When have you felt rejected by me? Is there something I do that I may not even be aware of which makes you feel rejected? What do you do when you feel rejected? Discussing these questions may be the basis for a new understanding in your marriage.

Even though the potential for rejection follows us throughout our lifetime, there is comfort in knowing that as children of God we are always acceptable to Him. He says, "Never will I leave you; never will I forsake you" (Hebrews 13:5).

Jesus Christ definitely knows the sting of rejection. Your feelings are no surprise to Him. John recorded, "He came to His own, and His own did not receive Him" (1:11, NKJV). Jeremiah 31:3 reads, "The Lord appeared to us in the past, saying: 'I have loved you with an everlasting love.'"

Because of God's unconditional acceptance, we can learn how to open our lives and risk giving our partner greater acceptance regardless of the past. And when you accept one another, you feel free to become all that God has for you.[3]

FEBRUARY 6

*It is not good for the man to be alone. I will make
a helper suitable for him* (Genesis 2:18).

God's design for marriage involves the equality of a man and a woman, learning to live in intimacy, and then discovering and living the specific roles He has given to us. The first woman was created to respond to the first man. He was the initiator, she was the responder. However, Adam was also designed to meet Eve's need for strength and love. A husband and wife need each other. This is what God's Word teaches: "Woman is not independent of man, nor is man independent of woman" (1 Corinthians 11:11). When God talks about "a helper suitable" for Adam, *suitable* actually denotes equality and adequacy.

Many individuals have reacted against God's original design. As a result, a blurring of roles has occurred along with a resistance among men and women to being either an initiator or a responder. In marriage, both assume those roles.

Have you ever wondered what it was like for Adam and Eve in the garden? Have you ever wondered what they did all day, how they spoke, or how they worked out the roles God assigned to them? They had the ideal balance of the roles which we struggle with so much today. Adam initiated his interaction with Eve, not abusively, patronizingly, or as a tyrant snapping out orders; but rather in a strong, yet loving manner. He was confident, yet gentle. In return, Eve was competent and willing without holding a grudge or feeling resentful.

Sin marred the relationship and created an imbalance. The power struggle which exists today in many marriages reflects the destructive residue of the fall of man. But because of Jesus Christ, God's gift to us, we can not only be restored to Him, but also live restored and redeemed lives in our marriages.

FEBRUARY 7

*I will give you a new heart and put a
new spirit in you* (Ezekiel 36:26).

Imagine you are living between 1900 and 1930. You open a news-paper and read that doctors are going to take the living heart from one person and transplant it into another. Would you believe it? Probably not. It's still difficult to fathom such a thing today, and yet human heart transplants are quite common.

But you know, everybody alive today needs a heart transplant because we were all born with a sinful nature. We have a problem with our hearts. The prophet Jeremiah said, "The heart is deceitful above all things and beyond cure" (17:9). We have no hope of curing the sinful heart by our own efforts.

The deceitful human heart manifests itself in our marriage relationship from time to time. We all exist with a diseased heart and desperately need a transplant. Fortunately, God promised to give us a new heart and a new spirit. June Hunt describes it this way:

> Slowly, after this divine transplant, healing begins and, as promised, your new heart becomes capable of perfect love. Your self-centeredness is now Christ-centeredness. There is healing to replace the hatred; there is a balm for the bitterness. You can face the world with a freedom and a future you have never known before.
>
> "Create in me a clean heart, O God, and renew a steadfast spirit within me" (Psalm 51:10). Once you have a changed heart, you have a changed life. You can love the unlovable, be kind to the unkind, and forgive the unforgivable. All this because you have a new heart—you have God's heart![4]

The operation is simple. It's painless. It's free. All you must do is accept it. It's a wonderful gift.

FEBRUARY 8

The husband should give to his wife her conjugal rights—
goodwill, kindness and what is due her as his wife; and
likewise the wife to her husband (1 Corinthians 7:3, AMP).

Lord, I know what sex is—
   It is body and spirit, it is passion and tenderness,
It is strong embrace and gentle hand-holding,
It is open nakedness and hidden mystery,
It is joyful tears on honeymoon faces, and
It is tears on wrinkled faces at a golden wedding anniversary.

> Sex is a quiet look across the room, a love note on a pillow, a
>   rose laid on a breakfast plate, laughter in the night.
> Sex is life—not all of life—but wrapped up in the meaning
>   of life.
> Help me to see that I can be sensual and pure, happy and holy,
>   sexual and spiritual.
> Thank you, O Redeemer, for letting me express love through
>   sex.
> Thank you for making it possible for things to be right with
>   sex—that there can be beauty and wonder between
>   woman and man.
> Thank you, Lord, for a love that stays when the bed is made.
> Help me to keep my marriage bed undefiled—
> To see it as an altar of grace and pleasure.
> Thank you, Lord, for making me a sexual being.
> Thank you for showing me how to treat others with trust and
>   love.
> Thank you for letting me talk to you about sex.
> Thank you that I feel free to say:
> "Thank God for sex!"[5]

FEBRUARY 9

Most assuredly, I say to you, whoever commits sin
is a slave of sin....Therefore, if the Son makes you
free, you shall be free indeed (John 8:34,36, NKJV).

The words of our Lord are the foundation for our status, our security, and our strength. That's quite a gift. But like so many gifts, it must be received and then made a part of our lives.

What is your status at this particular time in your life? When you reached 18, you became an adult. That was a new level of status for you. When you married, your status changed again. Similarly, your status changed when you invited Jesus into your life. You became a justified, forgiven person, accepted by God. The guilt you carried was taken away. You are no longer condemned; you are free. As you consider your freedom in Christ, relinquishing the plaguing thoughts of your life can become a reality. You can become a free person in your thought life!

Remember: Jesus Christ is within you. You are now His possession. When you focus on that fact, fear and worry begin to loosen their hold upon you. Remember Jesus' words when you are feeling the bondage of insecurity: "Surely I am with you always" (Matthew 28:20). Speak those words aloud several times a day. They're true.

There is another reason for your sense of freedom: the strength of Jesus Christ. He can give you power to counteract your negative thoughts and to face the issues of your life. How? Being free comes from thinking the truths that Jesus shares with us in His teaching, and claiming His power each day. Perhaps when you pray together as a couple you can say, "Lord, thank You for the status, security, and strength You give us. We claim Your power in our lives to guide our thoughts and actions. We believe in You and Your Word. Thank You."[6]

FEBRUARY 10

Through love be servants of one another
(Galatians 5:13, RSVB).

D id you grow up in a home with servants? Probably not; few of us did. But imagine that you received a phone call, and the voice on the other end told you that you were being assigned a person who would be your servant. The servant would be available to you for the remainder of your life. How would you feel? How would you like this person to serve you?

Can you imagine having a lifetime servant? You should be able to, because it's already happened. It started the day you shared your wedding vows with one another. The calling to be married is the calling to be a servant to one another. Does that surprise you?

The word *servant* comes from the Greek word meaning *slave*. The word reflects a person who is not at his own disposal, but is the property of the person who owns him. Our first priority as a servant is in our relationship to our Lord. We are to be at His disposal at all times; He has a work for us to do. As He modeled servanthood at the Last Supper by washing the disciples' feet, He asks us also to reach out and minister in very practical ways to other believers. This includes your partner.

Difficult? Yes, at times. Degrading? It shouldn't be. Embarrassing? No. Demanded of us by our partner? Definitely not! A spouse is never to demand this response from his or her partner. It is each person's own decision to respond in this loving way. In fact, humanly speaking, it's difficult—sometimes impossible. That's why we need the presence of the Holy Spirit in our lives. You and your partner are students in the school of love and servanthood. The instructor and motivating power in your life is the Holy Spirit. The attitude of servanthood is something to be developed.

Think of three ways you could serve your partner today. Share your ideas with each other and see if your partner agrees. Discover the joy of serving one another and others.

FEBRUARY 11

So whether you eat or drink or whatever you may do,
do it all for the glory of God (1 Corinthians 10:31).

Two corporate executives were sitting and talking in a conference room. One of them was very persistent in his questioning of the other. He kept saying again and again, "But, why are you doing what you are doing?" Finally, in exasperation the second man said, "What are you looking for with that question? Why do you keep asking it?" The first man replied, "I'm just trying to determine who really benefits by what you are doing. That's all."

That's a good question—who does benefit? Have you ever asked yourself, "Why am I doing all that I do?" Why do we, as a married couple, do all that we do? What's the purpose? Who benefits?

Paul's words speak to us about our motives for what we do. Many of us behave in a way that reflects a Christian lifestyle, but have inner motives which are not consistent with the actions. Often we respond out of fear or desire for recognition. Paul is calling each one of us to look at what we do and to be sure it is being done for the glory of God. There are no limitations to this call. The way you decorate the house, the selection of new furniture, the way you interact with your neighbors, the way you drive and respond to inconsiderate drivers, how you handle rude clerks in the store all fall under the category of living to bring glory to God. Paul is saying, "Do *everything* to His glory."

But what about your marriage? What do you do as a couple for the glory of God? What about your daily communication pattern, sexual relationship, fulfillment of each other's emotional needs, and the quality of your spiritual relationship? What a wonderful opportunity you have to draw other people to Jesus Christ through your marriage! Share with each other how you think your marriage is bringing glory to God.

February 12

*Consider it pure joy, my brothers, whenever
you face trials of many kinds* (James 1:2).

The words *joy* and *rejoice* are used 14 times in Paul's letter to the Philippians, more than in any other of Paul's writings. When Paul talked about joy, he was describing a settled state of mind characterized by peace. Joy is an attitude that views the world with all of its ups and downs and insecurities in the confidence which is rooted in faith.

Joy is more than a mood or an emotion. For Paul, it was an understanding of existence which encompasses both elation and depression. Joy is an attitude that can accept events which bring either delight or dismay. How? By allowing us to look beyond any upset or crisis to see our Lord. Then we realize that He is with us in every situation. Joy is a matter of learning to take our problems and the crises of life in stride and to use even painful circumstances to bring glory to God.

When James instructed us to consider trials a joy, he was challenging us to adopt the attitude which would allow the negative circumstances of life to affect us positively. In other words, you have a choice. He is saying, "Make up your mind to regard adversity as something to welcome or be glad about." Joy is a decisive action, not a passive surrender to circumstances.

You will confront upsets during your married life which have the potential to devastate you or even destroy your marriage. But by walking in the Spirit and allowing the Spirit to have His way in your life, joy can be the result. This doesn't mean that you deny or ignore hurt and grief. But eventually this sense of joy takes root in your life, and you are able to say, "Yes, there is pain and hurt, but the sense of gladness called joy is there as well." Thank God for that!

FEBRUARY 13

*Therefore, as we have opportunity, let us do good
to all people, especially to those who belong to
the family of believers* (Galatians 6:10).

I would sure like to avoid the middleman. I could save a lot of money."

Perhaps you've made a statement like that. But being in the middle is not always something to be avoided. In fact, you are a person in the middle whether you realize it or not. As Christians, we stand between God and others as those privileged to give to people around us what God has given us. In Paul's instruction in Galatians 6:10, we are told to share God's goodness with others as He has shared it with us. Goodness is really reflected by doing good to others. It involves being generous with everything including time, interests, strengths, money, and even energy. Paul instructed Titus, "Remind the people…to be ready to do whatever is good" (3:1).

Often marriage ends up being a contract. We are willing to be good to our partner when he or she is good to us. But if he or she doesn't perform to our expectations, we withhold our goodness. Perhaps there are times when your partner doesn't deserve what you give to him or her, but why should that surprise you? None of us are deserving of what God has given to us. It is only by His grace that we receive His goodness. True goodness means giving without taking into account what the receiver deserves.

W. Phillip Keller suggests that if we have goodness in our hearts, we are called to "help the downtrodden, bind up the broken hearts, set prisoners free, lift the fallen, feed the hungry, comfort the confused, bring the 'oil of joy' to those who mourn, spread light and cheer where there is darkness, share the good news of God's gracious love to the lost."[7]

How could you and your partner fulfill this calling to other people? Identify some people who need you to share God's goodness. Then make your plans. Allow the Spirit to enable you to express the fruit of goodness.[8]

FEBRUARY 14

Now it is required that those who have been given
a trust must prove faithful (1 Corinthians 4:2).

Faithfulness can only be accomplished by God's grace and by walking in the Spirit. It means maintaining your priorities, keeping appointments, returning things when you say you will, keeping promises, completing assignments, and maintaining fidelity in your marriage relationship.

Fidelity is a calling which includes every person who marries. Fidelity, however, is more than just reserving your sexual drive for your partner. Fidelity is a calling to faithfulness in every area of your married life. It is being faithful in developing friendship in marriage. It is being faithful to see your partner as a child of God, a joint heir, and to treat him or her accordingly.

Remember the phrase in the old wedding ceremony, "I pledge thee my troth"? *Troth* is an old English word which reflects a pledge to be true, faithful, loyal, and honest. Troth also means trust, reliability, and integrity in marriage. That's fidelity. Fidelity means putting forth the energy it takes to make a marriage work. It means never neglecting the little things in marriage which are important to your partner. This is what you promised at the altar when you pledged your troth.

Fidelity in marriage means protecting your relationship by not becoming over-involved in work, TV, hobbies, children, or even church. Fidelity means not allowing anything to drain away the time and energy which rightfully belong to the marriage relationship.

Fidelity is a positive quality which is based upon God's faithfulness to His people. God was faithful to Israel regardless of their unfaithfulness to Him. God's fidelity was a commitment for the good of His people and their development. It was meant to be a blessing. Fidelity is a blessing for you and your marriage as well!

FEBRUARY 15

How long, O Lord, must I call for help, but
you do not listen?...Why do you make me
look at injustice? (Habakkuk 1:2,3).

"Why?" The age-old question which comes from our lips to voice our confusion. The prophet Habakkuk cried it aloud. Job asked the question 16 times during his trials. The sudden shock of adversity opens the door of questioning within us. We ask why in an attempt to make sense of something which seems senseless to us. Do you hear the questions? Do you hear them calling from the hearts of husbands and wives, fathers and mothers?

"Why was our son born mentally handicapped?"

"Why did our child end up dying in the hospital? The surgery was such a simple procedure."

"Why did my partner die at such a young age?"

"Why did our house have to be the one hit by a tornado?"

What are the "why" questions in your life? What "why" questions do you think your partner struggles with? You may not receive an answer to all your "why" questions immediately. Perhaps some of them won't be answered in this lifetime. But it's perfectly all right for us to ask those questions again and again. And it is all right not to have an answer. Why? Because there probably isn't a logical answer which would satisfy you anyway. Even if God were to give you an answer right now, would you accept it? Probably not. Waiting without an answer gives us an opportunity to learn to live by faith. Perhaps that doesn't ease the hurt, but it does help us discover some benefits to the struggle. None of us can ever know all the answers anyway. God doesn't always explain Himself. And that's all right too. Paul said, "Oh, the depth of the riches of the wisdom and knowledge of God! How unsearchable are his judgments, and his paths beyond tracing out!" (Romans 11:33).

Eventually you will come to the place where you won't need to ask God why. Habakkuk did. Read his response to his "why" questions in Habakkuk 3:17-19. It could help you.

FEBRUARY 16

A joyful heart makes a cheerful face, but when the heart is sad, the spirit is broken....A cheerful heart has a continual feast (Proverbs 15:13,15, NASB).

Think about the couples you know. How many of them are serious-looking most of the time? How many of them always seem to be wearing contagious, cheerful smiles? A ready laugh, a warm smile, a mischievous twinkle in the eye, the ability to laugh at oneself, the desire to see the humor in the seriousness of life—all of these are qualities which build a marriage. When was the last time you really laughed together as a couple?

Laughter has a healing quality to it. People have recovered from serious diseases by learning to laugh each day. As people endure experiences of loss and grief in life, there will be times when laughter comes in as a welcome respite from the heaviness of their losses. A home where laughter is forbidden or absent is the breeding ground for depression, physical illness, and a critical spirit. There is much in life to laugh about. You may have to look for it, but it's there.

The writer of the book of Proverbs keeps talking about the cheerful heart. In Proverbs 17:22 he declares, "A cheerful heart is good medicine, but a crushed spirit dries up the bones." Good medicine actually refers to a cause of healing.

You can lighten your load in life and draw others to you by learning to have a cheerful heart. When you begin to laugh at life and at yourself you will gain a new perspective on your struggles. You begin to see a speck of light at the end of the tunnel. Perhaps laughter can begin today in your relationship with some pleasant words, a friendly smile, and the question for each other at the end of the day, "What was something worth laughing about in your life today?" Think about it, talk about it, then laugh about it. And have a joyful heart!

FEBRUARY 17

*For we all stumble in many ways. If any one does not
stumble in what he says, he is a perfect man, able to
bridle the whole body as well* (James 3:2, NASB).

How embarrassing! You are strolling casually along a level path
when suddenly—for no apparent reason—you stumble. You
quickly glance around to see if anyone is watching, and you can tell
by their silent smiles that they did indeed observe your momentary
clumsiness.

Many times when people laugh in those situations, they are not
really laughing at you. They are embarrassed because they know how
you feel; it has happened to them also. We all have stumbled at one
time or another.

But there is another kind of stumbling which is even worse than
tripping on the sidewalk. It has to do with a different kind of walking—
our Christian walk. As Christians, we know what the Word of God says,
and we have committed ourselves to follow it. But often we stumble,
and we violate the teachings of God. We do just the opposite of what
we are committed to doing. We don't want to get angry, yet we lose
our temper. We commit ourselves not to gossip, but we gossip anyway.
We vow to always be patient, kind, and understanding with our spouse,
then we slip up. It really doesn't matter what silent resolution we have
violated, once it happens, we're guilty. James said, "For whoever keeps
the whole law and yet stumbles at just one point is guilty of breaking
all of it" (James 2:10).

When your partner stumbles as a believer, how do you respond? Are
you quick to help him or her recover? Or do you let him or her just wallow
around for a while and try to get back up without your help? God's Word
says: "The steps of a man are established by the Lord; and He delights in
his way. When he falls, he shall not be hurled headlong; because the Lord
is the One who holds his hand" (Psalm 37:23,24, NASB).

Let God help you recover from your stumbling. And be ready at
all times to lend a forgiving, helping hand to your partner when he or
she stumbles.[9]

FEBRUARY 18

Therefore encourage one another and build each other
up, just as in fact you are doing (1 Thessalonians 5:11).

Do you know what the word *encourage* means? It's simple. It means to give courage to another person. It also means to inspire with courage, give spirit or hope, spur on, or stimulate. In Hebrew the idea is to put strength into someone's hands, arms, or body so he or she can handle pressure.

Where does encouragement come from? It begins with a heart of love and caring, and it is shared through words, attitudes, and actions. Someone has said, "Words that encourage are inspired by love and directed toward fear." We have a choice in what we say to people. Discouraging words cripple, but encouraging words inspire. Proverbs 12:18 (NASB) states, "There is one who speaks rashly like the thrusts of a sword, but the tongue of the wise brings healing."

How do you want to be encouraged? How does your partner want to be encouraged? Have you ever talked about it? Encouraging your partner is the process of believing in him or her, and there are many different ways of expressing this: "You are really capable"; "Just give it your best shot. I know you will do well!"; "Go ahead, do it at your pace and not mine. It's all right for us to operate at different speeds."

Pointing out your partner's abilities and strengths can build his or her esteem, self-confidence, and feelings of worth. Focus on your partner's value in God's eyes.

You can also encourage your partner by looking for and affirming the positive side of his or her liabilities. It's better to be potential-oriented than mistake-oriented. As you look for undeveloped potential in your partner, you are playing the role of a talent scout.

In what ways do you encourage your spouse? What will you do about it today?

FEBRUARY 19

*Carry each other's burdens, and in this way you
will fulfill the law of Christ* (Galatians 6:2).

There is a term which is often used among Christians today—*burden.*
Years ago it was associated more with animals than with people. The
phrase "a beast of burden" referred to a mule or horse used to carry a
heavy load. For the Christian, burden-bearing is a reflection of walking
in the Spirit and serving one another in love. Perhaps one of the most
important and most difficult arenas in which to be consistent in this
quality is in daily interaction of marriage.

Galatians 6:2 tells us to share our loads with one another. In marriage, as well as in other relationships, we are to carry each other's
burdens and get involved in each other's difficulties. As you read
on, you'll find that burden-bearing means going even further. We're
to help and support others to the extent of restoring them when they
fail in some way.

Think about sharing burdens with your partner by discussing the
following questions together:

- What are some burdens you can help your partner carry? How
  would your partner like you to assist him or her?

- What burden would you like some assistance with? What would
  be the best way for your partner to assist you?

As you help one another, remember:

- Helping does not always mean giving advice; many times it
  simply means listening!

- When helping with each other's burdens, avoid saying "I told you
  so."

- Watch out for the attitude of superiority. Burden-bearing should
  be carried out with gentleness, remembering that you've had
  similar problems and made mistakes.

Every load is easier to carry when both of you help.

FEBRUARY 20

Since we have been justified through faith, we have peace
with God through our Lord Jesus Christ (Romans 5:1).

Many couples remember back to the excitement of their courtship days and how special they felt because of the individual attention and high regard they received from their partner. Sometimes this high regard tends to fade the longer a couple is married. Some people have said, "The more you get to know your partner, the more they seem to fall out of your favor." This doesn't have to happen, however.

Contrary to how you often view your partner, God looks upon you with favor! Fortunately, God's favor is consistent! Consider this description of the peace and favor that you enjoy with God which Paul describes in Romans 8:

> Therefore, there is now no condemnation for those who are in Christ Jesus....The Spirit himself testifies with our spirit that we are God's children. Now if we are children, then we are heirs....And we know that in all things God works for the good of those who love him....Those he justified, he also glorified....If God is for us, who can be against us?...Who will bring any charge against those whom God has chosen?... Who shall separate us from the love of Christ?...For I am convinced that neither death nor life, neither angels nor demons, neither the present nor the future...will be able to separate us from the love of God that is in Christ Jesus our Lord (vv. 1,16,17,28,30,31,33,35,38,39).

What would happen if you said to your partner, "Let me share with you a description of the peace you have with God," and then read these verses to him or her? Regardless of what happens in your life, you can be constantly content because God favors you. May you always look upon your spouse with the favor he or she enjoys in God's eyes.

FEBRUARY 21

So in everything, do to others what you would
have them do to you, for this sums up the
Law and the Prophets (Matthew 7:12).

The very thought of living out the Golden Rule in marriage strikes terror in the hearts of many. As one person said, "If I were to do that, everyone else would control me and take advantage of me." But is that really true? No, just the opposite occurs. If we wait around for our partner to make the first move, and respond after we've seen what he or she has done, we're allowing that person to dictate our action and our response.

Jesus gave us a very simple truth. He said, "Go ahead, take the initiative, and treat others the way you want to be treated." Is this passage in practice in your marriage today? Can you think of at least three occasions from the past week when you lived out the Golden Rule in your marriage?

The Golden Rule applies to both major and minor responses in your daily interaction with your partner, such as

- serving your spouse a cup of coffee or a piece of cake;
- picking up an item for your spouse at a store which is a bit out of the way;
- turning down the volume on the TV when your partner is on the phone without being asked;
- helping to dress the children when your partner is running late;
- not turning on the lights or noisily dropping coins on the dresser when you come to bed late.

These are examples of simple daily responses in living out the Golden Rule in God's Word. But there is one more element—attitude. These responses work best when we do them humbly, not drawing attention to what we've done, even if our partner doesn't reciprocate.

FEBRUARY 22

In the true spirit of humility (lowliness of mind)
let each regard the others as better than and
superior to himself (Philippians 2:3, AMP).

Who's in charge here? Who's in control of this project?"
These questions are asked thousands of times each day, especially in business and industry. However, they are rarely asked or even discussed in the marital relationship, and yet they should be. The issue of control is one of the major conflicts which can develop in a relationship. It usually surfaces in some kind of power struggle between partners.

If you've ever watched the interaction of puppies, you've probably noticed that power struggles are quite common. One puppy rises up to control and rule the rest of the pack. And if this puppy is taken from the litter first, another power struggle ensues until one puppy dominates. It's not very different from what we see occurring between humans. The desire to be in control and take charge of one's life has been evident in people since the Fall. Why is this? Why is the drive to be in control of everyone and everything so dominant in some people that their life is one pilgrimage after another for power?

Have you ever met a controller? Such a person must be right, must win, must be in charge, and must appear blameless. Ironically, gaining control doesn't satisfy the controller. He or she is usually unhappy, afraid of rejection, and unable to be intimate.

The pattern of controlling is counter to the scriptural pattern for marriage. The attitude needed in marriage is reflected in Matthew 20:26-28; 23:11; Mark 9:35; 10:43-45; Luke 9:48; 22:26,27. Read these passages aloud. What do they say to you about the husband and wife roles in marriage? How do these tie in to today's key verse above? All these passages reflect a way of life that Jesus says is better for individuals and couples. And He's right!

FEBRUARY 23

A faithful man shall abound with
blessings (Proverbs 28:20, AMP).

Imagine for a moment that your wedding to your partner is taking place today. If you were to rewrite your wedding vows now, what would you commit to and promise to do? Before you think of your own answers, consider these that other couples have written.

- "My commitment to you is to listen to your concerns each day for the purpose of having the kind of marriage we both want."

- "I realize that our love will change. I will work to maintain a high level of romance, courtship, and love in our relationship."

- "I pledge myself to confront problems when they arise and not retreat like a turtle into my shell."

- "I commit myself to you in times of joy and in times of problems. We will tackle and share our problems together."

- "I promise that I will never be too busy to look at the flowers with you."

- "I will respect your beliefs and capabilities which are different from mine and will not attempt to make you into a revised edition of me."

- "I will be open and honest with no secrets, and I desire you to be the same with me."

- "I will reflect the Word of God in my relationship with you."

Which of these would you select for your marriage? Take a few moments and write out some new and additional vows. Many couples do this each year as they celebrate their wedding anniversary. It adds a new dimension to the commitment of marriage. With all the interference and distractions we encounter each day, we need lots of reminders to make our marriage a priority for the glory of God.[10]

FEBRUARY 24

*The tongue is a fire....It is a restless evil and full of deadly
poison* (James 3:6,8, NASB); *There is one who speaks
rashly like the thrusts of a sword* (Proverbs 12:18, NASB).

What power! It can incite riots. It can sway a nation. It can destroy
a marriage that took more than 30 years to build. What is this
power-packed device? It is the tongue. Your tongue is a necessary part
of your anatomy, but it is also a potential danger. James calls it a fire.
Dr. Chuck Swindoll comments:

> Verbal cyanide. A lethal, relentless, flaming missile which
> assaults with hellish power, blistering and destroying at will.
> And yet it doesn't look anything like the brutal beast it is.
> Neatly hidden behind ivory palace gates, its movements are an
> intriguing study of coordination. It can curl itself either into
> a cheery whistle or manipulate a lazy, afternoon yawn. With
> no difficulty it can flick a husk of popcorn from between two
> jaw teeth or hold a thermometer just so.
> But watch out! Let your thumb get smashed with a
> hammer or your toe get clobbered on a chair and that slip-
> pery creature in your mouth will suddenly play the flip side
> of its nature.
> Not only is the tongue untamed, it's untamable. Meaning
> what? Meaning as long as you live it will never take control
> of itself.[11]

Words of healing, comfort, empathy, and enticing love go far to
maintain and build a marital relationship. Words of bitterness, caustic
putdowns, ridicule, and personal slurs leave their own unique mark
upon a marriage as well. You may need to edit your thoughts for a
few seconds before you express them in words. Kind words go further
than harsh, attacking words. Chuck Swindoll says it simply and consistently: "Make your words like that nationally advertised shampoo,
concentrated and richer."[12]

FEBRUARY 25

Come to me, all you who are weary and burdened,
and I will give you rest (Matthew 11:28).

It's one of the major plagues that can kill a marriage: weariness, exhaustion, fatigue. We give and give until we have nothing more to give physically, emotionally, or mentally. We're too tired to talk, let alone listen; too exhausted to make love or even think about it. Have you fallen victim to weariness in your marriage?

The Word of God talks much about this state of exhaustion and the many factors which can bring it about. Sometimes waiting is the reason for our weariness. The psalmist said, "I am weary with my crying; my throat is parched; my eyes fail while I wait for my God" (Psalm 69:3, NASB). Constant criticism or harassment by others can also induce weariness: "I am weary with my sighing; every night I make my bed swim, I dissolve my couch with my tears. My eye has wasted away with grief; it has become old because of all my adversaries" (Psalm 6:6,7, NASB).

Often, mental or emotional weariness is the cause of our physical weariness. We attempt to take on the worries of the world, thus overloading ourselves mentally or emotionally.

What's the answer to this problem? Part of the solution is being aware when your partner is weary. Listen when your partner needs to unload. Maybe you can shoulder some of the load. But the real answer is found in Scripture: "Come to me, all you who are weary and burdened, and I will give you rest. Take my yoke upon you and learn from me, for I am gentle and humble in heart, and you will find rest for your souls. For my yoke is easy and my burden is light" (Matthew 11:28-30). By spending time with our Lord in prayer and just resting in His presence, you can discover how He can refresh you. Let Jesus Christ be your source of strength. "Consider him…so that you will not grow weary and lose heart" (Hebrews 12:3).

FEBRUARY 26

Take my yoke upon you and learn from me, for
I am gentle and humble in heart, and you will
find rest for your souls (Matthew 11:29).

In the old days of training horses, some of them were ridden for hours until they gave in to the control of the rider. Gentleness was produced through force. But animals such as oxen were tamed by placing a young untrained animal in a yoke with a mature ox who became an example for the younger one. That is the picture today's Scripture provides of the gentle nature of Jesus. He doesn't ride us like a broncbuster to produce gentleness in us. Rather He teaches us gentleness by His example. Jesus was gentle, and we are expected to be gentle also. Paul said that our spiritual wardrobe should include a garment of gentleness: "Therefore, as God's chosen people, holy and dearly loved, clothe yourselves with compassion, kindness, humility, gentleness and patience" (Colossians 3:12).

How can gentleness be displayed in your marriage? One of the best ways is through your communication. Be gentle in the choice of your words. Gentle words are comforting, soothing, and encouraging. Be gentle in your tone of voice; its impact is far greater than your actual words. Harshness in your words can grate like coarse sandpaper.

Our conduct is another way in which we can reflect a gentle spirit. Paul said, "If someone is caught in a sin, you who are spiritual should restore him gently" (Galatians 6:1). Spouses sin against one another in many ways. Holding a grudge or putting down your mate is not a reflection of gentleness. Faults should be handled with gentle forgiveness and restoration. Our goal in marriage is to exercise gentleness toward our spouse. May gentleness be reflected in your marriage relationship![13]

FEBRUARY 27

How can a young man cleanse his way? By taking
heed according to Your word (Psalm 119:9, NKJV).

Do you remember playing hide and seek when you were a child? A lot of excitement was generated by trying to outsmart the person picked to catch you.

Some people are still accustomed to hiding from others, but it's no longer a game. They hide their Christian beliefs when they are with a group of non-Christians. They hide their abilities for fear they will be asked to perform. They hide who they really are from others because they are afraid other people won't like them. Many men have a tendency to hide their feelings because they never learned to share them as they were growing up. When we hide our feelings, patterns of deception and mistrust develop, especially in a marriage. Hiding as a game has its place. Hiding as an adult has no place in a relationship.

But what does this talk about hiding have to do with the Scripture passage about cleaning up one's life by obeying God's Word? Well, hiding some things in our lives creates problems which need to be cleansed. But Psalm 119:11 gives us a legitimate and healthy example of hiding, even as an adult. It reads, "Your word have I hidden in my heart, that I might not sin against You" (NKJV). If you want to hide something, this is it—God's Word! Hide it in your heart by memorizing it. Verses committed to memory have a way of popping into your mind just when you need them most. God's Word will be reflected in your marital interactions when it is hidden in your heart and mind.

What verses have you and your partner memorized in the last year? Why not select some—perhaps from the meditations in this book—and commit them to memory this week. This could be a breakthrough in your marriage. God's Word can help cleanse you from negative habits of hiding in your life. What do you have to lose?

FEBRUARY 28

*A soft answer turns away wrath, but harsh
words cause quarrels* (Proverbs 15:1, TLB).

Some marriages are characterized by the tranquility of a serene lake.
Others are much like the turbulent rapids which feed Niagara Falls;
the swirling whitecaps are always present. A marriage relationship
carries the potential for both calmness and turbulence.

Differences between spouses are inevitable in any marriage. Why
should anyone be surprised? When two people who have lived separate
lives for 20 or 30 years bring together their family backgrounds and
their own preferences, habits, metabolisms, values, and inner clocks,
what else would you expect!

But Proverbs 17:14 (TLB) gives the remedy for these inevitable
clashes: "It is hard to stop a quarrel once it starts, so don't let it begin."
It's one thing to disagree, but quite another thing to behave disagree-
ably. A quarrel is the verbal strife caused when our emotions take over
a disagreement and attack the other person instead of the problem.
When a quarrel is over, there is usually hurt or strain.

Learning to handle your spouse's different opinions, values, beliefs,
and behaviors can be done for the glory of God. That may be a new
concept to you, but it's possible. If it isn't possible, why does the Word
of God have so much to say about not quarreling?

Conflict—healthy, nonattacking, problem-solving conflict—can be
a constructive experience in marriage. It is an opportunity for you and
your spouse to learn a different perspective or a new way of doing something. When you disagree without quarrelling, you learn to listen under
pressure. This discipline has the potential for the growth of humility
in your life. As you consider all these potential benefits, disagreement
doesn't seem so bad, does it?

February 29

*Having been freed from sin and enslaved to God, you
derive your benefit, resulting in sanctification, and
the outcome, eternal life* (Romans 6:22, NASB).

The idea that all of us are slaves sounds a little far-fetched, doesn't it? The word slave sounds so demeaning and limiting. Many of us pride ourselves in our independence and freedom. But in reality, every husband or wife is a slave—hopefully not to his or her spouse, however! The word which is used in this passage actually means bond servant. At one time we were bond servants to sin; sin was our master. Because of our relationship with Christ, we are now bond servants to Him. This means obeying and serving Him with undivided loyalty.

How does the concept of being Christ's bond servants relate to a marriage relationship? Perhaps it means evaluating how you think about and respond to your partner in light of the question, "How does my Master, Jesus Christ, want me to think and behave?" It means living a righteous life in respect to your partner. It means doing what Jesus wants you to do in your marriage even when you feel like doing something else. Lloyd Ogilvie puts it like this:

> Through the Savior we are made right with God. That reconciliation sets us free to desire to live a righteous life. Our righteousness is bringing all of life into agreement with the Lord. It means adjusting the totality of our life to be an expression of His love, His commandments, and His will revealed to us in prayer and reading of the Scriptures....Our freedom grows when we dedicate all our intellectual, emotional, volitional, and physical energies to serve Him.[14]

How can you adjust the totality of your life to express righteousness in your marriage? What might you do different? Think about it. Pray about it. Commit yourself to it with the power He gives to you. You will like the results.

MARCH

*There must be no "if" clauses in our relationships
with others, no conditions attached to becoming
involved with them. There is one love which breaks
down all barriers—the love of Jesus Christ.*

MARCH 1

It is not good for the man to be alone....This is now bone
of my bones and flesh of my flesh (Genesis 2:18,23).

As part of His design for us, God allows us and even calls us to enter six different levels of intimacy with our partner.

Emotional intimacy brings you a feeling of closeness with and trust in your partner. You are able to share feelings and emotions without fear of reprisal or ridicule.

Social intimacy occurs between friends who share common activities and learn to work together. This level of intimacy grows out of accepting your personality differences and using them in a complementary way.

Sexual intimacy is achieved through learning your partner's likes and dislikes in lovemaking. It means learning his or her love language and how he or she likes to be romanced.

When you are intellectually intimate with someone, you share ideas in depth with each other. You value your partner's opinions, he or she values yours, and you can both accept your differences of opinion.

Recreational intimacy involves having fun together. You like to play together, and you discover many similar interests.

Perhaps the level of closeness that is lacking in many relationships is spiritual intimacy. This involves sharing your deep beliefs and being willing to talk about similarities and differences together. Worshiping together, sharing God's Word together, encouraging each other spiritually, and praying for one another are all part of this process.

Yes, it's a bit scary to be intimate with another person. But there is a safeguard which protects you as you open yourself up to your husband or wife. It's called God's love. Mike Mason writes: "The only thing which can shield a couple through the searing experience of self-revelation they are to undergo is God's love....Only love can drive out the constant threat of condemnation and rejection that otherwise haunts and spoils all experiences of intimacy."[1]

MARCH 2

Do not be afraid. Stand firm and you will see the
deliverance the Lord will bring you today (Exodus 14:13).

If you sometimes feel like a failure, join the rest of the human race. If you have failed, congratulations: you're human and normal. It's the fear of failure that can be the real problem. Fear immobilizes us, stalls us, cripples us, and bogs us down. The fear of failure is one of the main reasons why perfectionists tend to procrastinate!

God has some words to help us overcome the fear of failure. When Moses led the Israelites out of Egypt, Pharaoh's chariots, horsemen, and troops pursued them. When the Israelites saw the enemy coming they began complaining to Moses and blaming him for their plight. They said they would rather serve the Egyptians than die in the desert. They were ready to give up.

Sometimes couples get to the place where they are afraid to work on their marriage anymore. They think, "It's not going to do any good anyway," and that attitude keeps them from any attempts at enhancing and enriching their marriage.

Some of your attempts to improve your marriage may indeed fail. Some of your attempts to promote change may not work the way you want them to. But don't let that stop you from trying a new approach. For example, let's say that your partner is very quiet. You are frustrated with that and increase the pressure on him or her to open up. But even more silence occurs, and you throw up your hands in despair. Don't give up. Perhaps you can discover a new way to improve his or her communication. Don't let the fear of future failure rob your marriage of its potential.

The words of Moses, "Do not be afraid," should give you the encouragement to keep trying in your relationship. Ask God for wisdom. Read books on the subject area you're concerned about. Share with each other where you might be frustrated and how you want your marriage to grow. And then share your concerns together in prayer. That can be the breakthrough.

MARCH 3

And this I pray, that your love may abound yet
more and more (Philippians 1:9, AMP).

Is the word *abound* in your love vocabulary? Abound comes from the Latin word meaning to overflow like the breaking waves of the sea. When you stand by the ocean and see a wave begin to build, you know what the outcome will be. There is no way in the world to hold that wave back. When the wave finally crests and crashes, the water and spray permeate everything around it. That's the way your love for your partner is to flow. Humanly speaking, it is sometimes difficult for us to let our love abound. Selfishness often restricts our love for our partners to a trickle instead of allowing it to flow like a flood. But when we are being led by the Spirit, the possibility for loving with abounding love unfolds.

Storge, one of several Greek words for love, depicts a sense of natural affection and belonging in a relationship. Marriage partners who find in each other the assurance of loyalty and emotional refuge experience storge love. Marriages flourish when storge love abounds.

Phileo, also translated love, is friendship love, one of the highest priorities in marriage. Phileo is a companionship type of love. It's the kind of love that communicates as friend to friend. It means you enjoy eating a meal together without reading the paper or watching television. It means you may even enjoy shopping together (occasionally!) just because you are together. Phileo describes the sheer enjoyment of being in one another's presence sharing your thoughts, feelings, and dreams.

Phileo is also a cooperation kind of love. It means you can sit down together and work out a new budget after the washer and dryer give out. If ever a love needed to abound between marriage partners today, it's friendship love.

Perhaps you could take a few minutes now and share with each other what friendship love means to you. And however you define it in your relationship, let it abound!

MARCH 4

Husbands ought to love their wives as their own bodies.
He who loves his wife loves himself (Ephesians 5:28).

Caring for a wife is a matter of cherishing her. It not only involves showing her that she is special, but shielding or protecting her from all types of harm. How can a husband manifest this quality? Here's an example.

A young couple planned to attend a church potluck. Although Mary wasn't really known as an outstanding cook, she still decided to bring a homemade custard pie to the potluck. She baked it, and as she and Sam drove to the dinner, her fear began to mount. They both could smell the charred crust and scorched custard.

When they arrived, Mary's pie was placed on the table along with the other food dishes. Before anyone came to the table, Mary sliced a small piece of the pie and asked her husband to sample it. The look of horror on his face confirmed her deepest fears. She was devastated. What would her friends think of her for bringing such a horrible-tasting pie to the potluck?

But before anyone came back to pick up dessert, Sam grabbed Mary's pie from the table and announced to the group that he was going to make a pig out of himself and eat Mary's pie by himself. He noted that there were plenty of other pies and cakes available, and after all, how often did he get his favorite dessert!

Mary later remarked, "Sam sat in a corner courageously eating the whole pie so no one else would be able to taste it and find out how bad it was." She went on to say how special this response was from her husband. It was confirmation that she had married a man who would be sensitive enough to rush in and protect her. His act of love was a sacrifice, but it was deeply appreciated.

When a wife is cherished and cared for, she is secure, safe, and free from fear. How is this quality expressed in your marriage?

MARCH 5

What causes fights and quarrels among you?
Don't they come from your desires that battle
within you? You want something but don't get
it.... You quarrel and fight (James 4:1,2).

According to these verses, our desires are a major source of quarrels in our relationships, including marriage. The word *desires* comes from a Greek word which we often translate *hedonism*. It is aptly reflected in the phrase, "I want what I want when I want it." When both partners in a marriage are operating by this selfish guideline, watch out!

Not all desires are bad or sinful, nor must their expression always lead to quarrels. They only become bad when we violate God's plan for us. For example, food is a gift from God, and our desire to eat is normal. But some people have made food their god. The sex drive is God's gift, and sex was designed by God for our pleasure. That's a fact! But it must be expressed within marriage to be in God's plan. However, even within marriage some people feed on films and books which distort His plan. Material possessions are also a blessing from God. But when they draw us away from God instead of becoming part of His plan for us, they are a problem.

The apostle James goes on to say, "You adulterous people, don't you know that friendship with the world is hatred toward God? Anyone who chooses to be a friend of the world becomes an enemy of God" (v. 4). James calls his readers adulterous people because of their friendship with the world. He is saying they were committing spiritual adultery by following their desires more than following God. When you have a love affair with the world, you are committing spiritual adultery! What do you think of that concept? Can a marriage relationship be more in sync with the world than with God? What happens to the relationship and each partner when husband and/or wife prefer friendship with the world? How can you guard your marriage against this danger? Talk about it.[2]

MARCH 6

"God opposes the proud but gives grace to the humble." Submit yourselves, then, to God. Resist the devil, and he will flee from you (James 4:6,7).

One of the main themes of the book of James is pride versus humility. That's a conflict that creates tension in many marriages today as well. In James 4:6-10 there are five exhortations designed to eliminate pride and encourage humility.

First, James tells us to submit ourselves to God. Bowing down to God is the first step to eliminating human pride.

Second, James tells us to resist Satan and "come near to God" (v. 8), which causes God to draw near to us. You don't have to be afraid of rejection from God. Unfortunately, many people wait until their lives or their marriage is a shambles before they draw near to God.

The third exhortation requires a change of the external: "Wash your hands, you sinners" (v. 8). Washing hands was an external sign of cleansing, a symbol of resisting Satan and of drawing near to God.

The fourth step involves an internal change: "Purify your hearts, you double-minded" (v. 8).

The last exhortation can be summed up in one word—repent: "Grieve, mourn and wail. Change your laughter to mourning and your joy to gloom" (v. 9). James is not talking about going around feeling guilty. He's talking about godly sorrow. When you realize that you have sinned, and are sorry for it *before* getting caught, you are repentant. That's godly sorrow, and it's the best way to avoid pride and develop humility. And the result: God will give you grace (v. 6). That's quite a promise. Think about it.[3]

MARCH 7

*Do not slander one another. Anyone who
speaks against his brother or judges him speaks
against the law and judges it* (James 4:11).

Slander involves words which may not be true but which can cut a reputation and even ruin a life just the same. Yes, slander happens in marriage relationships because of disbelief and misinformation. Have you felt the sting of a false yet slanderous statement?

Dr. Gene Getz comments on four passages from James which deal with our speech:

> James 1:19,20: As a Christian I should always listen carefully and objectively and get as many facts as possible before I draw conclusions. Furthermore, I should not speak out until I develop more objectivity by carefully thinking about what I've learned; and when I speak, it must not be motivated by quick-tempered anger that is vindictive.

> James 2:12,13: As a Christian I will be judged by God for the way I use my tongue. If I am not merciful, I will not be shown mercy. Practically speaking, this means I will be treated the way I treat others—even in this life. Critical people breed counter-criticism toward themselves.

> James 3:2: I will never be perfect in what I say. However, the degree to which I follow God's guidelines in what I say and the way I say it, reflects my level of spiritual maturity.

> James 3:9: If I praise God with my words and at the same time I am hurting and tearing down other Christians by what I say, I am in violation of the will of God.

Which of these statements would most help your marriage? [4]

MARCH 8

Brothers, do not slander one another....Who are
you to judge your neighbor? (James 4:11,12).

What harmony there would be in our homes if we didn't have such a problem with our tongues. But we're all guilty of uttering slander—false, damaging, judgmental statements about each other. Here are four good reasons why we should not slander.

1. *We are brothers and sisters in Christ.* We are to avoid speaking ill of other Christians even when their lifestyle is repulsive to us. Why? Because we are related to them in Christ. Rather, Paul said that we are to "be devoted to one another in brotherly love" (Romans 12:10).

2. *We are to be examples of love.* Even if others are slandering, we are to be examples of loving speech. You may experience pressure from others whose tongues are not under control. And you may be tempted to speak against the obvious faults of others. Perhaps family members, in-laws, church members, or even pastors have offended you in some way. It is so easy to lash back at them verbally. But slander is definitely not the will of God for His people.

3. *We are to submit to the Word of God.* When we slander others, we mock the Word of God. We may be obeying God's Word in other areas, but when we disobey it in regard to slander, we have shown disrespect for it instead of completely submitting to it.

4. *We are to humble ourselves before God as well as others.* Why did James write about slander right after the passage on pride (4:6-10)? Pride is often an inflated feeling covering feelings of insecurity. One way to build up ourselves is to tear down someone else with slander!

Is there someone in your life whom you are tempted to speak against slanderously? Have you ever been slandered? How did it feel? How did you handle it? How might a spouse slander his or her partner? Perhaps this discussion isn't the most enjoyable, but it can be productive!

MARCH 9

You ought to say, "If it is the Lord's will, we
will live and do this or that" (James 4:15).

Life is uncertain. We make our plans and dream our dreams, but they may not be the same plans that God has for us. And being a Christian is no guarantee that all will go as you want or that you will live to be 85! Many couples plan as if they know for certain that all will work out. And when it doesn't, they are crushed.

Using the phrase in our planning, "If it is the Lord's will," does not reflect a pessimistic fatalism. Instead, it recognizes the fact that life is uncertain and God is the only One who knows the future. None of us knows for certain what will happen tomorrow. You may lose your job tomorrow. One of you may be crippled or killed in an auto accident. Your plans for that extensive vacation to another country may be canceled because of a revolution there. That's the life and times in which we live.

So what is James saying to you as a couple? First, include God in all of your planning. Not only include Him, put Him first. Ask for His guidance.

Second, realize that all you have and are came from Him. He is the one to receive credit for what you do.

Third, if you are blessed with wealth, use it for the glory of God.

Now it's time to discuss. How can today's meditation change your life and perspective at the present time?[5]

MARCH 10

The Lord is my shepherd, I shall not
be in want (Psalm 23:1).

Before continuing with this meditation, read the remainder of Psalm 23 aloud together from your Bible.

One of the dangers in marriage is expecting too much from your partner. Some people marry looking to their spouse to provide all they have missed during their growing up years. This places an unrealistic burden upon the marriage. Your partner is not your shepherd. The Lord is, and His promise is that you shall lack nothing. When Jesus was here on earth He referred to Himself as a shepherd. He is called "the good shepherd" (John 10:11,14), "the Chief Shepherd" (1 Peter 5:4), and "that great Shepherd of the sheep" (Hebrews 13:20).

You've probably read Psalm 23 many times. When we read about walking through the valley of the shadow of death, we tend to apply it to the time of our physical death. But this valley has also been called the valley of deep gloom, representing those difficult experiences in life when it appears that there is no hope or solution. Sometimes we see how non-Christians live and the way everything seems to fall into place for them. We begin to doubt and question God. When crises come in the marriage relationship and the losses of life begin to hit us we wonder, "Where is God in all of this?" Psalm 23 assures us that He is with us. We don't have to fear.

Sometimes it's easier to trust in our own abilities or the resources society makes available. After all, we can see them and touch them. Trusting in the promises of God requires faith in something we can't see. And we want an answer right now, not tomorrow. The promise of the psalm is that there will be neither want nor fear for the couple who trusts in the Great Shepherd.

At what times of your life has this psalm meant the most to you? Which verse has the greatest meaning to you at this time in your life? Take a few minutes and share your answers with each other. When you finish, read the psalm aloud one more time.

MARCH 11

It is not good for the man to be alone (Genesis 2:18).

You and I were created for companionship. Friendship is a fulfilling part of our lives. We value friends as we grow up. We continue with fewer but closer friends throughout adulthood. Do you enjoy your mate's presence, thoughts, and communications? Do you enjoy working side by side with your spouse as a friend?

Friendship is part of God's intention for marriage. Hopefully your friendship as a couple started prior to your marriage. If your friendship matures during marriage, you will have the stability to weather the crises of change which will happen over the years.

Years ago Lois Wyse described marital friendship this way:

> Someone asked me to name the time
> Our friendship stopped and love began.
> Oh, my darling, that's the secret.
> Our friendship never stopped.[6]

Friendship is reciprocal. Both partners must invest time and energy in the relationship. Friendship is based upon trust which is built over much time and many experiences. A friend is one you can call upon to support you and stick by you. As you already know if you've been married for a while, your friend and lifelong partner does not always agree with you. And that's all right. Solomon said, "Faithful are the wounds of a friend, but the kisses of an enemy are deceitful" (Proverbs 27:6, NKJV). Your relationship can become deeper because of your discussions over differences. Out of mutual respect for one another, friends do not attempt to control or dominate each other.

Reflect together on the friendship you have in your marriage. And if you would like it to grow, talk about your plans to make growth a reality.

MARCH 12

The man and his wife were both naked, and
they felt no shame (Genesis 2:25).

Friendship and companionship in marriage has the potential for greater depth than in any other relationship, for in marriage there needs to be no covering of any kind. Still it takes time for trust to develop so you can fully reveal yourself. How is that trust developed? Perhaps it is best stated by Colleen and Lou Evans, Jr.:

> And what is a friend? Many things….A friend is someone you are comfortable with, someone whose company you prefer. A friend is someone you can count on—not only for support, but for honesty.
>
> A friend is one who believes in you,…someone with whom you can share your dreams. In fact, a real friend is a person you want to share all of life with—and the sharing doubles the fun.
>
> When you are hurting and you can share your struggle with a friend, it eases the pain. A friend offers you safety and trust….Whatever you say will never be used against you.
>
> A friend will laugh with you, but not at you….A friend will pray with you…and for you.
>
> My friend is one who hears my cry of pain, who senses my struggle, who shares my lows as well as my highs.[7]

Is this a description of your marriage now? If it isn't, what steps could you take to make it a reality? In what way could the presence of Jesus Christ help to make it a reality?

Don't wait for your partner to reach out to you in a gesture of friendship. Perhaps your taking the initial step will free your spouse to respond to you. Ask God at this time how He would like you to become more of a friend to your partner. Ask Him for the consistent strength and power to make it happen.

MARCH 13

As God's chosen people, holy and dearly loved, clothe
yourselves with...kindness (Colossians 3:12).

Have you ever met someone with a kindness thermostat? This kind of person only turns up the kindness when it's to his or her advantage. When others discover this tendency, they begin to think, "I wonder what he (or she) wants this time."

Kindness is reflected in many ways. We see it when a cup of cold water is offered in the name of Christ (Matthew 10:42). We see it when people consider others as more important than themselves (Philippians 2:3,4). We see it happening when someone shows kindness to the person who has caused offense. Kindness means being polite to the salesperson on the phone, even when the call has interrupted your dinner!

Kindness in marriage is one of the best places to discover whether we are really walking in the Spirit or not. The longer you're married, the easier it is to take one another for granted. We tend to ask, request, and demand more from our partner than we offer to help. Kindness may inconvenience us a bit. But that's one of the characteristics of kindness—it costs. Phillip Keller says: "Kindness is more than running a bluff on beleaguered people. It is more than pretending to be concerned by their condition. True kindness goes beyond the play acting of simulated sighs and crocodile tears. It is getting involved with the personal sorrows and strains of other lives to the point where it may well cost me pain—real pain—and some inconvenience."[8]

It certainly cost the Father and the Son something to extend their kindness to us. Begin to visualize each day how you will extend yourself in kindness to your partner in ways which will meet his or her needs. Don't be surprised if you begin to discover some real benefits to this lifestyle![9]

MARCH 14

*I...appeal to and beg you to walk (lead a life) worthy
of the [divine] calling...with behavior that is a credit
to the summons to God's service* (Ephesians 4:1, AMP).

You've probably received many calls in your life. You were called to
be married, called into a specific vocation, and as a believer you
have a spiritual calling as well. But if someone were to ask you to
describe your calling as a Christian, what would you say? Paul helps
you out in chapters 1–3 of Ephesians where he spells out the calling for
the believers at Ephesus. He said:

- They were chosen in Christ "before the creation of the world" (1:4).
- They were predestined to be adopted as God's children (1:5).
- In Jesus Christ they had redemption through His blood and the forgiveness of sins (1:7).
- They were guaranteed eternal life by the presence of the Holy Spirit in their lives (1:13,14).
- They had hope in Christ—a glorious inheritance (1:18).
- They had experienced the power that had raised Jesus from the dead (1:19,20).
- They were the recipients of God's incomparable grace which had saved them (2:8,9).
- As Gentiles they became one in Christ with Jewish believers (2:15,16).
- In Christ they had "access to the Father" (2:18).
- In Christ they had the potential to know the love of Christ (3:19).

That was their calling. That is your calling. That is your partner's
calling. To live a worthy life means to walk a certain path, to follow a
prescribed way designed and planned by Jesus Christ.[10] Do you know
what that way is? Scan Ephesians 4 sometime today. List what you find
and then talk about your findings as they apply to your marriage.

MARCH 15

*Be completely humble and gentle; be patient, bearing
with one another in love* (Ephesians 4:2).

What Paul asked the Ephesians to do in this verse was totally contrary to the self-centered pagan world of their day. It may even be a bit contrary to the way many of us live today.

If there was ever a foundational verse for a marriage relationship, this is it! Look at the same passage in the Amplified Bible. And as you read it, consider ways in which this would apply in your daily interaction together: "Living as becomes you—with complete lowliness of mind (humility) and meekness (unselfishness, gentleness, mildness), with patience, bearing with one another and making allowances because you love one another."

Lowliness does not mean developing low self-esteem or becoming a doormat. It means to have a true estimation of yourself, not thinking of yourself in either an inflated or deflated manner. It also means not looking down at other Christians because of their problems, position, or deficiencies. Perhaps the best way to describe biblical humility is with the words of Jesus after He had washed His disciples' feet following the Last Supper: "Now that I, your Lord and Teacher, have washed your feet, you also should wash one another's feet. I have set you an example that you should do as I have done for you" (John 13:14,15). Humility is most clearly seen in servanthood.

To be patient means not allowing yourself to become provoked by what others do or say. What a difference patience makes in marriage! Perhaps you have seen a puppy playing with an older dog. The puppy growls and nips, but the larger dog, who seemingly could devour him with one bite, just patiently endures. Patience accepts insult and even injury without becoming bitter and without complaining. It is an attitude which can express graciousness toward someone who is unpleasant. Patience is difficult to produce by yourself, but possible with Jesus Christ.

MARCH 16

So I tell you this, and insist on it in the Lord, that
you must no longer live as the Gentiles do, in the
futility of their thinking (Ephesians 4:17).

If you want to know what Paul means when he urges us to live a life worthy of our calling (Ephesians 4:1), look at what he tells us in 4:17-19. We are to turn our backs on our old way of life. Just as single people cannot take their single lifestyles into the marriage relationship, so believers cannot bring their lives of sin into the Christian life and walk. In verses 18 and 19 Paul described the people as darkened in their understanding and futile in their thinking. He didn't mince words. The original language implied that the people were vain, foolish, purposeless, and empty. Their goals were worthless. And it all started in the mind.

In verse 18 Paul makes reference to the hardening of their hearts. There is an important progression described here. In verse 19 he says, "They, having become callous, have given themselves over to sensuality, for the practice of every kind of impurity with greediness" (NASB). How does something like this happen?

First, we refuse to admit that we need to learn, and we resist spiritual truths. Then we become insensitive to spiritual truths. This issue is prevalent in a number of marriages. One partner continues to grow in his or her understanding and application of the Scriptures while the other resists. Soon there is distance between the couple spiritually. And it all starts in the mind or thought life.

This is the life we are called to leave—the life of futile, unspiritual thinking. Take a look at your life and your marriage. Is there any behavior which is more reflective of the old life than of the new life in Christ? What can you do to bring about change?

MARCH 17

*Lay aside the old self....Be renewed in the spirit of your
mind and put on the new self* (Ephesians 4:22-24, NASB).

One way to illustrate what Paul is saying in this verse is with the
example of shopping for clothes. When you go out to buy a new
outfit, chances are good that you won't select the first item you try
on. When you enter the dressing room, you take off the clothes you're
wearing and try on the new outfit. You may go through this process
several times before you are satisfied. But you don't mind the process
because it leads you to the outfit you really like.

In the Christian life we need to go shopping every day. Christian
growth is a daily process of taking off attitudes, beliefs, and behaviors which reflect the old lifestyle and putting on those which reflect
the presence of Christ in our lives. This passage teaches that the only
way any of us can progressively succeed in this daily process is by
being renewed in the spirit of our mind. The renewal described here
is basically an act of God's Spirit powerfully influencing man's spirit,
attitude, state of mind, and disposition with respect to God and spiritual truths.

What thoughts do you or your partner struggle with that reflect
more of the old self than the new self? Have you ever shared and prayed
about these together? One of the joys of marriage is to share your spiritual struggles together and encourage each other spiritually. Did you
know that two of the best ways to renew your heart and mind are
studying God's Word regularly and learning from a knowledgeable
teacher?

Where are you today in your spiritual understanding compared
with where you were one or two years ago? What are your plans for
growing together spiritually during this year? This discussion may be
the foundation of an interesting dinner conversation in a quiet setting.
It may also make for a great date!

MARCH 18

Be imitators of God, therefore, as dearly loved
children and live a life of love (Ephesians 5:1).

You order a new appliance for the home. You purchase a new car. Your boss installs a new computer for you. What do all of these items have in common? They all come with a set of instructions. That's the first item most people look for when they buy a new product—the operating instructions. Ephesians 4:25–5:2 contains the instructions we need in order to know how to walk worthy of our calling (Ephesians 4:1). These are instructions for living a life of love. Take a moment to read this passage aloud together.

Paul begins by identifying traits which reflect the former life. The first one is dishonesty. He said, "Therefore each of you must put off falsehood and speak truthfully to his neighbor, for we are all members of one body" (4:25). Honesty and truthfulness are characteristics of a true Christian. A marriage relationship must be built on truthfulness and trust. Sometimes a husband or wife fails to tell his or her partner about a personal problem until after it has done damage to the marriage. This erodes trust. Sometimes a partner withholds some information, causing the other partner to believe something other than the truth. This too erodes trust.

We also need to be truthful in the questions we ask our partner. "Honey, how do you like the new dress?" or "What did you think of the job I did in the garage?" are loaded questions. Does your partner have the freedom to give you an honest answer? Questions shouldn't be asked unless you are willing to hear an honest response!

Remember that the main reason for being honest is that "we are members of one body." We belong to each other, and we are to help one another grow spiritually. Honesty helps this process happen. It's a better way to live.[11]

MARCH 19

Be angry, and yet do not sin; do not let the sun go
down on your anger (Ephesians 4:26, NASB).

Anger! It's an emotion that will occur in every marital relationship. It's normal. Some people experience it occasionally, others frequently. Some people are openly volatile and abusive while others are only passively aggressive.

Paul tells us to be angry but not to sin. How is this possible? The word used in this verse is the same one used to describe Jesus' anger at those who frowned on healing on the Sabbath (Mark 3:5). It means an abiding, settled attitude which is slowly aroused under certain conditions against evil and injustice. The purpose of anger is to cause us to do something about evil in the world. But like so many emotions, the way we express this emotion makes all the difference in how it is received by others. Stating, "I am really angry and upset over this situation, and here is what would help the problem," is healthier than a verbal attack on a partner.

Paul also says, "Do not let the sun go down on your anger." The word used for anger here means irritation, exasperation, or bitterness. When that kind of anger invades a relationship, damage occurs. And when it lingers, it gives Satan a foothold in the relationship (v. 27). A person whose life reflects an abundance of anger does not reflect a life worthy of God's calling!

What can you do about misdirected anger in your marriage? First, remember that most anger is caused either by hurt, fear, or frustration. Deal with the initial cause rather than expressing your anger. Next, look to the Word of God for guidance. Proverbs states, "He who is slow to anger has great understanding" (14:29, NASB). Nehemiah said, "When I heard their outcry and these charges, I was very angry. I pondered them in my mind and then accused the nobles and officials" (Nehemiah 5:6,7). Do you slow down enough to ponder the cause of your anger? It can make the difference. Talk with your partner right now about how you can help each other control your anger.

MARCH 20

He who has been stealing must steal no longer, but
must work....Do not let any unwholesome talk
come out of your mouths, but only what is helpful
for building others up (Ephesians 4:28,29).

When Paul wrote these words, stealing was a way of life in society. He countered this tendency with constructive guidelines for thieves who had become Christians. Perhaps you may feel that these words do not apply to your marriage. But think about this: Stealing is not limited to taking a tangible object. It could be the theft of time, energy, or attention which rightfully belongs to our partner. It's also easy to steal from God when it comes to time invested in His work and activities. The lack of tithing to His work has been labeled embezzling by many.

Unwholesome talk is certainly an issue today. Language that used to be banned from radio and television is now commonplace in the media. The unwholesome content of stories, jokes, and conversations today reflects our non-Christian society. Unwholesome talk is inappropriate for those who know Jesus Christ as Savior. It may cost you to keep your language pure, especially in the business community. Refusing to use profanity and to tell, listen to, or laugh at certain jokes and stories may make your coworkers uncomfortable around you. Profanity is a reflection of the content of one's thought life. Perhaps, then, your thought life is the place to begin work.

How can your words help to build up another person? How will other people be different because of what they hear you say or talk about? Discussing this as a couple may be enlightening for you.[12] Take a few minutes to discuss what you've read today.

MARCH 21

Do not grieve the Holy Spirit of God, with whom you
were sealed for the day of redemption. Get rid of all
bitterness, rage and anger (Ephesians 4:30,31).

In Ephesians 4 Paul gives several guidelines for the way we are to walk as Christians. Here are three more specific sins which are a reflection of the old self and which grieve the Holy Spirit: bitterness, rage, and anger. Take a minute right now to discuss together what each of these words mean to you. As you may already know, each person has his own inner dictionary based on personal experiences with these terms.

Bitterness is a disposition which often is expressed by a person with a tongue as sharp as a razor. Resentment is alive and well in this person, and it is often reflected in how he or she needles others. He or she is ready to fly off the handle very quickly with a response that bites or stings. You can imagine the result of that kind of response.

The Greeks defined bitterness as a long-standing resentment which refuses to be reconciled. Many people nurse their hurts and anger. In time the actual offense is blown out of proportion. These people have not yet learned forgiveness.

The anger described here is different from the anger we discussed in Ephesians 4:26 on March 19. There are six different Greek words for anger in the New Testament. The word used here describes a strong feeling of antagonism which is expressed in a strong physical or verbal outburst. This type of anger blazes up into a sudden explosion. It is similar to a match which quickly ignites and then burns out.

Can you imagine the effect upon a marriage or a family when rage and anger are present? Anger is bound to occur when you have two imperfect people living side by side. But the problems mentioned in Ephesians 4:30,31 are not conducive to a healthy marriage. Usually they are brought into the marriage as part of a person's psychological baggage.

What tendencies toward bitterness, rage, or anger did you bring into your marriage? Do you need to get rid of some of this baggage? Your marriage will benefit from such a step.

MARCH 22

*Do not grieve the Holy Spirit of God, with whom
you were sealed for the day of redemption. Get
rid of all...brawling and slander, along with
every form of malice* (Ephesians 4:30,31).

In this passage Paul mentions three more negative characteristics
which must be evicted from Christian individuals and marriages:
brawling, slander, and malice.

Brawling is the violent, abusive, negative verbal outburst directed
at another person by someone who has completely lost his cool. There
seems to be a correlation between the volume and the destructiveness of
the words. Some people attribute this kind of verbal abusiveness to their
family background. They blow up because that is how their parents
handled interpersonal conflict. That may be, but here are two questions
to consider about verbal brawling: What does it accomplish in a positive
way? Is it in keeping with the Word of God? What we have learned in
our original family can be unlearned, and a new pattern can be learned.
The Scriptures, rather than our family, should be our guide.

Have you ever been slandered? It hurts; it cuts. It's hard to defend
against. Results can linger for years even when the slanderous statement was false. Slander is abusive talk against another person or against
God. Lawsuits are filed daily in our country by people who have been
slandered. Before we believe or say anything against someone, especially our spouse, we must verify it with the person in question.

Malice is a strong word. It reflects our motives or intent. It has
been defined as the evil inclination of the mind or the perversity of the
disposition that finds pleasure in hurting another person. The phrase,
"You hurt me, and I will make you pay for it," is malicious and has no
place in a marriage, no matter how bad the offense may have been.

Are any of these still residing in your marriage? Let them go, give
them up, and replace them with the response found in Ephesians
4:32.

MARCH 23

Be kind and compassionate to one another, forgiving each other, just as in Christ God forgave you (Ephesians 4:32).

In this verse Paul gives us a pattern for living which will cement relationships rather than divide them. Kindness is actually goodness of heart, in contrast to the malice discussed in verse 31. When a kind person hears something negative about another person, his or her first response is compassion instead of the desire to share the account with others. He or she verifies the information first and then attempts to help. Think of six to ten ways you could express kindness in your relationships with others around you, especially with your partner.

The participants in one large adult class were asked to write how they saw themselves putting Ephesians 4:32 into practice in their family life during the coming week. After a few minutes one woman stood up and shared a profound, life-changing response which touched a nerve in everyone: "This week I will speak to my family members as kindly as I speak to people outside the home." Frequently we are more polite, sensitive, and courteous to strangers or acquaintances than we are to our family members. In fact, we often wouldn't get away with speaking to others outside the home the way we speak to our family. The greatest opportunity we have to walk worthy of our calling (Ephesians 4:1) is within the family.

To have compassion means to be tenderhearted. Your acts of kindness come from your compassion (see also Colossians 3:12 and 1 Peter 3:8). Compassion reflects a deep feeling of concern for others.

Spend a few minutes talking about kindness and compassion. Ask your partner: "How can I express kindness to you in a way which will help you?"; "In what ways could I become a more compassionate person?" Listen to what your spouse has to say, and then thank him or her for the suggestions.

MARCH 24

Be kind and compassionate to one another, forgiving each other, just as in Christ God forgave you (Ephesians 4:32).

You've heard about forgiveness before, but look again at this passage. How are we to forgive? "Just as in Christ God forgave us"! What does this mean? Quite simply it means to forgive just as freely, generously, wholeheartedly, spontaneously, and eagerly as God has forgiven us. We haven't been spit upon; Jesus was. Yet He forgave. We haven't worn a crown of thorns; Jesus did. Yet He forgave. We have not been crucified; Jesus was. Yet He forgave. (See 1 Peter 2:21-25.)

Many marital partners cling to their hurts and nurse them instead of forgiving their spouse for offending them. Not to forgive means we allow resentment and bitterness to gain a foothold in our lives. Unforgiveness can be compared to destructive termites which slowly and steadily feast their way through the inner structure of a house. By the time their work reaches the surface, the destruction is often irreversible. So it is bitterness and unforgiveness.

Lewis Smedes says about vengeance and forgiveness:

> Is it fair to be stuck to a painful past? Is it fair to be walloped again and again by the same old hurt? Vengeance is having a videotape planted in your soul that cannot be turned off. It plays the painful scene over and over again inside your mind. It hooks you into its instant replays. And each time it replays, you feel the clap of pain again. Is it fair?
>
> Forgiving turns off the videotape of pained memory. Forgiving sets you free. Forgiving is the only way to stop the circle of unfair pain turning in your memory.[13]

Forgiving means you no longer allow what has happened in the past to influence you. You are free. The person who hurt you is free. You are both free to love each other.

MARCH 25

Do not be afraid, for I am with you (Isaiah 43:5).

Fear! It makes us prisoners within ourselves. It makes life a chore. It disables and cripples our relationships with others. Fear saps our energy and interferes with our progress in life. Oh, it's true that some fears are useful, but many more are useless and debilitating. What about you? What are the fears in your life? What are your partner's fears? Do you know? Have you ever talked about them?

Let's take it one step further: Are there any fears that hinder the progress of your marriage? That's not a strange question, because many couples live with fear in the marriage relationship: the fear of trusting, the fear of rejection, and the fear of being embarrassed by a partner. The marriage relationship is supposed to offer the ultimate in closeness and security, but it is often torn by fears.

Like so many of the problems and struggles in life, fears are managed best when two people work together to confront them. The irony is that people seem to be driven by fear instead of drawn by hope. They allow the fears of life to control them and dictate their responses. Does any of this sound familiar? It may seem a bit risky to share some of your hidden fears with your partner, but he or she is there to comfort and support you. Listen to one another when fear strikes.

Christians are not exempt from fear. Fear even invades the lives of people of faith. The way to overcome our fears is to take them to God, pray together about them, confront them together, and go forward in spite of them. You will be afraid at times, but fortunately we don't have to abound in fear because "God did not give us a spirit of timidity [fear], but a spirit of power, of love and of self-discipline" (2 Timothy 1:7).

MARCH 26

Do not be afraid, for I am with you (Isaiah 43:5).

"How's your marriage?" one man asked another.

"Compared to what?" his friend answered.

"Compared to a year ago. Is it any different? Has there been any growth or change?"

That kind of a question borders on meddling!

So how's *your* marriage? Marriages do change in several ways. For some couples change is slow, and for others it is rapid and radical. For some change just happens, but in others the partners make it happen. They are willing to look at their marriage, evaluate its strengths and weaknesses, and make plans for change. It involves risk. It involves upsetting the comfortable status quo. But too much comfort and no change can lead to complacency and eventually to stagnation.

Risk—a word that strikes fear in the hearts of some people. It means exchanging a known for an unknown. It means moving from predictability to unpredictability. Risk-takers sometimes leave a sign around to remind them of the necessity of risk and change. The sign says, "Remember the turtle. It only makes progress when it sticks its neck out."

In what area in your marriage do you need to take some risks in order to effect a necessary change: communication, sex, dating, decision-making, dealing with in-laws? There may be some practical fears facing you right now—the fear of buying another house before your present home sells, the fear of leaving the security of a weekly salary to start your own business. Everyone can become a risk-taker. Talking about your fears of trying something new can alleviate some of them.

Confront your fear of risking with the confidence that comes from your relationship with Jesus Christ. The words "fear not" are stated in God's Word 366 times. Let them echo again and again in your mind: Fear not, fear not, fear not!

MARCH 27

And the Lord said to Moses, "I...am pleased with
you and I know you by name" (Exodus 33:17).

"I am pleased with you."

Some of us were fortunate to hear these words from our parents. Some of us heard them from teachers, friends, and other relatives. These words are very important in the marital relationship. They convey love. They convey acceptance. They counter the fear of rejection. They are healing words. The phrase, "I am pleased with you not just for what you do, but for who you are," can make your partner's day so much brighter! Words such as these are not spoken often enough between married couples. But they are spoken constantly to you by God our Heavenly Father. He tells you that you are worthy, competent, and of value. He tells you that you were bought with a price (1 Corinthians 6:19,20).

God knows you through and through. He knows your partner the same way. He knows each of us by name: "Before I formed you in the womb I knew you, before you were born I set you apart" (Jeremiah 1:5); "I am the good shepherd; I know my sheep and my sheep know me....I lay down my life for the sheep" (John 10:14,15).

J.I. Packer writes about what it means to be known by God:

> There is tremendous relief in knowing that His love to me is utterly realistic, based at every point on prior knowledge of the worst about me, so that no discovery now can disillusion Him about me....
>
> He wants me as His friend and desires to be my friend, and has given His son to die for me in order to realize this purpose.[14]

God is pleased with you. Tell your partner that God is pleased with him or her. Tell your partner that you too are pleased. It will make for a better day.[15]

MARCH 28

In Him you have been made complete
(Colossians 2:10, NASB).

Remember the TV miniseries *Roots* of many years ago? Perhaps you read the book by Alex Haley. It was a fascinating story of a black man searching for his roots and heritage. His journey took him back to Africa.

Many of us are interested in our genealogy. Doing a historical search of your partner's family and heritage can help you understand him or her in a new way. Looking at your own roots can help you also. But as Christians we enjoy an additional heritage. Our roots are found in the fact that we were created in the image of God. And God wants His work to be complete in us. Enjoy the following description of your heritage in Christ:

> This, then, is the wonder of the Christian message: that God is this kind of God; that He loves me with a love that is not turned off by my sins, my failures, my inadequacies, my insignificance. I am not a stranger in a terrifying universe. I am not an anomalous disease crawling on the face of an insignificant speck in the vast emptiness of space. I am not a nameless insect waiting to be crushed by an impersonal boot. I am not a miserable offender cowering under the glare of an angry deity. I am a man beloved by God Himself. I have touched the very heart of the universe, and have found His name to be love. And that love has reached me, not because I have merited God's favor, not because I have anything to boast about, but because of what He is, and because of what Christ has done for me in the Father's name. And I can believe this about God (and therefore about myself) because Christ has come from the Father, and has revealed by His teaching, by His life, by His death, by His very person that this is what God is like: He is "full of grace."[16]

MARCH 29

Do not be afraid. Stand firm…Be
still…Move on (Exodus 14:13-15).

We all need words of encouragement. Life is full of obstacles and sudden unpleasant surprises. Dr. Lloyd Ogilvie offers some practical advice from Exodus 14:13-15:

1. "Do not be afraid." Fear is usually the first reaction to our impossibility. Don't be afraid of fear. It reminds us we are alive, human. Like pain, it's a megaphone shout for God—a prelude to faith. The same channel of our emotions through which fear flows can be the riverbed for trust and loving obedience. Fear is only a hairbreadth away from faith. When we surrender our fear, telling God how we feel, we allow faith to force out fear.

2. "Stand firm." Stand your ground. Don't give in to your fear and run away. Face your fear, allow yourself time to calm down, and then see the fear from God's perspective.

3. "Be still." Sometimes we are so frantic and noisy with our fear that we override God's direction, God's peace, and God's presence in our lives. We can be helped by quietly listening for His voice to guide us.

4. "Move on." This is what God said. When confronted with something we fear, we can run from it and give it control over us. Or we can face it, move toward it, and eventually neutralize it. When we fail to move on, we procrastinate, and procrastination is not God's plan for us. Procrastination is fear that has forgotten the promises of God. It is our effort to make life stand still for a while when God has clearly instructed us to keep moving.[17]

Take a few minutes to discuss how these thoughts can help you in your marriage and parenting. But be sure you "move on."

MARCH 30

They...cried out in fear. But immediately Jesus
said to them, "Take courage! It is I. Don't
be afraid" (Matthew 14:26,27).

"Pay attention!" "Look at me!" "Give me your undivided attention!" These are common phrases which teachers, parents, and even spouses say to each other. Focusing your attention on a person helps you receive what that person has to offer. It keeps you from being distracted.

One of the greatest distractions in life is worry. The tendency to ask "what if?" again and again keeps us from resolving problems. What are some of your worries? One wife said that she was worried that she worried and worried that her husband would discover that she had the problem of worrying!

As Jesus walked on the water toward His disciples, He called Peter to climb out of the boat and walk to Him, which he did. Peter was doing just fine until he lost his focus and became distracted. He looked at the waves of the storm instead of keeping his eyes on Jesus. His fear rose and he began to sink.

Peter's situation has something to say to each of us. If he had kept his eyes upon Jesus, who was the source of his strength, Peter would have been all right. But his eyes strayed, and he was overwhelmed by the problem and crumbled.

Worry is like that. We concentrate too hard on the problem and forget the solution. This creates more difficulties. Some problems won't go away. Some concerns are legitimate. Sharing those concerns with Jesus and asking for His guidance will give us the ability to weather the storm.

Discuss together what tends to distract you from relying upon the Lord and how you could help each other trust God more. Listen to your partner. He or she may have a good idea.[18]

MARCH 31

Now to Him who is able to keep you from stumbling,
and to make you stand in the presence of His glory
blameless with great joy... (Jude 24, NASB).

Do you listen to the benediction at the end of the sermon? To many people it only signifies the conclusion of the worship service and the opportunity to get on with the rest of the day. What is a benediction? It literally means "good words." A benediction is a promise, a prayer, a good word to every person who hears it. Remember this: The minister is not the only person who can pronounce a benediction. You can be a living benediction to your partner!

One of the most commonly used benedictions from the Bible is Jude 24,25 (NASB): "Now to Him who is able to keep you from stumbling, and to make you stand in the presence of His glory blameless with great joy, to the only God our Savior, through Jesus Christ our Lord, be glory, majesty, dominion and authority, before all time and now and forever. Amen." This passage tells you what Jesus Christ does for you every day. He guards you, protects you, looks after you, and keeps you from stumbling. When you rely upon Him, you will not stumble.

These words also tell you what Jesus will do for you in the future. He will present you to God blameless with great joy. Tell your partner what this promise means to you and how it makes you feel! Today Christ keeps you from stumbling, and tomorrow you will be presented to God blameless. When we fail—and often we do—God keeps no record of it. God does not deal with us according to our sins (Psalm 103:10), but He accepts us in Christ. Because of the work of Jesus on the cross, you are accepted as blameless.

Perhaps one of your most important callings in marriage is to follow the model of Christ by being a living benediction to your partner. Help keep your mate from stumbling, and when he or she does fall, don't keep track of it. Scorekeeping isn't a part of marriage; however, forgiveness is.

APRIL

*Many athletes in training soon discover that
their commitment requires more discipline than
they bargained for. Isn't marriage the same?*

APRIL 1

Come to Me, all you who labor and are heavy
laden, and I will give you rest. Take My yoke
upon you and learn from Me,...and you will find
rest for your souls (Matthew 11:28,29, NKJV).

Burnout! Exhaustion! Working 70 hours a week for several months or struggling with the night shift of a newborn baby for weeks on end can be wearying. We begin to bend under the burden. But there are other burdens we place upon ourselves which are like yokes of slavery.

Those who are legalistic place yokes upon themselves as well as others. Critical parents or spouses abuse others and often themselves by the yoke of criticism. They don't know the meaning of the word affirmation. Striving to please other people is one of the yokes of slavery. Seeing your performance as the basis for your security is a yoke, as is looking to your appearance as the basis for your self-esteem. Holding unrealistic standards of behavior and achievement for your children or spouse is another slavery yoke.

Take a good look at your personal life. Do you feel free or burdened with a yoke? Look at your marriage. Do you feel free or burdened with a yoke? Look at your relationship with the Lord. Do you feel free or burdened with a yoke?

In Jesus' time, a training yoke was used to train a young oxen. The older, wiser, and stronger ox was matched with the younger one. The size of the yoke was different as well. The older ox shouldered more of the load and guided the younger one in making sure the furrows were straight. When you feel exhausted, remember the words of our Lord, "Take off that yoke. Come and join me in mine. Let me shoulder the burden. I will carry your weight." God helps us with the necessary burdens of life and assists us in throwing off the unnecessary yokes of slavery which we place upon ourselves.

APRIL 2

We do not dare to classify or compare ourselves with some who commend themselves. When they measure themselves by themselves...they are not wise (2 Corinthians 10:12).

Let's compare notes and see if we agree." That's a healthy way of sharing information and insights. But there are comparisons in life that are less than healthy. Unfair comparison occurs when you place one person beside another for the purpose of emphasizing their differences. This happens quite frequently in marriages: "Your mother sure cooks differently than my mom does"; "Your family really has some strange ideas"; "How come you don't hang up the towels in the bathroom the way I do?" The underlying message in these statements is, "You and your family are different; therefore, you and your family are wrong."

What kind of comparisons occur in your marriage? What behaviors, skills, or attitudes in one another do you judge as different (and therefore wrong)? How do you compare yourselves with other couples? Do you compare your clothes, home, car, where you live, or where you vacation with those of other people? If so, what does it accomplish? Two things can happen when you compare yourself with someone else. You may end up feeling proud or even self-righteous if you perceive others as inferior to you. Or if others fare better than you in the comparison, you could end up with an inferiority complex.

The message here is stop making comparisons. Someone always ends up feeling bad or acting defensive. Instead, try to focus on who you are and who your partner is in the sight of God. Try to realize that the reason everyone is different is because God made us that way. No wonder your partner is different from you! This is healthy! The only standard you have to be concerned about is measuring up to the plan God has for your life. The security that comes from being in God's plan can eliminate the need for any other comparisons.[1]

APRIL 3

Pursue love (1 Corinthians 14:1, NKJV).

One of the most overused, misunderstood, and misused words in the English language is the word love. You may love your work, love your dog, love to eat, and love your spouse. But hopefully love means something different to you in each of these settings! When Paul instructs us to "pursue love" he implies a strenuous activity. Let's consider two words which are used in the Bible to help us understand the kind of love God wants couples to pursue.

Did you know that the first word used to describe marital love is not translated love in the Bible? The word is *epithumia*, which refers to a strong desire of any kind. It means to set your heart on something. You can set your heart on a bigger house, a flashier car, or a better job. Some desires are good, others are not. Whenever epithumia is used in the Bible in a negative way it is translated lust. But in a marriage relationship it refers to the strong physical desire a husband and wife have for one another. We must flee lust, but we are free to strongly desire our husband or wife. Have you thanked God for the desire He has placed within you for your partner?

Your God-given epithumia for your partner may be stronger at some times than at other times. Perhaps you are like many husbands and wives who must learn to channel their own desires in order to synchronize with their partner's desires.

Another word for love is *eros*. Eros describes someone who is strongly affected by sexual desire. Eros can be controlled and positive, as in a marriage relationship, or uncontrolled and negative, as in an extramarital affair. The word is not used in the New Testament, but its Hebrew counterpart is found in the Old Testament. When you finish this meditation, turn to the Song of Solomon and read some of its passages to one another. Many married couples have experienced enjoyable moments pursuing the beauty of erotic love in this book from the Word of God.

APRIL 4

If you faint in the day of adversity,
your strength is small (Proverbs 24:10, RSVB).

This is a quiz. Which do you prefer, prosperity or adversity? Easy question. Let's try a difficult one. Which condition is easier to handle or live with? You may be surprised at the answer. Chuck Swindoll responds this way:

> Adversity is a good test of our resiliency, our ability to cope, to stand back up, to recover from misfortune. Adversity is a painful pedagogue.
>
> On the other side is prosperity. In all honesty, it's a tougher test than adversity. The Scottish essayist and historian, Thomas Carlyle, agreed when he said: "Adversity is sometimes hard upon a man; but for one man who can stand prosperity, there are a hundred that will stand adversity."
>
> Precious few are those who can live in the lap of luxury…who can keep their moral, spiritual, and financial equilibrium…while balancing on the elevated tightrope of success. It's ironic that most of us can handle a sudden demotion much better than a sizable promotion.[2]

During prosperity we tend to forget about being dependent upon God. But when we are plunged into the depths of adversity, there is only one thought on our mind: survival! And we tend to pull together with those around us.

When prosperity hits, all too often integrity seems to erode. If you are experiencing prosperity, whom do you thank for it? How can it be used to glorify God?

What will adversity do to your marriage? Better talk about it now, for adversity hits all of us at one time or another. In adversity, you need resilience. But in prosperity, you will need integrity. With these vital qualities, you can make it through both situations.[3]

APRIL 5

*Love endures long and is patient and kind; love
never is envious nor boils over with jealousy; is
not boastful or vainglorious, does not display
itself haughtily* (1 Corinthians 13:4, AMP).

How would you define a loving relationship, the kind of love which should be the foundation of marriage? Which of the following definitions do you like best? Why?

A loving relationship is one in which individuals trust each other enough to become vulnerable, secure that the other person won't take advantage. It neither exploits nor takes the other for granted. It involves much communication, much sharing, and much tenderness.

A loving relationship is one in which one can be open and honest with another without the fear of being judged. It's being secure in the knowledge that you are each other's best friend and no matter what happens you will stand by one another.

A loving relationship is one in which the individuals involved grow in their understanding and acceptance of each other's differences and encourage each person to reach out and share as much beauty and love as possible.

A loving relationship is one which offers comfort in the silent presence of another with whom you know, through words or body language, you share mutual trust, honesty, admiration, devotion, and the thrill of being together.

A loving relationship is one in which the loved one is free to be himself—to laugh with me, but never at me; to cry with me, but never because of me; to love life, to love himself, to love being loved. Such a relationship is based upon freedom and can never form in a jealous heart.[4]

APRIL 6

So then let us pursue the things which make for peace and
the building up of one another (Romans 14:19, NASB).

D r. Ed Wheat has an excellent suggestion for marriage. He says that
one of the ways to keep your marriage alive is to bless your spouse.
But what in the world is a blessing? The word in the New Testament
is based on two Greek words translated *well* and *word*. Blessing your
spouse literally means to speak well of him or her. You can speak well
of your partner to others, and you can speak well *to* him or her through
compliments, words of encouragement, and the small courtesies of life
which tend to fade after the days of courtship. Blessing your partner
also involves edifying or building up as Romans 14:19 states.

How is this done? Dr. Wheat has a number of suggestions. Which
of these are presently true of your relationship? Which ones need to
be implemented?

> 1. Make a decision to never again be critical of your
> partner in thought, word or deed. This should be a decision
> backed up by action until it becomes a habit that you would
> not change even if you could.

> 2. Spend time studying your spouse so you develop a sen-
> sitivity to the areas in which the person feels a lack. Discover
> creative ways to build your spouse up in those weak areas.

> 3. Spend time thinking daily of positive qualities and
> behavior patterns you admire and appreciate in your spouse.
> Make a list and thank God for these.

> 4. Consistently verbalize praise and appreciation, and do
> this in a specific and generous manner.

> 5. Recognize what your spouse does, but also who your
> spouse is. Let him or her know that you respect them for what
> they accomplish.[5]

APRIL 7

For where your treasure is, there your
heart will be also (Matthew 6:21).

The book of Ecclesiastes causes questions for some people and confusion for others. Some wonder why it's even in the Bible. In his helpful book *The Rhythm of Life,* Richard Exley suggests that Ecclesiastes reflects the thoughts of a workaholic who was coming to the end of his life. It's the portrayal of a man who had invested his life in work rather than relationships and then discovers—too late—the futility of a life lived for things rather than people.

The man's success at work is obvious, for he says, "I became greater by far than anyone in Jerusalem before me" (Ecclesiastes 2:9). But he didn't find any pleasure in that life: "I hated life, because the work that is done under the sun was grievous to me. All of it is meaningless, a chasing after the wind" (2:17). Have you ever felt that way about what you do? Have you ever caught yourself wondering, "Isn't there more to life than this?"

At the end of his life, this man discovered that he had no significant person in his life to whom he could leave his accumulated wealth. How tragic. Yes, he had children, but they were like strangers to him because he had failed to cultivate a relationship with them.

Are you living the kind of life that will give you fulfillment at its end? In what are you investing your time and energies?[6] Fulfillment in marriage at retirement occurs only through fulfillment during the seasons of marriage beforehand. Dr. James Dobson says: "I have concluded that the accumulation of wealth, even if I could achieve it, is an insufficient reason for living....I will consider my earthly existence to have been wasted unless I can recall a loving family, a consistent investment in the lives of people, and an earnest attempt to serve the God who made me. Nothing else makes much sense."[7]

APRIL 8

I saw God face to face, and yet my life
was spared (Genesis 32:30).

"What did you get out of the worship service?"
That's an interesting question. Have you ever asked your partner that question after a service? It assumes that we go to worship in order to get something out of it. But is that the purpose of worship? Webster's Dictionary doesn't think so. Worship means reverence to God. Worship means acknowledging God for who He is and recognizing Him. The focus of worship is not supposed to be on us, but on God! When Simeon took the baby Jesus in his arms, he worshiped God by saying, "Sovereign Lord, as you have promised, you now dismiss your servant in peace. For my eyes have seen your salvation" (Luke 2:29,30). His worship focus was God, not himself.

Jacob's claim of seeing God face to face is really the core of worship. We can attend church but not worship. We can sing the hymns but not worship. Our thoughts may be on the dinner cooking at home or on whether the children are behaving in children's church. Our eyes may be looking at a friend's new outfit or at the crack in the sanctuary ceiling. In worship our spiritual eyes and our physical eyes should be directed at God.

Worship can occur at church or at home. It's encountering God face to face as you focus upon Him. It can be done in prayer, thoughts, or even as you listen to a praise song.

Think for a moment about the significant times in your spiritual life. When did you experience significant moments of worship in which you knew you encountered God? Does your partner know about them? Would he or she be able to describe them for another person from what you have told him or her?

Talk about worship in your personal and marital life. How can you help your partner worship? Share your concept of God with each other. Yes, it may be a new thought for him or her. Yet focusing on God can not only enrich your life, but your marriage as well. Now, there's a radical thought!

April 9

Therefore each of you must put off falsehood and speak truthfully to his neighbor (Ephesians 4:25).

You've been called into court to testify in a trial. As you take your place in front of the courtroom, you are asked, "Do you swear to tell the truth, the whole truth, and nothing but the truth, so help you God?" When you answer yes, you are giving your vow or pledge of truth. If you break that pledge in a court of law you are committing perjury, which itself is a crime!

People of truth are such an endangered species today that the credibility gap has become a sad hallmark of our generation. But there is no place for a credibility gap in marriage. Trust can only occur when you can depend upon your partner's word in the small things as well as the large. Think about these common, everyday promises which are often forgotten instead of carried through:

"Sure, I'll pick up the dry cleaning on the way home."

"Okay, I'll clean the garage on Saturday, right after I get home from golf."

"All right, we'll sit down and talk sometime this week."

Continual violations of even small promises like these generate mistrust. This mistrust can cause such doubt in your partner's word that you may feel you must constantly remind and nag him or her to follow through. And in time your partner develops a deaf ear!

What does God have to say about the credibility gap? "And whatever you do, whether in word or deed, do it all in the name of the Lord Jesus" (Colossians 3:17); "It is better not to vow than to make a vow and not fulfill it" (Ecclesiastes 5:5). How can you apply these passages in your marriage? It takes genuine integrity! What better place to see this happen in your marriage than by following through with the small, seemingly insignificant promises you make to each other each day. Build a backlog of trustworthy responses that your partner can depend upon.

APRIL 10

Blessed is the man who does not walk in
the counsel of the wicked....His delight is
in the law of the Lord (Psalm 1:1,2).

Before continuing with this meditation, read the remainder of Psalm 1 aloud together from your Bible.

The Book of Psalms is the oldest hymnbook of the church. The psalms actually reflect the music of the heart of man. Whatever spiritual mood you may be experiencing, you will find it expressed verbally within the Psalms.

Psalm 1 has a message of guidance for each person today. It presents a clear distinction between two kinds of people: the righteous and the wicked. The first and last words of this psalm reveal the ultimate destiny of each group. The righteous are "blessed" (v. 1) and the wicked "perish" (v. 6).

In verses 1-3 you find a description of the righteous person. The righteous person does not seek or follow the advice of those who live a lifestyle which is counter to the Word of God. Nor does he spend time with these people. When a person ignores the guidance of these verses, the impact of associating with the ungodly often seeps into a marriage relationship. It may not be apparent at first, but soon attitudes and eventually behaviors begin to change and a spiritual erosion takes place.

The godly use the Word of God as their guide for life, and they meditate upon it. The heart of meditation is studying and reflecting upon the meaning of Scripture and how it applies to our lives. God's Word is to be our guide for life; we're not to replace it with the opinions of talk show hosts, the Wall Street Journal , trendy self-help books, or the advice of our coworkers in the office.

What are the results of focusing your life and marriage on the Word of God? Like a tree planted by streams of waters, you will be strengthened and refreshed each day. It's a guaranteed benefit available to you!

What about you? Whom do you spend time with and listen to? Talk about how the two main categories in Psalm 1—the righteous and the wicked—influence your life and your marriage.

APRIL 11

You have collected all my tears and preserved
them in your bottle! You have recorded every
one in your book (Psalm 56:8, TLB).

Did you know that God notices your tears? He created you with the capacity to weep, knowing that crying is a major part of the healing process for your body. Some people cry silently and inwardly; they stifle their tears. Others are more fortunate and can let the tears flow. Charles Swindoll tells us, "A teardrop on earth summons the King of Heaven. Rather than being ashamed or disappointed, the Lord takes note of our inner friction when hard times are oiled by tears. He turns these situations into moments of tenderness: He never forgets those crises in our lives where tears were shed."[8]

Tears can express many feelings. There are tears of joy and happiness, tears of heartache and sorrow, and tears of frustration and anger. Tears often communicate your feelings to a spouse in a way words cannot.

What prompts you to tears? Perhaps it's the joy of a newborn baby. The singing of a much-loved hymn may bring back a flood of memories. Some people cry when they pray. Others cry when the memory of a loved one comes to mind. Do you consider tears an enemy rather than a friend?

When was the last time you cried in front of your partner? Did your partner know why you were crying? When do you feel like crying but fight to hold back the flow? When have you cried together as a couple? How do you want your partner to respond to you when you cry?

Jesus wept. So did David when he lost his son Absalom. In other words, strong people weep as well as weak people. It is a sign of strength and wholeness to cry over something that deeply moves you. Don't apologize for your tears. After all, why apologize for a wonderful gift from God? Your tears are an important part of your communication. Let them flow.

APRIL 12

And he [Peter] went outside and
wept bitterly (Luke 22:62).

Max Lucado is one of the most gifted Christian writers of our time. In the excerpt below he talks about some of the often overlooked attendants at the cross when Christ died.

There was one group in attendance that day whose role was critical. They didn't speak much, but they were there. Few noticed them, but that's not surprising. Their very nature is so silent they are often overlooked. In fact, the gospel writers scarcely gave them a reference. But we know they were there. They had to be. They had a job to do.

Yes, this representation did much more than witness the divine drama; they expressed it. They captured it. They displayed the despair of Peter; they betrayed the guilt of Pilate and unveiled the anguish of Judas. They transmitted John's confusion and translated Mary's compassion.

Their prime role, however, was with that of the Messiah. With utter delicacy and tenderness, they offered relief to His pain and expression to His yearning.

Who am I describing? You may be surprised.

Tears. Those tiny drops of humanity. Those round, wet balls of fluid that tumble from our eyes, creep down our cheeks, and splash on the floor of our hearts. They were there that day. They are always present at such times. They should be, that's their job. They are miniature messengers; on call 24 hours a day to substitute for crippled words. They drip, drop, and pour from the corner of our souls, carrying with them the deepest emotions we possess. They tumble down our faces with announcements that range from the most blissful joy to darkest despair.

The principle is simple; when words are most empty, tears are most apt.[9]

APRIL 13

*We pray this in order that you may live a life
worthy of the Lord…being strengthened with all
power…so that you may have great endurance
and patience* (Colossians 1:10,11).

Have you ever watched a small child plant and tend his first garden? Each day he runs to the spot where the seeds were planted and looks to see if they've broken ground. He soon learns that there is nothing he can do to hurry up the seeds. He is beginning to learn the patience exercised by the professional farmer who knows not to harvest his crops too soon or they won't be ripe. An impatient farmer will be a poor farmer!

Impatiently pushing or hurrying your spouse can prove just as costly in a relationship. Learning to patiently adjust to your partner's pace will build your marriage relationship.

Patience helps us persevere. James wrote, "Brothers, as an example of patience in the face of suffering, take the prophets who spoke in the name of the Lord" (5:10). Isaiah and Jeremiah were persecuted for their stand, yet they patiently endured the pressure and continued to speak God's Word. Jesus' life was filled with obstacles, yet He also persevered patiently.

Patience helps us persist. But what is the difference between perseverance and persistence? Perseverance seems to imply enduring and waiting even when it is difficult. Persistence suggests a bulldog-like tenacity and grip that helps us carry out what God wants us to do.

Are you patient in this way with yourself? with your partner? There are some practical ways to show patience with one another. For example, give your spouse the time he or she needs to think of an answer to a question. Explain yourself again if he or she needs it, even though you may think you are perfectly clear. Gently remind, instead of being critical, when your partner forgets. This is true patience, and it only comes when we are walking in the Spirit.

APRIL 14

Brace up your minds; be sober....Do not conform
yourselves to the evil desires (that governed you)....Be
holy in all your conduct (1 Peter 1:13-15, AMP).

Warning! This substance is dangerous to your health. Defects and breakdowns can occur with continued use." Sound familiar? We often find warnings on certain product labels about possibly dangerous side effects.

In the passage above, Peter warns us about three problems which can create defects and breakdowns in our moral and spiritual lives. Can you find the three warnings in this passage?

The first is a warning to strengthen your thought life. "Brace up your minds" means to exert mental activity. Each Christian is called to put out of his or her mind anything that would hinder progress in the Christian life. There are times when our thoughts about our partner can hinder the development and progress of our Christian life. Can you think of any thoughts that need to be evicted from your mind?

The second warning is to "be sober." When you are sober, you are alert, responsible, in charge of all of your senses, and able to make good, rational decisions.

The last warning is to not let yourself be conformed to a non-Christian lifestyle. It's really easy to become distracted by the values and concerns of our society. It takes a person with strength of character and integrity to say no to the lifestyle of non-Christians.

Peter calls us to be holy because of the hope we have of glory with Jesus Christ. In this translation, it's called "divine favor" (v. 13). Perhaps you and your partner can talk about what being holy means to each of you. God wouldn't ask us to be holy if it wasn't possible.

APRIL 15

The Lord gave and the Lord has taken away; may
the name of the Lord be praised (Job 1:21).

Did you worship today? No matter what day of the week it is, you can worship God. Worship doesn't stop when we leave the church sanctuary. What happens there can assist us to worship wherever we are.

We meet God in worship through times of joy and celebration. Many couples have told me that the birth of their child was a worship experience. They rejoiced in God's creation. They shared that special moment with Him. That's worship.

The difficult experiences of life can be opportunities of worship as well. As we go through the various seasons of life we discover that joy can come from loss and pain as much as from pleasurable experiences. God is there both in the happy occasions and in times of crisis. Richard Exley writes:

> I am not suggesting that God sends adversity to enhance our appreciation of life or to make us more aware of His nearness. Nor am I implying that the fullness of life comes only to those who have passed through deep waters. Rather, I am saying that God is present in all of life, including its tragedies. His presence transforms even these agonizing experiences into opportunities for worship....
>
> We don't worship God because of our losses, but in spite of them. We don't praise Him for the tragedies, but in them.[10]

Even when we don't feel His presence, God is there. Perhaps this thought may help you today, next month, or three years from now. Allow the promise of God's nearness to lead you to worship Him in tough times as well as good times.

APRIL 16

If any of you lacks wisdom, he should ask God,
who gives generously to all without finding
fault, and it will be given to him (James 1:5).

"You can't make it without it. It just won't work. You've got to have it!"
A hyped-up television commercial? No, just some words of wisdom
about wisdom. Wisdom is essential if you are going to make it in life
and marriage.

In today's passage wisdom means having full knowledge or broad
intelligence. And it wasn't only James who emphasized our need for
wisdom. Solomon prayed, "Give your servant a discerning heart to
govern your people and to distinguish between right and wrong"
(1 Kings 3:8,9). Also, read what Paul said about wisdom in Ephesians
1:17-19, Colossians 1:9-12, and Philippians 1:9-11. In the last passage,
Paul defines wisdom as depth of insight and the ability to discern what
is best.

How do you recognize wisdom in action? Look at what James says
in 3:13: "Who is wise and understanding among you? Let him show
it by his good life, by deeds done in the humility that comes from
wisdom." Humility and wisdom go together, and the two of them must
work in tandem to produce the kind of good deeds which will nurture
a marriage relationship.

The wisdom James talks about comes from God. He amplifies his
description in 3:17: "The wisdom that comes from heaven is first of
all pure; then peace-loving, considerate, submissive, full of mercy and
good fruit, impartial and sincere." True wisdom will be reflected in
behaviors which are talked about all through the Word of God. The
wisdom that God gives us enables us to live according to His will, and
it comes out of our heart. Above all, wisdom reflects the character of
God and the lifestyle He has for us.

Aren't there times when you wish you had more wisdom? Perhaps
you're facing that challenge right now. What are the characteristics of
wisdom in your life at this time? in your marriage?[11]

APRIL 17

*If any of you lacks wisdom, he should ask God....But
when he asks, he must believe and not doubt, because
he who doubts is like a wave of the sea* (James 1:5,6).

Wisdom is evidenced in your life by behaviors and attitudes which reflect God's character. All of us can have the wisdom described by James. But how do you get it? You ask for it. Yes, ask for it with a strong belief that your request will be answered. James gives us a very realistic illustration of the doubter. He is not talking about someone who occasionally doubts, but about the person who has a lifestyle of wavering, someone who is as unsettled about following God as a storm-tossed wave. When you have a settled confidence in God, you can ask for wisdom and receive it.

How do you get wisdom? You also get it through the Scriptures. The Bible is God's revealed truth and wisdom. How frequently do you read the Scriptures as an individual? as a couple? Most of us struggle with being consistent in this area at some time in our lives. The more you read, the more wisdom you receive and the more your life changes. Consider this: If you read aloud the same chapter from the Word of God every morning and evening for one month, that chapter will be yours for life! Try it. What do you have to lose?

How do you get wisdom? You also get it through other mature and growing Christians. We cannot exist in isolation from one another. The body of Christ is a source of wisdom.

How do you get wisdom? Life's experiences also provide lessons which cause us to grow in wisdom—that is, if we let them. What have you learned from others and from life? Share this with your spouse.

APRIL 18

*The brother in humble circumstances ought to take
pride in his high position. But the one who is rich
should take pride in his low position, because he
will pass away like a wild flower* (James 1:9,10).

Isn't this an interesting verse! It seems like a contradiction, but it's not.
Think about this: Who are the exceptions in the world—the rich or
the poor? Perhaps in America we think it's the poor—but is it? There
have always been more poor people in the world than rich people—in
Jesus' day and in ours. And when the people in the first century became
Christians, they soon discovered that inviting Jesus Christ into their
lives did not necessarily solve all their economic problems. Often the
poor remained poor.

You need to be wary of those who teach that faith in Jesus Christ
automatically results in economic blessings which will turn you into a
wealthy person. Even many supposedly prosperous upperand middle-
class Christians today don't really own what they possess. Someone
else actually owns their homes and cars, and they simply make the
payments.

James said, "You may not have a lot of money, and you may live
in poverty, but you do have a high position in Jesus Christ." How? If
you know Jesus Christ, you are a child of the King. You're an heir of
God and co-heir with Christ (Romans 8:17). That's the source of true
wealth.

James is telling us not to be intimidated by those with money, and
not to be ashamed of what we have. In Jesus Christ we are all equal. It
is not wrong to be rich or to become rich. The Word of God gives us
many examples of godly people who were wealthy. But there are some
problems which come to Christians who are wealthy. What do you
think some of them are? Talk about it.[12]

APRIL 19

For the sun rises with scorching heat and withers the
plant....In the same way, the rich man will fade away
even while he goes about his business (James 1:11).

Are you rich? Yes, in spiritual terms you are. But are you rich in the world's terms? Do you plan to be wealthy 5, 10, or 20 years from now? Would you like to be rich? If we're honest, most of us wouldn't mind trying it for a while!

There is a cost to being wealthy. Wealth is often a means of exercising undue power or control over others. Some who are wealthy rely on their wealth for security and happiness instead of relying on God. Wealth can lead to sin. Paul wrote, "The love of money is a root of all kinds of evil. Some people, eager for money, have wandered from the faith and pierced themselves with many griefs" (1 Timothy 6:10).

What does James mean when he says, "But the one who is rich should take pride in his low position" (1:10)? He is trying to communicate to the wealthy this concept: Let people know that your riches are not the most important thing in the world to you. Let them know this by giving of what you have to help the needy. Let others know that your peace and security come from your relationship with Jesus Christ rather than from your wealth. Let them see this by actions and business decisions which reflect biblical teachings and values rather than by the amount of money you can make for yourself on a deal. Let them know that storing up riches in heaven is far better than what can be accumulated here on earth.

All of us, regardless of how much we have, are called to be good stewards of what God has given us. If you would like something to talk about together today, here's a thought: Discuss how much money you give to God and others and when you will be able to double what you are now giving. That's something to think about![13]

APRIL 20

*Try to stay out of all quarrels and seek to live a
clean and holy life* (Hebrews 12:14, TLB).

Puppies and kittens are a delight to watch. They seem to play constantly. They growl and snarl, jump at each other, cuff one another, roll, tumble, grab, and chew. They can do this happily by the hour. But occasionally one of them either goes too far, gets too rough, or doesn't know when to quit. And that's when the fur starts to fly. It's no longer friendly banter; it's serious confrontation. Lighthearted play is replaced by the intent to overpower, to hurt, to get even, and to win the battle. The growls are no longer playful but harsh. The atmosphere changes from pleasant to intense and volatile. Often the mother dog or cat has to break up the scuffle by stepping in to give her young a sound cuffing.

Does this description sound familiar to you as a married couple? Couples often end up quarreling when their differences get out of hand and each defends his or her turf by swinging at the other verbally. Quarrels are symptoms that a husband and wife are competing with each other instead of complementing each other.

Quarreling is our choice, not God's. His choice is peace. Quarreling leads to retaliation and recrimination, peace leads to intimacy and closeness. Paul was against quarreling: "Quarreling, harsh words, and dislike of others should have no place in your lives" (Ephesians 4:31, TLB); "Don't quarrel with anyone. Be at peace with everyone, just as much as possible" (Romans 12:18).

Instead of lashing out at each other, take time out to decrease the intensity of the situation, reflect, reevaluate, and discover the areas where you actually might agree. As a believer in Christ, be patient in working out solutions. When there are two Christians in a marriage, there is a third party present in every disagreement. Have you invited Him recently to give His opinion? It might be the best one available!

APRIL 21

With humility of mind let each of you regard one another as more important than himself (Philippians 2:3, NASB).

You have probably heard about Tony Campolo through his speaking and writing ministry. Consider some thoughts on marriage from the pen of his wife, Margaret:

> Remember how much you enjoyed looking terrible in the funny mirrors at amusement parks when you were a child? It was fun because you knew you really did not look like that. You could always find a real mirror and be sure you were you.
>
> In marriage, each partner becomes the mirror for the other....Often a problem in a bad marriage is that one or both of the mirrors is working like those old amusement park mirrors. A spouse begins to reflect ugly things, and the other one feels that his or her best self isn't there anymore.
>
> Mirrors reflect in simple ways; people are far more complicated. We choose what we reflect, and what we choose has much to do with what the other person becomes. One of the most exciting things about being married is helping your partner become his or her best self by reflecting with love.
>
> Positive reflecting will make your spouse feel good about himself/herself and about you, but it will also change the way you feel. As you look for the positive and overlook the negative, you will become happier about your marriage and the person you married. This will happen even if your spouse does not change at all!...
>
> In a difficult marriage, as in the difficult times of a good marriage, ask God for understanding and the ability to do what is humanly impossible. Jesus is our model. And in reflecting our marriage partners positively we are following His example.[14]

APRIL 22

*Watch out! Be on your guard against
all kinds of greed* (Luke 12:15).

Greed is like a slithering snake. It creeps around us relentlessly. It is never satisfied. Feed it and its hunger increases. It is born to consume. Greed's cry is, "It's never enough." You've seen it in others and felt it in yourself: just one more piece of pie, one more hour of work, one more new dress or suit. In his second letter, Peter talks about "a heart trained in greed" (2:14, NASB). Greed is the underlying theme of the so-called good life.

The three keys words of greed are more, more, and more. The Greek word in today's verse actually means "wanting more." In the ancient world greed was considered one of the deadly vices. Greed is condemned in the New Testament.

In Luke 12:16-21, Jesus told a simple story about greed. A rich man harvested a bumper crop, so he decided to rip down his barns and build even bigger ones to hold everything he owned. He decided to party and take life easy. He had it made, and his desire was, "More, I want more." What he got instead was not what he expected. God said to him, "You fool! This very night your life will be demanded from you. Then who will get what you have prepared for yourself?" (v. 20).

The drive to accumulate more leads to a feeling of dissatisfaction. Greed makes us cut corners. It makes us distort our values. We sell out our integrity to get something we want. Greed causes us to lose more than we ever gain, because in the drive to acquire we have to neglect other aspects of our lives. How many marriages have failed because of the drive for more money or a top position in the company? How many relationships falter because of the burden of the inflated house payment? We may call it "moving up," but perhaps the honest word is greed. At the end of our lives, what can we really take with us? Only the best thing—our faith in Jesus Christ. And it's a free gift!

APRIL 23

Husbands…be considerate as you live with your wives…
so that nothing will hinder your prayers (1 Peter 3:7).

Married couples report different results in their efforts to blend their personal prayer lives into a genuine and meaningful prayer life together. Some share prayer just before going to bed in the evening. Others say that morning or evening mealtimes provide their best opportunity for common prayer, though couples with children often find themselves delegating table prayers to children, especially very young ones. For many couples prayer is an intensely personal experience. Each partner prays privately and often silently, but each is aware of the power of the other's prayers.

Here are a few helpful suggestions which may improve your prayer experiences together:

1. *Prayer is effective only when you are treating each other considerately.* If your prayers together are hindered (that is, if you can't bear the idea of praying with each other), examine closely the way you treat one another. There may be offenses which need to be discussed, confessed, and forgiven.

2. *Prayer does not have to be verbal.* When a severe crisis strikes, we are often rendered speechless with shock. We can simply hold each other in our arms and be silent as we count on the Holy Spirit to pray for us (Romans 8:26).

3. *Prayer does not have to concern "religious" subjects.* A healthy sexual union between husband and wife, for example, is cause for thanksgiving to each other and to God.

4. *Pray when you are separated even more than when you are together.* Any time of separation is a time for some heavy-duty praying.

5. *Talk about your prayer life in light of Scripture.* Lay aside all shyness with your partner, and dare to discuss your prayer life and your love life as frankly as Scripture does.[15]

APRIL 24

*So if the Son sets you free, you will
be free indeed* (John 8:36).

S lavery has been a plague on society ever since the beginning of man.
Slavery was a blight in the early history of our nation, and it has
been a problem throughout the world. When one nation takes over
another through an act of war, some kind of slavery is often the result.
We were not meant to live in bondage to others.

Sometimes slavery is imposed upon us and other times we make
ourselves slaves. Think about it for a minute: Are you a free person? Are
you really free? Most Americans assume they are free. Perhaps there are
degrees of freedom. Total freedom doesn't exist even in this country.

There can be slavery and bondage in a marriage relationship. Many
wives and even some husbands live under the yoke of domination and
control by the other spouse and are very restricted in their personal lives.
Some individuals are addicted to the master of perfectionism; others to
the master of pleasing everyone else to the neglect of their own life. Any
form of addiction is slavery whether it be to drugs, alcohol, tobacco,
television, pornography, food, power, spending, constant activity, or
even church traditions.

As you reflect upon you own life, is there anything which tends
to make you a slave? Are you allowing something to dominate you?
Is there any activity in your marriage which is out of control and to
which you feel enslaved?

The emancipation proclamation of Abraham Lincoln was really
nothing compared to the emancipation proclamation we have received
from God. Wherever you live and whatever your circumstance in life,
you are a free person because of Jesus Christ. Are you and your partner
living in freedom today? Are you both enjoying the benefits of your
freedom, or are you still struggling in the bondage of slavery to something or someone?

APRIL 25

It will also come to pass that before they
call, I will answer; and while they are still
speaking, I will hear (Isaiah 65:24, NASB).

I'm really hesitant to go and talk to that person. I'm just not sure what I'm going to say to him. I have no idea how he will react. He could be taken aback by what I will ask!"

You've probably heard words of concern like these. Perhaps you've used them in your own hesitancy to make a request of another person. You may even be hesitant to bring up a subject with your partner from time to time. We all have this hesitancy occasionally.

But there is one person with whom we need never hesitate to make a request. What did God say to us about coming to Him? In today's verse He says that the answer to your prayer is already prepared before you pray. Your prayers don't surprise Him in the least. Prayer does not begin with what we ask but with what God has prepared. Lloyd Ogilvie has some insightful words to share with us on this idea:

> God has more prepared for us than we are prepared to ask. We need to spend as much time seeking what God wants us to ask for as we do asking. Then our asking will be in keeping with His will. Prayer is seeking God with all our hearts. God can use our imaginations to give us a picture of His future for us, but with one qualification: that we seek Him with all our hearts. Prayer is the time to let God paint the mind picture of what we are to be and do.[16]

Take a few minutes today and discuss with one another these questions: Are you ever hesitant to bring a request before the Lord? Why? How can you as a couple better discover what He wants you to pray about together? Try this approach to asking and discover what your prayer life together can become!

APRIL 26

Where there is no vision, the people are
unrestrained (Proverbs 29:18, NASB).

When you married, did you have a vision for what your marriage would become? Did you have a dream? It's all right to dream, for many dreams are translated into a vision for the future and pursued in a realistic way. Marriage itself is a dream. David Augsburger writes: "Marriage is the pursuit of a dream. A dream of loving and being loved; of wanting another and being wanted in return, of melting into another and being eagerly embraced, of understanding another and being understood, of feeling secure and guaranteeing another's security, of being fulfilled in fulfilling another's needs."[17]

Some say dreams are just for dreamers and not for people who live in the real world. Really? The lack of dreams and visions for the future may lead to feelings of futility. Think about the words of the following poem:

The Dream

> may be modest or heroic,
> vaguely defined or crystal clear,
> a burning passion or a quiet guiding force,
> a source of inspiration and strength or of
> > corrosive conflict.
> My life is enriched to the extent that
> > I have a Dream and give it
> > appropriate place in my life
> > —a place that is legitimate and viable
> > for both myself and my world.
> if I have no Dream or can find no way to live it out,
> > my life lacks genuine purpose or meaning.[18]

Turn your dreams into reality with the power and presence of Jesus Christ in your life.

APRIL 27

Gentle words cause life and health (Proverbs 15:4, TLB).

How do you convey your love to one another—through your eyes, body language, looks, what you do, or what you say? Regardless of your answer, it's still called communication. A marriage is no better than the quality of the couple's communication! And your marital strength will come from the honesty of your communication. The most revealing signs of marital health will be the level of honesty, openness, and directness that the two of you create together. Communication is a bridge that you each walk across in order to meet one another. Sometimes the bridge is difficult to cross because the path leading to it may be steep and have some boulders in the way, but you must cross the bridge all the same.

Have you ever considered how your communication patterns reflect the family from which you came? Think about it: When it comes to communicating, who are you most like in your family—your mother or your father? Did you expect the communication pattern of your parents to be present in your own marriage?

Many communication patterns in marriage are based upon questions and statements. Some people are more adept at persuading and some at clarifying. Even thought questions and statements have their place. There is one other style of communication which has more impact and gives more meaning to a relationship. It's called the invitation. Invitations are statements like, "Tell me about..." or "I'd like to hear your thoughts or feelings about..." Invitation statements do not lead, trap, guide, control, or command. They give the other person total freedom to express himself or herself in his or her own way. Invitations free the other person rather than control him or her. When you give an invitation to your partner you are welcoming his or her thoughts and feelings.[19] And that's healthy communication. Practice by inviting one another to share your thoughts right now.

APRIL 28

A friendly discussion is as stimulating as the sparks
that fly when iron strikes iron (Proverbs 27:17, TLB).

We can't say enough about the concept of intimacy in marriage because it is truly the bonding element of any relationship. Many writers have expressed their thoughts on this topic. Here's what David Augsburger has to say:

> Intimacy is the courage to be vulnerable, the necessary strength to be weak together. There is no way to avoid hurt in a relationship, although we should try to minimize the possibility and grow in our ability to reduce its intensity, spread, and duration by working through the injury as soon as possible. Being vulnerable, as one fallible human with another, means that hurts are inevitable but not irreparable. We will be hurt by each other if we live with each other. Since both pleasure and pain are essential to being alive, we must learn to handle our hurts to enrich our joys. In fact, working through our hurts, we deepen our love.[20]

How else can we describe intimacy? Intimacy has a history, but it is also a moment of closeness. Intimacy has stability, but it is also open to change and growth. Sameness kills intimacy. Intimacy is self-giving and serving, but it is also being who you really are. Intimacy is caring and accepting, but it is also differing and confronting. Intimacy is openness, but it is also privacy for it honors secrets and respects space. Intimacy involves great amounts of time, and yet there are brief peak moments. Intimacy requires mutual transparency, but it also respects the timing of the other person. Intimacy recognizes and accepts the weakness and frailty of one another, but it is hopeful that love will always be present.[21]

Share together: Which of these descriptions reflect your thoughts and feelings about intimacy?

APRIL 29

We have not stopped praying for you and asking God
to fill you with the knowledge of his will through all
spiritual wisdom and understanding (Colossians 1:9).

Answer honestly: Would you prefer to fit into your partner's plans or have your partner fit into your plans? That's a loaded question, because we all tend to want others, including our spouse, to fit into our plans instead of us fitting into theirs.

We have the same conflict when we pray. Instead of praying that we will fit into God's plans, we often bring to God our own plans and ask Him to accommodate Himself to them. In contrast, consider the prayer of Paul in Colossians 1:9-12 for the Colossian Christians. He prayed that God would give them spiritual wisdom and understanding. They could probably have used some prayer for strength, wealth, security, well-behaving children, and better relationships with in-laws as well. But that's not what Paul asked for. He asked God to give them wisdom and understanding so that they would walk in a manner worthy of the Lord and please Him with their lives.

He also prayed that they would be strengthened so they would be steadfast, patient, and joyful, giving thanks to the Lord. You can read about the benefits of this prayer in verses 10-14. Take a look at these verses and consider how the results would help your own life at the present time.

Paul was really asking that these people would fit into God's plan. That's interesting. Too often we attempt to use God for our own benefit rather than ask Him for the wisdom and spiritual understanding we need to serve Him—wisdom which will actually assist us in answering our other concerns. Some people pray for their will to be done rather than for God's will to be done in their lives.

Where do you need spiritual wisdom and understanding at this time in your life? How will you apply it when it is given? to what situations? Think about these questions during the day and talk to each other about your thoughts before you retire for the night.[22]

APRIL 30

*If I rise on the wings of the dawn, if I settle
on the far side of the sea, even there your
hand will guide me* (Psalm 139:9,10).

Have you had a good crisis lately—you know, when a whirlwind sweeps through your life, throws you around, and disrupts all of your best laid plans. Those crises make us feel like we're in a barrel rolling downhill, being thrown all about. All of us will have crises come into our lives. But except for adrenaline addicts, not too many of us really like to have our lives invaded by crises. Before crises come, it's important to burn into your memory the fact that you will have an opportunity for more spiritual growth during a crisis than at most other times. It is during a time of crisis that God wants to do something in your life.

The promise of today's passage is that no matter where you are, God will lead you. In Isaiah 43, the Lord declares that He will be with you through your times of crisis. Turn to that chapter right now and read it aloud before you proceed.

Did you notice the number of times God said "I will"? It appears more than ten times. Go back and notice what the "I will" statements apply to in this passage. A comforting thought is that He will not remember our sins. That is encouraging, since for some of us there's a lot for God to forget!

Many people feel that one of the most comforting "I will's" is in verse two: "I will be with you." Will you remember that when you are discouraged? Will you remember it when you are faced with a difficult ethical dilemma at work? Will you remember it when you feel that you have nothing left to give in your marital relationship? Will you remember it when you feel that you're all alone and no one else cares? These are words of comfort which can lift us at any time.[23]

MAY

When we rejoice in the Lord, we begin to see life from God's point of view. Praise is our means of gaining new perspective and guidance for our bogged-down lives.

MAY 1

A man's mind plans his way, but the Lord
directs his steps (Proverbs 16:9, RSVB).

Self-control is usually thought of in terms of restraint. Perhaps another way in which it can be considered concerns the self-control or discipline needed in setting and attaining goals—especially marital goals. Unfortunately, goal-setting is one of the most neglected essentials in marital growth. A goal is something you would like to achieve or to have happen. Stating a goal involves faith because you are declaring something you would like to see occur in the future. "Faith is the substance of things hoped for" (Hebrews 11:1, NKJV).

In many ways, the way a couple leads their life together is determined by their goals—or lack of goals. Clearly defined goals give direction to the marriage, but muddled, hazy, and unclear goals lead to confusion.

What about you? What goals have you established for your marriage? Are they clear? Have you worked them out together? What do you want your marriage to reflect? What do you want it to say about you as a couple and about the presence of God in your lives? These are questions you should talk about. Goals can lift you from present difficulties by placing your focus on positive hopes to come. As Christians, we live both in the present and the future. Paul says to each of us, "Forgetting the past and looking forward to what lies ahead, I strain to reach the end of the race" (Philippians 4:13,14, TLB).

Spend time now talking about the questions raised in this meditation. One last suggestion: Discussing the fruit of the Spirit in Galatians 5:22,23 might be a good place to start. What would it be like if love, joy, peace, patience, kindness, goodness, faithfulness, gentleness, and self-control were reflected in your marriage daily? What would that mean for you? What would it mean for the glory of God? What goals can you set to achieve this?

MAY 2

Consider it pure joy, my brothers, whenever you face
trials of many kinds, because you know that the testing
of your faith develops perseverance (James 1:2,3).

The book of James is an interesting book. It is practical and insightful.
If its guidelines are followed, they can make a radical difference in
our lives.

James talks to us about trials. The trials he refers to are the many
kinds of difficulties that come into our lives. Some of them happen
because of circumstances beyond our control, and others we bring on
ourselves because of sin. When he talks about joy, he's not talking
about happiness or pleasure. Joy is a sense of gladness. It is the ability
to look beyond the problem or difficulty and see the opportunity for
growth. It means discovering how God can be glorified through what
we are experiencing.

James tells us to consider trials a joy. "Considering" is a matter of
attitude, making a choice about how you will respond to your trials.
It is a decision to endure because of your desire to do the will of God.
It is a choice to complete the will of God in spite of what it costs you.
You're not denying the trial, but instead you're realistically facing it and
in time turning the heartache into joy. And the result is perseverance
or endurance.

Yes, it is possible to actually experience an inner peace while the
world is crumbling around you. Think for a moment: What are the
trials you are facing at the present time? What makes it hard to persevere? How could you view your situation differently in light of this
passage? Use these questions to discover how you can help each other
through the difficult times.[1]

MAY 3

And now these three remain: faith, hope
and love (1 Corinthians 13:13).

Where did you get your model for a marriage—from parents, friends, church, society, the Bible? We all enter marriage with some idea of what a marriage is meant to be, but where did that idea come from? Some say the Bible, and yet the Bible does not really give us detailed models for marriage relationships. What it does give are principles for living that can shape a marriage into something positive and fulfilling which brings glory to God.

Here are four virtues which give us a basic model for healthy marital relationships: faith, hope, love, and justice. David Augsburger comments:

> Faith is the commitment to creative fidelity; it is faithfulness to each other before God. Faith is both a way of perceiving and of acting; it is believing and doing.
>
> Hope is the call of creative trust; it is hopefulness with each other before God. Hope is both a push from within the "hopeful" hoper and the pull from the possibilities of the future.
>
> Love is the choice to see the other partner as equally precious; it is loving-kindness that acts in equal regard. Love is a way of seeing, feeling, thinking, and acting toward another.
>
> Justice is the commitment to work out mutually satisfactory and visibly equitable sharing of opportunities, resources and responsibilities in living with others; it is a creative drive for fairness in all covenantal relationships. Justice goes beyond retribution for injuries, and redistribution of resources to a redemptive and releasing discovery of what is truly right, good and beautiful.[2]

MAY 4

O Lord, our Lord, how majestic is your
name in all the earth!...What is man that
you are mindful of him? (Psalm 8:1,4).

B efore continuing with this meditation, read the remainder of Psalm
8 aloud together from your Bible.

Here is an easy way to remember this psalm. It's divided into three
parts. Part 1 (vv. 1,2) reflects the recognition of the majesty of God's
name and all His works. God is glorified by the simple faith of children.
Sometimes as adults, we make our faith complicated and miss out on
the delights of praising God in a simple way. What have you praised
God for recently?

Part 2 (vv. 3,4) conveys the comparative insignificance of mankind.
In verse 4, the psalmist asks, "What is man?" What does it mean to be
a man or woman, a creation from God? Talk about it together. Perhaps
you have experienced this sense of smallness as you stood outside on
a clear summer night in the mountains. Looking toward the heavens,
you watched a light show made up of millions of stars and planets. And
the more you gazed upon the vastness of the heavens, the more insignificant you felt. Perhaps you said, "I feel so small. Who am I and how
do I fit in to all that God has made?"

But in Part 3 (vv. 5-8) we discover the great significance God has
placed on His human creation. When you are distressed and discouraged, or when your self-esteem is at an all-time low, turn to this passage
and read it. God values you highly and has a place for you in His
plan!

Now read Ephesians 1:19-23 and 1 Corinthians 15:24-27. These
passages describe the complete dominion of Jesus Christ, whose work
on the cross has restored us to our rightful position with our Creator.

Finally, read Psalm 8 aloud again, but this time face your partner
and read it to him or her. Share the depth of God's magnificence and
His love together.

MAY 5

*For the Law was given through Moses; grace and
truth came through Jesus Christ* (John 1:17).

Let's think about grace in a new way:

We use grace to describe many things in life: a well-coordinated athlete or dancer; good manners and being considerate of others; beautiful, well-chosen words; consideration and care for other people; various expressions of kindness and mercy.

Those examples remind me of Christ. What a perfect illustration of grace! Think of several examples with me. He stood alongside a woman caught in adultery. The Law clearly stated, "Stone her." The grace killers who set her up demanded the same. Yet He said to those self-righteous Pharisees, "He who is without sin, let him cast the first stone." What grace!…

When He told stories, grace was a favorite theme. He employed a gracious style in handling children. He spoke of the Prodigal Son in grace. As He told stories of people who were caught in helpless situations, grace abounded…as with the Good Samaritan. And instead of extolling the religious official who spoke of how proud God must be to have him in His family, Christ smiled with favor on the unnamed sinner who said, "God, be merciful to me, a sinner."

Even from the cross He refused to be angry toward His enemies. Remember His prayer? "Father, forgive them…" No resentment, no bitterness. Amazing, this grace! Remarkable, the freedom and release it brought. And it came in full force from the only One on earth who had unlimited power, the Son of God.

My plea is that we not limit it to Him. We, too, can learn to be just as gracious as He. And since we can, we must…not only in our words and in great acts of compassion and understanding but in small ways as well.[3]

MAY 6

Love must be sincere. Hate what is evil;
cling to what is good (Romans 12:9).

Let's tackle a problem which plagues us throughout life. It's called comparison. Consider the words of Chuck Swindoll:

> Most of us fall short when it comes to letting others be because of two strong and very human tendencies: we compare ourselves with others (which leads us to criticize or compete with them) and we attempt to control others (which results in our manipulating or intimidating them).
>
> Christians seem especially vulnerable when it comes to comparison. For some reason, which I cannot fully discern, we are uneasy with differences. We prefer sameness, predictability, common interests. If someone thinks differently or makes different choices than we do, prefers different entertainment, wears different clothing, has different tastes and opinions, or enjoys a different style of life, most Christians get nervous....
>
> Who wrote the "let's compare" rulebook? Will you please show me from Scripture where God is pleased with such negative attitudes? Comparison fuels the fire of envy within people. It prompts the tendency to judge...it makes us prejudiced people. The worst part of all is that it nullifies grace. It was never God's intention for all His children to look alike or embrace identical lifestyles. Look at the natural world He created. What variety!...
>
> Before we will be able to demonstrate sufficient grace to let others be, we'll have to get rid of this legalistic tendency to compare. Legalism requires that we all be alike, unified in convictions and uniform in appearance, to which I say, "Let me out!" Grace finds pleasure in differences, encourages individuality, smiles on variety, and leaves plenty of room for disagreement. Remember, it releases others and lets them be, to which I say, "Let me in!"[4]

MAY 7

To one he gave five talents of money, to another
two talents, and to another one talent, each
according to his ability (Matthew 25:15).

Do you remember the parable of the talents? You can read it in its entirety in Matthew 25:14-30. In the New Testament, large amounts of silver and gold were measured by weight in talents. The parable is about a master distributing tens of thousands of dollars to his servants, discovering what they did with the talents of money they received, and rewarding them accordingly. It's a story illustrating how we should put to use the different gifts and abilities God has entrusted to each of us.

We use the word talent today to describe some special ability that might qualify you for a talent show—singing, tap-dancing, ventriloquism, etc. But in the context of the parable, talent consists of whatever God has entrusted to you in order to live out your faith and touch the lives of others. It may appear to you that some Christians have been blessed with many abilities while you have to struggle just to find one! Do you feel this way? Does your partner feel this way? But as the parable illustrates, it's not how many talents you have but what you do with them that's important. Your talent, no matter how insignificant it may seem to you, is not to be buried but used to minister to others.

Sometimes in a marriage, one partner has a well-developed ability to trust God and has learned many lessons during the years. His or her partner may not be at that level. What the weaker partner needs is not to be badgered to "just have more faith," but patient support, instruction, and guidance so that his or her faith has an opportunity to grow and develop.

Perhaps it's time for each of you to take inventory of your special abilities and gifts as well as what God has entrusted to you in terms of your faith in Him. Every Christian has been entrusted with at least one talent: knowing who Jesus Christ is and responding to His call. That's a talent the whole world can use! With whom will you share your talent this week?

MAY 8

*Do not worry about what to say or how to say it. At
that time you will be given what to say, for it will
not be you speaking, but the Spirit of your Father
speaking through you* (Matthew 10:19,20).

"What in the world will I say?"

At some time in life we're all confronted with this challenge. Even in marriage we struggle for the appropriate words to share a thought or concern with our partner. And when pressure situations occur, sometimes our minds tend to shut down and we don't know what to say.

In today's passage Jesus is talking about our concern over what to say when we are faced with giving testimony about Him in a setting which is hostile to the Christian faith. He assures us that the Holy Spirit will give us the thoughts, the words, and the courage which we so often lack. During your marital journey there may be times when you are concerned about sharing your faith in Christ with someone or when you are challenged in your faith by other people. Rely upon the fact that God is the source of your thoughts and words at those times. Dr. Lloyd Ogilvie says:

> Our only task is to open our minds in calm expectation of wisdom beyond our own capacity. We were never meant to be adequate on our own. It is when we think we are adequate that we get into trouble. A Christian is not one who works for the Lord but one in whom and through whom the Lord works. We are not to speak for God but to yield our tongues to express the thoughts the Lord has implanted.[5]

What can we draw from these words? Listen to the Lord before you speak and, after you have heard Him, speak with confidence and concern. Perhaps today you can identify an area of concern in both your lives regarding something you need to say to someone. Pray for this situation and then ask God for the words and the confidence you need.

MAY 9

*The wrong desires that come into your life aren't
anything new and different. Many others have
faced exactly the same problems before you. And no
temptation is irresistible* (1 Corinthians 10:13, TLB).

Life is full of decisions. We have to make many of them each day—small, insignificant decisions as well as life-changing ones. Do you remember some of the significant ones you've made over the years? Once upon a time you decided to marry your partner. You are renewing that commitment daily as you decide to honor and serve your partner. When you make a decision, what causes you to make it? What or who influences you? Sometimes we make wise decisions, especially when we seek the Lord's guidance. Sometimes we make unwise decisions, especially when we trust our own wisdom.

Some couples develop difficulty in their marriage because of decisions based on what they see. They are enthralled by what others have accumulated: a new, spacious home, a sharp BMW, a ski boat. Remember Lot? He was prompted to make a bad choice because of what looked good to him (Genesis 13:10). Our eyes can mislead us to focus on what we want but cannot afford. Why is it that the number one conflict during the first year of marriage for a majority of couples is finances? Evaluate what you see! Is it a necessity or a luxury? How will your life be different by having it? Evaluate it in writing and you may be surprised!

Some couples make decisions based upon what they hear. Whom do you listen to, and what are they saying? Listening to others gripe and complain about their partner could begin to influence your perspective of your own partner. Listening to others rationalize their behavior could have an erosive effect upon your values.

What do you see and hear that is building your marital relationship? What do you see and what do you hear that may create problems in your marriage? Discover what your partner has to say about this.

MAY 10

This is love for God: to obey his commands (1 John 5:3).

Wouldn't you like to be able to listen in on what others say about your marriage? Well, perhaps not. It could be threatening, surprising, revealing, or even shocking. Are there any guidelines that a couple can follow which will create a positive witness and perhaps even encourage other Christian couples or draw others to Jesus Christ? Let's consider a few. Think about how these biblical principles could be reflected in your marital life:

1. "Make it your ambition to lead a quiet life, to mind your own business and to work with your hands, just as we told you, so that your daily life may win the respect of outsiders and so that you will not be dependent on anybody" (1 Thessalonians 4:11,12). What does this passage mean to each of you? How can it be expressed in your marriage?

2. "Be wise in the way you act toward outsiders; make the most of every opportunity. Let your conversation be always full of grace, seasoned with salt, so that you may know how to answer everyone" (Colossians 4:5,6). What does this passage mean to each of you? How can it be expressed in your marriage?

3. "So whether you eat or drink or whatever you do, do it all for the glory of God. Do not cause anyone to stumble, whether Jews, Greeks or the church of God—even as I try to please everybody in every way. For I am not seeking my own good but the good of many, so that they may be saved" (1 Corinthians 10:31-33). What does this passage mean to each of you? How can it be expressed in your marriage?

4. "Owe nothing to anyone except to love one another" (Romans 13:8, NASB). This final passage may serve as a long-range goal for you. It's a difficult guideline to follow in today's society, but it is possible. How can it be fulfilled in your marriage?

MAY 11

Be careful that you do not forget the Lord your God,
failing to observe his commands, his laws and his decrees
that I am giving you this day (Deuteronomy 8:11).

Consider the words of a couple who at one time had Jesus Christ at the center of their married life:

> As we started our marriage we made sure that we prayed together and were involved in worship and helping at our church. Jesus Christ was very real to each of us. As the years progressed we noticed something happening. We both worked and made excellent money. Soon we began to acquire things and our level of living really rose. But as it climbed, our relationship with our Lord diminished. The more we made and acquired, the more difficult it was to maintain our focus upon God. Does everyone have that problem?

That's a good question. It's a struggle to maintain our focus upon God when the temptation to maintain an affluent lifestyle is so prevalent. Moses warned the children of Israel about the dangers of prosperity before they entered the Promised Land. Perhaps we need the same warning today:

> For the Lord your God is bringing you into a good land...where bread will not be scarce and you will lack nothing.... When you have eaten and are satisfied, praise the Lord your God for the good land he has given you. Be careful that you do not forget the Lord your God....Otherwise, when you eat and are satisfied...then your heart will become proud and you will forget the Lord your God (Deuteronomy 8:7,9-12,14).

It's easy to worship our possessions rather than the One who makes them possible. Is this a temptation in your marriage? Think about it and talk about it today.

MAY 12

We have a building from God, a house not made
with hands (2 Corinthians 5:1, NASB).

God's Word tells us that we are aliens—temporary visitors on earth—and that our eternal home is in heaven with God. Perhaps realizing what awaits us in the future will affect how we think, what we do, and how we do it each day. Saturate yourself with the central thought of the following passages: our future home. Then discuss how you will apply these passages to your life as a couple:

> For our citizenship is in heaven, from which also we eagerly wait for a Savior, the Lord Jesus Christ; who will transform the body of our humble state into conformity with the body of His glory (Philippians 3:20,21, NASB).

> But you are a chosen race, a royal priesthood, a holy nation, a people for God's own possession, that you may proclaim the excellencies of Him who has called you out of darkness into His marvelous light; for you once were not a people, but now you are the people of God; you had not received mercy, but now you have received mercy. Beloved, I urge you as aliens and strangers to abstain from fleshly lusts, which wage war against the soul (1 Peter 2:9-11, NASB).

> For here we do not have a lasting city, but we are seeking the city which is to come. Through Him then, let us continually offer up a sacrifice of praise to God, that is, the fruit of lips that give thanks to His name. And do not neglect doing good and sharing; for with such sacrifices God is pleased (Hebrews 13:14-16, NASB).

How can you and your partner be a living sacrifice? Discuss how you can do good and share today.

MAY 13

Who am I? (Exodus 3:11).

Have you ever asked yourself, "Who am I?"? Sounds ridiculous, doesn't it? But it isn't. At some time or another in our life most of us raise that question: "Who am I really?"

Many people answer with, "I'm not sure I know. I'm uncertain. I don't feel secure about myself. The only thing I am sure of about myself is that I feel inferior. Whoever I am, I'm inferior!" That's a mouthful! Have you ever felt inferior about yourself because of uncertainty about who you are? This tendency keeps us from reaching out to others, hinders us from responding to God, and inhibits us from becoming all that we can be.

If you feel inferior, you're not alone. Moses struggled with feelings of inferiority. He had a very interesting interaction with God. God wanted him to lead the people. Moses was full of resistance because of how he felt about himself. Listen to his responses to God: "Who am I?...What shall I tell them?...What if they do not believe me or listen to me?...I have never been eloquent....I am slow of speech and tongue" (Exodus 3:11,13; 4:1,10).

What have you said when God called you to do something for Him? Many of us have a pattern of resistance. But when God asks you to do something, He doesn't leave you on your own. He told Moses He would be with him. He told Moses what to say. He gave Moses signs to perform for the people. God said that He would be Moses' mouth.

Moses struggled with feelings about himself. But at least he talked to God about it. Then he received answers and help. What about you? Are there feelings about yourself that need to be expressed to God? It's the first step in allowing Him to give you some answers. Give it a try. When He calls you to do something, He will also give you the resources.[6]

MAY 14

In the same way the Spirit also helps our weakness;
for we do not know how to pray as we should, but
the Spirit Himself intercedes for us with groanings
too deep for words (Romans 8:26, NASB).

I just don't know what to say when I pray. Sometimes I'm at a loss for words."

If you've ever felt this way, you're not alone. We've all felt like this at some point. Often it's when we attempt to pray that we become very conscious of the spiritual struggle in our life. As we sit down to pray our minds wander. Every few minutes we sneak a look at the clock to see if we've prayed enough. Often prayer is more of a task or an "ought to" experience than an experience of joy and delight. Have you ever felt limited in prayer in this way? Has your partner felt this way? Have you discussed your struggles with prayer together?

The Holy Spirit is God's answer when we don't know how to pray. You and I cannot pray as we ought to pray. We are often crippled in our prayer life. That's where the work of the Holy Spirit really comes into play. He helps us in our prayer life by showing us what we should pray for and how we ought to pray. That's quite a promise!

J.B. Phillips translates today's verse in this manner: "The Spirit also helps us in our present limitations. For example, we do not know how to pray worthily, but his Spirit within us is actually praying for us in those agonizing longings which cannot find words. He who knows the heart's secrets understands the Spirit's intention as he prays according to God's will for those who love him." When you feel helpless and hopeless and unable to pray, turn to this passage and remind yourself of the power you have available to you. When you are weak in prayer, the Holy Spirit picks up the slack. That's a wonderful promise of assistance, isn't it!

MAY 15

In the same way the Spirit also helps our weakness;
for we do not know how to pray as we should, but
the Spirit Himself intercedes for us with groanings
too deep for words (Romans 8:26, NASB).

One of your callings in marriage is to assist your partner when he or she needs help. You are always to be listening for a call for assistance. Similarly, there is someone looking out for us when we need help in our prayer life: the Holy Spirit. Let's consider several specific ways that He helps us.

First, when you are oppressed by problems in life or feel down on yourself, the Spirit intercedes for you by bringing you to the place where you can pray. Your ability to begin praying is prompted and produced by the working of the Holy Spirit within you. There may be times when all you can do is sigh or sob inwardly. Even this kind of prayer is the result of the Spirit's work.

Second, the Spirit reveals to your mind what you should pray for. He makes you conscious of such things as your needs, your lack of faith, your fears, your need to be obedient, etc. He helps you see what your spiritual needs are and helps you bring them into the presence of God. He helps you by diminishing your fears, increasing your faith, and strengthening your hope.

Third, the Spirit guides you by directing your thoughts to the promises of God's Word which are best suited to your needs. He helps you realize the truth of God's promises. The discernment that you lack on your own has been given to you by the Spirit.

Finally, the Spirit helps you pray in the right way. He helps you sift through your prayers and bring them into conformity with the purpose of prayer.

When you are having difficulty praying, remember that you have someone to draw on for strength in developing your prayer life. That's quite a support system, isn't it![7]

MAY 16

There is a time for everything, and a season for
every activity under heaven (Ecclesiastes 3:1).

How about a second honeymoon—or a third, fourth, or fifth? Unrealistic? Not really. Consider the thoughts below and start planning!

Play is not so much escape as recreation, being created anew. Life stagnates when its routines sap it of originality and freshness. Even the best marriages get stale if they become too predictable. Play recharges our batteries, fills our gas tanks, and gives us a tuneup to prepare us for the next stretch.

So the second, third, fourth (and beyond) honeymoons should have a recreative purpose. They can refresh us and renew us. How about a fresh perspective on your job? Or a fresh perspective on your routines? A new look at meeting some tough times or hurts?

An extra honeymoon can give you the time and distance to take a fresh look at yourselves, individually and as a couple. Have I as the husband been helping my wife to be fulfilled as a person? Have I been as loving and kind as I should be to her? Have I as a wife been as supportive as I should? Have I been interested in my husband and his work? To these you can add a hundred new questions that will rejuvenate a tired marriage....

These honeymoons may last a week, or they may be just a lunchtime together. Do you ever set aside an hour or two to play—go on a hike, browse through antique stores, play a game, or whatever you like to do together? Try it sometime.[8]

MAY 17

If our hearts do not condemn us, we have confidence
before God and receive from him anything we ask
(1 John 3:21,22); *If we ask anything according*
to his will, he hears us (1 John 5:14).

There are two important *ifs* in this passage which have a direct bearing upon our prayer life. The first has to do with our feelings of self-condemnation. Isn't that an interesting concept John wrote about! He knew that we have a tendency not to use the power of prayer when we feel unworthy to go into the presence of the Lord. We project our own feelings of self-condemnation onto God and thus refuse to let Him lift our feelings about ourself. Have you ever experienced those feelings?

Did you notice the word *confidence?* In a way, that word tells us how to pray. The original Greek word actually means boldness. It means the freedom to speak boldly. But what gives us this confidence or boldness? The verse says "confidence before God." It's not your own confidence or boldness. Only because of what we have in Jesus Christ are we able to speak boldly to God. Our confidence before God should take precedence over our feelings of self-condemnation which keep us from prayer.

The second *if* concerns praying in God's will. Asking according to His will often seems to be a difficult issue. But it loses its difficulty when we begin praying for God to create a desire for His will within our hearts! Have you ever prayed this way?

God is accessible, and you need not be hesitant. You have been given the right to speak boldly. Are you taking Him up on His offer as individuals and as a couple? He really wants you to—even today.[9]

MAY 18

He who answers a matter before he hears the facts, it
is folly and shame to him (Proverbs 18:13, AMP).

L isten to me, please."
This is a common request because everyone, including your spouse, wants to be listened to. But there is more to wanting to be heard than experiencing good communication. Listening to your partner sends the message, "You are important to me, and I want to be involved in your life by welcoming you and what you say."

How well do you listen? How well does your partner listen? Today we will reflect on some thoughts about listening and the impact of listening on your marriage.

> It is impossible to overemphasize the immense need humans have to be really listened to. Listen to all the conversations of our world, between nations as well as those between couples. They are for the most part dialogues of the deaf.[10]

> If we would love, we must listen to one another. This is the first work of love. It is in listening that marriage matures.[11]

> Listening effectively means that when someone is talking you are not thinking about what you are going to say when the other person stops. Instead, you are totally tuned in to what the other person is saying.[12]

> Love is listening. Love is the opening of your life to another. Through sincere interest, simple attention, sensitive listening, compassionate understanding and honest sharing. An open ear is the only believable sign of an open heart. You learn to understand life—you learn to live—as you learn to listen.[13]

What did you hear these words saying for your marriage?

MAY 19

Perfect love drives out fear (1 John 4:18).

For Your Holy Spirit, God, I'm thankful!

Without Him, I'm nervous, anxious, fearful—
    too often thinking of me:

What will she think of me?
How will I impress him?
Will they think I'm weird?
What if they don't like my idea?

But oh, how happy I am with Your Holy Spirit!
He focuses my thoughts on You:
How may I best represent Jesus?
Will I be careful of His reputation?
What will be their response to His love
    through me?

Release! Support! Affirmation!
And then comes His serendipity!
In each person He shares with me He reveals
    His Son.
He enables me to enjoy their differences!
Because of what He paid for them;
Because of what He's doing within them;
Because He's promised to finish what He's
    started in each who chooses Him,
I can love them—actually enjoy them—
    each unique, special creation.

Thanks much, Lord, for replacing my fear
    with Your love, my anxiety with enjoyment,
    my doubt with hope.

Your Spirit is my stronghold!
He is my treasure, my precious friend.[14]

MAY 20

Dear friends, let us practice loving each other, for love comes from God and those who are loving and kind show that they are the children of God (1 John 4:7, TLB).

Couples who meet with ministers for premarital counseling are often asked to try to define the love that they have for each other. That's a good assignment, for it is important to clarify this feeling. Read the definitions of love listed below and talk about them together.

Is love not, in biblical terms, an emotion? It is an orientation, an attitude, of the total personality, "heart and soul and mind and strength." It is an outgoing concern for what is loved that seeks to serve and to give.[15]

To love somebody is not just a strong feeling—it is a decision, it is a judgment, it is a promise.[16]

Love is an activity; if I love, I am in a constant state of active concern with the loved person.[17]

It is in the very process of doing things for others that you begin to fall in love. It is also through the very process of doing things with and for others that you stay in love.[18]

When we open that hidden part of ourselves even for a moment, we need someone who will react with us. We need someone who will share our strong emotions. We need someone so involved that he will be afraid with us, be glad with us, be depressed with us; who will expose his own humanity as we expose ours. It is this contact between two human beings, revealing their common sensitivities, which draws them from loneliness and joins them together.[19]

Take a moment to complete together the statement "Love is..." in your own words.

MAY 21

Man looks at the outward appearance, but the
Lord looks at the heart (1 Samuel 16:7).

I just don't understand you!"
Have you heard that statement before? Maybe you hear it from
your partner occasionally. It's frustrating to be misunderstood. Your
message may be clear in your own mind, but for some reason the other
person can't make sense of what you say. Don't feel alone. Misunderstanding is part of life. It is inevitable. If you choose to walk in God's
grace and follow His will, prepare to be misunderstood. The world is
imperfect. So are you and your partner. But it's better to make a stand
and be misunderstood than to become a chameleon attempting to
please everyone. That is a sure way to lose your identity and your integrity and become a victim. Many people become approval addicts living
for the scraps of approval thrown by others.

Remember when you are misunderstood that Jesus was there too.
He understands what it feels like to be misunderstood. It is comforting
to know that even though people can't see past what you say to understand what is in your mind or on your heart, God can.

When you are the victim of misunderstanding with others, especially
your partner, don't be defensive. Just because people don't understand
you, you don't have to turn your back on them. You don't have to say,
"I don't care what you think." A misunderstanding is simply an opportunity for greater communication. Use that opportunity to clarify your
statement. The exercise will benefit both you and your listeners.

Here are some important questions about misunderstanding to
discuss with your partner: Who misunderstands you more than anyone
else? What do you not understand about your partner? What does
your partner not understand about you? What do you not understand
about God? As you communicate today, make sure there is no misunderstanding between you on these issues.[20]

MAY 22

In peace I will both lie down and sleep, for
you, Lord, alone make me dwell in safety
and confident trust (Psalm 4:8, AMP).

Sleepless nights—you know what they are like, especially those nights when you go to bed extra early because you have to get up at some unearthly hour. You lie there telling yourself to go to sleep. But sleep is like an elusive phantom. You toss and turn, disturbing your partner and causing him or her to wake up in a grumpy mood. We have all had to deal with sleeplessness at one time or another.

When you do sleep? Is your sleep restful? Is it a time of recouping your strength, or do you awake just as exhausted as you went to bed? If so, why? Some people have difficulty sleeping because they carry their fears and worries to bed with them. Have you experienced the peace the psalmist is talking about in today's verse? Do you give your fears and worries to Jesus Christ each night before you lie down? Do you say, "Lord Jesus, here are the burdens that I have carried all day long. I should have shared them with you earlier, but I do so now. I thank you that you will take my cares and that they don't have to plague my sleep. Thank you for the promise of your Word." If you haven't tried it, what do you have to lose?

Do you watch the news on TV just before you go to bed? If so, it may be having a negative effect on your sleep! Watching the bad news of the world isn't really conducive to rest. Talking about positive things together, listening to some soothing music, reading a book or passages of Scripture aloud to each other, or making love may make a difference in the way you sleep. Talk about it. What is your bedtime routine? Could it be better? God's Word can make the difference.

MAY 23

*Speaking the truth in love, we will in all
things grow up into him who is the Head,
that is, Christ* (Ephesians 4:15).

Truth, trust, freedom from fear, security—all these qualities go hand
in hand. Being truthful is a prized character quality in the Scriptures. Notice the following proverbs from The Living Bible: "To hate
is to be a liar; to slander is to be a fool" (10:18); "Lies will get any man
into trouble, but honesty is its own defense" (12:13); "A good man is
known by his truthfulness; a false man by deceit and lies" (12:17).

Strong words? Yes! Important words? Yes! Let's apply these words
now to your marital relationship.

> The practice of honesty and clear communication in marriage is likely to result in an extra dividend, for it encourages
> spouses to be generous, comforting, and consoling. If the
> spouses can be truthful and open about themselves, mutual
> support and helpfulness are possible.[21]

> Honesty is part of love. A couple should be able to be
> honest about their thoughts, fears, deeds, motives, and desires.
> To live behind a mask is to deny one's partner the privilege
> of knowing his inner self. It also robs one of the power of a
> single-minded life.[22]

> Wise is the spouse who learns how to listen so as to make
> it easier for his mate to speak. The corollary of speaking the
> truth in love is hearing it. This may rule out quick rejoinders,
> and involve receiving one's partner's words in silence, with a
> caress, or with a meaningful but unspecific statement such as,
> "The more I know you, the more I love you."[23]

> We can choose to give trust—if we really want to trust.
> Trust is love put in action. To love another is to be eager to
> trust, to extend that trust, to take risks in trusting.[24]

MAY 24

But while he was still a long way off, his father saw him
and was filled with compassion for him; he ran to his son,
threw his arms around him and kissed him (Luke 15:20).

Nonverbal expressions don't lie. They are so automatic that few of us ever learn to distort them. They're powerful. Their message has more impact than the spoken word. Jesus expressed them. He looked upon people with anger. His face reflected compassion. He communicated with a sigh.

We all use nonverbals continuously to express delight and dismay, satisfaction and smugness, consternation and compassion. Other people believe our nonverbals more than our words. And well they should, because nonverbal communication is the most accurate. Smiles, frowns, shrugged shoulders, raised eyebrows, crossed arms, extended arm, hands on hips—like the old song says, "Every little movement has a meaning all its own"! Do your nonverbals say, "Come to me, I love you, I want you close to me, I accept you." Or do they say, "Don't bother me, I don't want you near me, I'm threatened by you, I don't forgive you."

In the parable of the lost son (Luke 15:11-32), the father demonstrated for each of us how to reach out and accept another person. He did it first through his nonverbals. His wayward son didn't really deserve his father's acceptance. But the father looked up one day and saw the young man dragging himself home. Before his son could grovel for forgiveness, his father got up, ran to him, and threw his arms around the dirty, smelly, wayward lad. He accepted him, loved him, and said, "I take you the way you are right now. Welcome back!"

Whom do you need to welcome back into your life right now through your nonverbal expressions and words? Do you need to express acceptance to your partner in some way today? Each of us in our own way has played the part of the prodigal. And when we turned toward home, God smiled on us. Can we do any less toward those who need acceptance, forgiveness, and affirmation?

MAY 25

Therefore, rejecting all falsity and done now
with it, let every one express the truth with his
neighbor, for we are all parts of one body and
members one of another (Ephesians 4:25, AMP).

When we can depend upon the truthfulness and frankness of our partners, we feel safe and secure. In Proverbs we read: "It is an honor to receive a frank reply" (24:26, TLB); "In the end, people appreciate frankness more than flattery" (28:23, TLB).

Not only does truthfulness bring benefits to your marriage, think of what it does for you personally.

> What a release that is, to become a new, true person, to become the truth. And what a relief it is to be the truth. To be truly yourself before God, before others—and before yourself. No need to run and hide. No more games of hide-and-seek with your conscience. No more faking. No more playacting. No more false fronts or faces. You're free. Free to be the truth, the whole truth and nothing but the truth—by the help of God.[25]

Being truthful in your marriage relationship has many forms of expression, as David Augsburger relates:

> It is not enough—it is never enough—to simply talk of telling the truth. A man can tell the truth and be a liar still. All he has to do is select what truths to tell, or which half-truths to combine, and with a smattering of skill and "with a little bit of luck" he can be an "honest" liar. It is not enough to talk of telling the truth or even of telling the whole truth. We must be the truth. Be true persons. Be truly human. Be true to self, be true to others and be true to God, the source of all truth. It's one thing to say the truth—it's another to be it. That's what makes Jesus Christ stand out.[26]

MAY 26

The Lord longs to be gracious to you (Isaiah 30:18).

There is good news and there is bad news. Which do you want first? The good news is that God's grace is free and unlimited to you. The bad news is that so many of us try to earn grace through what we do. We perform and perform, thinking that we must in order for God to love us. We don't need to perform. When Jesus ministered to people, was it based on their goodness? Not at all. In fact, He instructed His disciples to offer what they had to those who lacked the means of repayment. And, as one author suggests, "God's grace operates in the same fashion today—not just for salvation but for all of life. He offers the inconceivable to the unworthy and withholds the expected from the deserving. Faith is not a system of proving our worthiness to Him, but the unadorned reception of what He offers focusing not on the strength of the receiver, but on the character of the giver."[27]

Sometimes we feel like we don't deserve God's grace. The truth of the matter is, we don't deserve it. But He gives it anyway. God's grace is available when everything in your life is going well. God's grace is available when everything in your life is not going so well. You will hit storms in your life. In Matthew 14:25-32, Peter hit a storm on the water. Jesus said to Peter and to us in the midst of the storm, "Come on, trust Me. I'll take you through this." Sometimes it's a hard choice to trust God in the midst of hard problems. But this trust is only made possible through God's grace.

In every circumstance, God's grace is there—not to take away the problem and ease the struggle, but to strengthen us and help us through the situation. And you know what? You don't have to deserve that grace. Just accept His gift.

How is God's grace a model for how husbands and wives should treat each other? Talk about how you will apply grace to your relationship today.[28]

MAY 27

*Be still, and know that I am God; I will be exalted among
the nations. I will be exalted in the earth* (Psalm 46:10).

Why is it that in most marriages one partner seems to run by a cal-
endar and the other by a stop watch? One operates slowly and
deliberately while his or her partner is quick, impulsive, and sponta-
neous. One partner is saying "Slow down!" while the other is urging
"Hurry up!" Pacing is an important adjustment for most couples.

Life is full of many situations which cause us to slow down whether
we want to or not. The high-powered, intense executive is often forced
to a snail's pace by a massive heart attack. You're in a hurry on the
freeway when gridlock slows you to 20 miles per hour. You have a
busy Saturday of yard work planned when a sudden storm sweeps in
and immobilizes you indoors. Such delays and schedule interruptions
are frustrating—especially when you can't control them. And when
they occur, you sometimes end up abusing the extra time instead of
using it!

But there is a better way of handling slow-downs that isn't so frustrating. Take charge of your life and slow it down yourself. Believe it
or not, all that you do and the rate at which you do it can be changed!
Think about it for a moment. What if you were immobilized for the
next two weeks and couldn't do anything. Would the world come to
an end? No. Could you use that time in a healthy positive way? Definitely yes. How? By being quiet in the presence of God, thinking about
Him, talking with Him, and asking for His guidance. Perhaps God
will get through to you sooner and clearer if you slow down and listen
to Him.

Jesus didn't hurry. He took time for rest, and He relaxed with
others. He didn't even hurry when Lazarus was dying! If God asks you
to be busy and hurry, go ahead. But if He isn't doing the asking, who
is—and why? Talk about the pace of your lifestyle together and your
need for quietness in God's presence.

MAY 28

But where sin increased, grace increased
all the more (Romans 5:20).

Do you remember the sharp sting of a personal failure? Do you recall the discomfort and heaviness that overcame you? Did you feel kind of like a leaky balloon gradually deflating and collapsing? Talk to each other for a few minutes about how you feel when you fail.

We have all failed. You forget an appointment. You blow up at a child who brings home a bad report card. You forget your main point in a speech. Your big sale falls through. When little failures accumulate we begin to see ourselves as a failure. But this is false thinking. No matter how often you fail, you are not a failure. The Bible is full of people who failed but who were anything but failures. Abraham lied, Moses committed murder, and David committed adultery and murder. But they all dealt with their failures and pressed on to serve God in the light of His grace. We need to do the same in our failures.

No matter why or how often we fail, our challenge is to understand each failure in the perspective of God's grace. We must allow Him to help us learn from the failure and use it for His glory.

Facing up to our failure is the first step. Admitting, "I blew it, I made a mistake, I'm responsible" is never easy. But it's necessary. Any kind of denial or cover-up not only raises a barrier between ourselves and others, it keeps us from seeing and accepting the comfort and support of God's grace. God's grace enables us to confront the pain and ask the question, "What was my responsibility in the failure, and what can I learn from it?" That's how we move on rather than get stuck. God says to us, "You're all right in my eyes when you succeed and when you fail."

Failure—yes, it's a part of life. Some call it a curse, but it's a curse that can be turned into a blessing![29]

MAY 29

He is also head of the body, the church; and He
is the beginning, the first-born from the dead; so
that He Himself might come to have first place
in everything (Colossians 1:18, NASB).

Two men met and one said, "What do you do?" The other didn't give an answer but in a friendly voice replied, "Who are you?" The other persisted in saying, "What do you do?" But he was met with the same reply, "Who are you?" Which question do you relate to more? Which of the two questions is more meaningful to your partner?

Some people go through life as doers, fixers, and accomplishers. They learn to juggle a multitude of tasks. Their life is made up of what they do, even for God. Their identity is wrapped up in what they do instead of who they are. As a result, sometimes chaos reigns because life is lopsided and out of balance.

Balance in life comes from letting Jesus Christ have first place in everything. Working for God doesn't bring more grace. He is more interested in who you are than in what you do! That is top priority with Him. Your value to God—and to your partner—is based on who you are in Jesus Christ, a person "accepted in the Beloved" (Ephesians 1:6, NKJV).

Where is the focus in your marriage? Do you accept each other for what you do or for who you are? What we do is to be an outgrowth of who we are. Our activity should be a reflection of inner values and beliefs. When Jesus Christ has been given His rightful place in our lives—the center—we begin to develop new character qualities. We discover our strengths and gifts, and what we do takes on new meaning. Activity becomes less intense and less frantic. Instead it expresses deeper concern for other people and their needs. There may be less emphasis on production and competitiveness but more on love, concern, and caring. That can only bring new life and health to you and your marriage.[30]

MAY 30

Just as you received Christ Jesus as Lord,
continue to live in him (Colossians 2:6).

Grow up!" This is a message many of us heard from well-meaning teachers or parents. Unfortunately, the words usually implied a rapid transformation: "Grow up right now!" But maturity at all levels of life is a gradual process. Farmers know that when the crop ripens slowly the flavor is better.

Growth and change in your spiritual life is a slow process too. Penelope Stokes writes: "Spiritual maturity is not a ladder that we climb or a goal that we aim for. It is, rather, the process of becoming all God has called us to be as individuals. We don't have to compete for the 'Mature Christian of the Year' award; we don't have to be hothouse tomatoes rushed to market on an arbitrary time schedule. We can, instead, ripen naturally on the vine, producing sweet fruit and good seed."[31]

Spiritual maturity is a journey, and we need the grace of God to sustain us on our way. The Word of God tells us that Jesus is the One who produces growth and spiritual maturity in our lives. He is "the author and perfecter of our faith" (Hebrews 12:2) as well as the One "who began a good work" in us and "will carry it on to completion" (Philippians 1:6).

In reality, spiritual maturity is a matter of growing closer to Jesus Christ and growing deeper in the understanding of God's Word and the Christian life. Maturity is a reflection of our walk with Christ. And because it's a walk, we do have some personal responsibilities. What are they?

First, don't compare your growth with that of other people or put your energy into making sure others (including your partner) are growing fast enough.

Second, take an honest look at your life, and allow the Holy Spirit to say, "Here's an area for some work."

Third, learn to be transparent and open before God and your marital partner. Admit your needs. What better place to reflect maturity than in your marriage?[32]

MAY 31

I consider that our present sufferings are not
worth comparing with the glory that will
be revealed in us (Romans 8:18).

Do you ever feel like not praying? How about when a shocking circumstance rudely crashes through the door of your life? Sometimes we don't feel like praying because we're too busy wondering why something happened: "God, why this? Why now? Why does it hurt so much?" God hears both your spoken and unspoken questions. Share with your partner the times when you've asked God why.

You can allow circumstances to control your interpretation of who God is, or you can allow God to control your interpretation of the circumstances. God is not the source of your pain. But He is the source of your comfort. Romans 5:2-4 states, "We rejoice in the hope of the glory of God. Not only so, but we also rejoice in our sufferings, because we know that suffering produces perseverance; perseverance, character; and character, hope."

Our society teaches us to avoid pain and look for pleasure. After all, happiness and fulfillment are what everyone is after. But people don't smile all the time. That's not realistic. There's a different perspective on life given in God's Word. If all things work for good (Romans 8:28), then something can be learned from the hard times of life. Penelope Stokes comments: "Those who suffer may have no heart to pray, no desire for fellowship, no peace in the midst of turmoil. But God's grace supports us even when we cannot comprehend it. He holds us up with invisible hands, never letting us go, waiting patiently until the time when we can see Him once again." [33]

So when you hit that time when you don't feel like praying, tell God about it. If there is a "why" question burning within your heart, go ahead and ask Him why. It's okay to be honest and real with God. Nothing you can say will surprise Him or shock Him. He already knows; why not get it off your chest and into the open. [34]

JUNE

⁓

*There is a substitute for criticism. It's called love.
Love heals. Love protects. Love builds up. And more
change occurs with love than with criticism.*

JUNE 1

Wives...be submissive to your husbands....Your beauty
should not come from outward adornment....Instead
it should be that of your inner self (1 Peter 3:1,3,4).

How do you feel when you read these words? Reactions vary. Interpretations vary. When Peter wrote these words he wrote them to a society in which wealthy women placed extreme importance on outward adornment. Naturally, a great deal of time went into the cultivation of this beauty. However, Peter contends that God is far more interested in the inner beauty of a woman than her outward appearance. But inner beauty also requires time and nurturing through daily involvement in the Scriptures and in prayer. In our society there is a tremendous imbalance between the amount of time we spend on outward appearance and the time we devote to inward development. Many women base their feelings of self-worth on how they look, whereas the true basis of self-worth should be on how God views us.

Peter mentions in verse 4 that inner beauty is reflected in an outwardly noticeable gentle spirit. Does this mean a Christian woman should never offer her opinions, solutions, leadership, or strength? Not at all. Nor does it mean that she is to be weak or incompetent. She is to use her God-given gifts and talents to the best of her ability. Gentleness is an attitude of thoughtfulness and servanthood. It means being willing to see God's pattern for marriage as the healthiest way to develop personal security and to reflect the presence of Jesus Christ in your marriage. A woman with a gentle spirit is one who has confidence as a result of relying upon God and using this gift to serve others.

June 2

*Husbands, in the same way be considerate as
you live with your wives, and treat them with
respect as the weaker partner and as heirs with
you of the gracious gift of life* (1 Peter 3:7).

A husband is responsible to choose a proper heart attitude toward his
wife. To be considerate as the initiator means to initiate in a loving
manner. Unfortunately, some husbands are very passive and allow their
leadership capabilities to either die or stagnate. Taking responsibility
and initiative is part of a husband's calling.

The King James Version of 1 Peter 3:7 instructs husbands, "Dwell
with them [wives] according to knowledge." The original language for
being considerate means seeking to know, to inquire, or investigate.
The implication here is for a husband to become an explorer and set
out on a lifetime expedition to discover his wife's likes, dislikes, needs,
the way in which she would like her needs met, her love language,
her strengths, weaknesses, moods, her sense of timing, and fears, and
then take all of this into consideration when he interacts with her. No
husband is a mind reader, so it is helpful when wives share their specific likes and dislikes with their husbands. From time to time it may
be helpful for a wife to identify for her husband 10 or 12 of her specific
needs and the best way he can meet them. A wife deeply appreciates her
husband when he really listens to her rather than merely tolerating her
viewpoint. When a husband is learning to respond to his wife from his
heart, his challenge is to attempt to see things from his wife's perspective and to understand her uniqueness.

And whenever it is obvious to a wife that her husband is making
this his goal, it is helpful that she recognize his attempts and affirm
him for seeking to live according to God's Word.

JUNE 3

Worship the Lord with reverence (Psalm 2:11, NASB).

Worship and marriage—are these themes related? Definitely. Life and marriage are full of surprises, and not all of these surprises are joyful. Some of them hurt. Some destroy. Some linger for years like an insidious cancer. What makes the difference in our marriages in the face of life's many surprises? Worship. Coming face to face with God and focusing on Him helps us handle life's surprises. Richard Exley comments:

> If you've lived for any length of time, you've probably had opportunity to see the different ways people respond to adversity. The same tragedy can make one person better and another person bitter. What makes the difference? Resources. Inner resources developed across a lifetime through spiritual disciplines. If you haven't worshiped regularly in the sunshine of your life, you probably won't be able to worship in the darkness. If you haven't been intimate with God in life's ordinariness, it's not likely that you will know how or where to find Him should life hand you some real hardships. But by the same token, if you have worshiped often and regularly, then you will undoubtedly worship well in the hour of your greatest need.[1]

As you worship during the good times, you are building your resources for the difficult times. That's why worshiping and sharing this intimate experience with God as a couple are so vital for the marriage relationship.

Most of the hymns we sing were written for worship. Do you have a hymnbook? Browse through some of the hymns. Select one which has words you and your partner want to express to God today. Sing or read the hymn aloud to Him. Your worship experience will definitely benefit your marriage.

JUNE 4

*Lord, who may dwell in your sanctuary? Who
may live on your holy hill?* (Psalm 15:1).

Before continuing with this meditation, read the remainder of Psalm 15 aloud together from your Bible.

What an interesting question! What are the conditions in which a person can dwell with God? The answer, which is given in verses 2-6, may not be very popular today. It can be summed up in one word: holiness. We can use another word to describe this quality: integrity. The psalm talks about our relationship with other people. We cannot expect to dwell in the presence of God if we are not treating other people properly. The psalmist describes people who do what is right and speak truthfully. He says people of holiness and integrity can be depended upon. They are concerned for others, not just for themselves.

To put it in today's context, people of integrity don't slander others or go around spreading gossip. They don't take unfair advantage of others. In today's society, many people are looking for some kind of advantage so they can gain the upper hand over others. They want to come out on top. We see it in marriages through the many power struggles which emerge. People who dwell with God are consistent in what they think, say, and do in their marriages. They can be depended upon to come through for their partner. Characteristics such as these are essential for trust to develop and remain within a marriage relationship.

The psalmist goes on to indicate that holy people are not afraid to share their disapproval when others do something wrong. They keep their promises, even when it puts them at a disadvantage. They are willing to accept the consequences. And they don't exploit others.

To sum up this psalm, the person who dwells with the Lord loves his or her neighbor. Your partner is your neighbor as well. As you focus on dwelling with God together in holiness and integrity, you will remain secure and stable throughout the ups and downs of life. That's not a bad promise, is it?

JUNE 5

*Be joyful always; pray continually; give thanks
in all circumstances, for this is God's will for you
in Christ Jesus* (1 Thessalonians 5:16-18).

Does your partner fulfill every request that you make of him or her? If so, you have a rare partner! And if you are honest, you must admit that you have denied some of his or her requests as well. That's just a normal part of life. Sometimes your request is not answered because your partner has more insight or wisdom than you at that moment. You often discover later that your partner's denial of your request was right, even though it was counter to what you wanted.

God's response to our prayers is the same. He does answer our requests, but when He answers and the way in which He answers may not be what we expect. Lloyd Ogilvie writes:

> Because God can see what we cannot see, and knows dimensions which we can never understand, He works out our answers according to a higher plan than we can conceive. We are to tell Him our needs and then leave them with Him. It's only in retrospect that we can see the narrowness of our vision and can see that His answer was far better than what we could even have anticipated.
>
> Prayer is not just the place and time we tell God what to do, but the experience in which He molds our lives. In the quiet of meditative prayer, we begin to see things from a different point of view and are given the power to wait for the unfolding of God's plan.[2]

There are times when our prayers need to include these words: "Lord, please give me the insight to know what I am to pray for and what You desire for my life. Give me the patience to wait for Your timing in answering my prayer. And give me the ability to handle answers which I did not anticipate."

Do you know what is at the heart of your partner's prayers at this time? Perhaps you could learn right now by asking.

JUNE 6

*Your word is a lamp to my feet and a
light for my path* (Psalm 119:105).

Your eyes strain to see. You squint, rub your eyes, and clean the windshield with a cloth. Nothing seems to work. You're driving in fog—that heavy, wet, misty, impenetrable haze. Many people avoid driving in it when they know it has descended in their vicinity.

Some types of fog can't be avoided. Often our lives seem to be shrouded in thick fog, a fog that exists in our mind. We can't think clearly. We're faced with momentous decisions as a couple and the clarity we seek is elusive. We're stymied by confusion and disorientation. We need a strong light which can penetrate the mist and give us clarity of mind and spirit.

The psalmist said that God's Word is both a lamp and a light which direct us in our times of clarity and our times of foggy thinking. John the apostle talked about another light which can lead us out of the fog: "In him was life, and that life was the light of men. The light shines in the darkness, but the darkness has not understood it....The true light that gives light to every man was coming into the world" (John 1:4,5,9). The Word of God reveals the light that can give clarity to any life, and this clarity is found in God's Son, Jesus Christ.

There's another use for this light, however. God wants us to share His clarifying, guiding light with others. We are to become rescue units penetrating the fog to discover others who are struggling. We are to let them know about the light that can change their lives. Do you know other couples who need this light? If so, how will you take the light to those people?[3]

JUNE 7

As far as the east is from the west, so far has he
removed our transgressions from us (Psalm 103:12).

"Just forget it, will you! If you could forget what happened we could move on in life."

This is an important request whether spoken in angry exasperation or as a plaintive plea. No doubt you have spoken this request to your spouse in the past, for marriage provides the greatest possibility for hurt and offense. But when we say, "Forget it, please," aren't we really saying, "Let me off the hook, give me a break, forgive me"?

What a relief that we don't have to plead, bargain, or become exasperated with God over our sins. All we have to do is follow 1 John 1:9: "If we confess our sins, he is faithful and just and will forgive us our sins and purify us from all unrighteousness." What does He do about our sinfulness? He forgives us. What does He do with our offenses? He forgets them. In Isaiah we read: "I, even I, am he who blots out your transgressions, for my own sake, and remembers your sins no more" (43:25). Jeremiah added: "'They will all know me, from the least of them to the greatest,' declares the Lord. 'For I will forgive their wickedness and will remember their sins no more'" (31:34). James Moffatt translates this last verse, "Their sin I never will recall."

If God is omniscient, He can't really forget anything. But He can and does choose not to recall sins that have been forgiven. We, as humans, tend to remind others of their transgression. God doesn't. What are our choices when others offend us? We can choose to forgive, but we can't really forget. So we can choose to remember with bitterness and indignation, or we can choose to remember with compassion. What about it? When it comes to forgiving and forgetting, will you give a blessing or a curse? It is your choice.[4]

JUNE 8

Religion that God our Father accepts as pure
and faultless is this: to look after orphans and
widows in their distress (James 1:27).

Religion is a rather vague word. What does James mean by it? Simply
this. He used it to describe a person's service to God and others
as a Christian. And then he goes on to describe how we can reflect our
faith in Jesus Christ in a very practical way.

The illustration he uses had an impact on his readers. The plight
of widows and orphans was a pressing need of that day. It was also a
concern in Old Testament times, and God had compassion for the
less fortunate: "Do not take advantage of a widow or an orphan. If
you do and they cry out to me, I will certainly hear their cry" (Exodus
22:22,23). Furthermore, God repeatedly instructed His people to take
care of aliens and strangers and not mistreat them (Exodus 22:21;
Deuteronomy 10:17-19). Jesus echoed the Father's concern in Mark
12:38-40.

These principles of caring for the less fortunate were not limited to
Bible times and culture. They are applicable for each one of us today.
God wants you and your partner to care for people who have physical
needs that cannot be cared for in any other way. Take a moment and
reflect: Who are the people who need you? Are they in Africa or China,
or do they live on your block? Could they be in your own church?
What are their needs? We have been called to care for the needs of
Christians and non-Christians alike.

God wants us to care for the needs of family members as well.
Sometimes it's difficult to see family members as people to be ministered to in this way, especially if they are unappreciative. You may have
to look carefully to discover some of the needs of your loved ones. They
may be embarrassed to let you know they have need, but you can find
them if you really look.

Living out our faith is very practical. It means making a difference
in another person's life. Who's first on your list?[5]

JUNE 9

*Religion that God our Father accepts as pure
and faultless is this:...to keep oneself from
being polluted by the world* (James 1:27).

Pollution—the very word strikes a dissonant chord whenever we hear it. Images of oil spills, smog, toxic waste, and gas leaks come to mind. Environmental pollution is all around us, and most of it can be prevented with thought and care.

There's a worse kind of pollution, however. It's personal pollution. James states that an important characteristic of true religion is keeping yourself from the pollution of the world. You live in a sinful world, and its influence is all around you. But who is influencing whom? Is the world polluting you or are you influencing the world for God? If you are allowing the world's pollution to affect you, its attitudes and beliefs will creep into your marriage as well.

God's Word is very clear about avoiding the contamination of the world: "Do not be conformed to this world....But be transformed (changed) by the [entire] renewal of your mind—by its new ideals and its new attitude" (Romans 12:2, AMP); "You adulterous people, don't you know that friendship with the world is hatred toward God? Anyone who chooses to be a friend of the world becomes an enemy of God" (James 4:4).

All right, then, but the big question is how do we keep from being polluted by the world? Again look to God's Word: "He has bestowed on us His precious and exceedingly great promises, so that through them you may escape (by flight) from the moral decay (rottenness and corruption) that is in the world because of covetousness (lust and greed), and become sharers (partakers) of the divine nature" (2 Peter 1:4, AMP). God's promises, written in His Word, are the antidote to personal pollution.

Share with each other some promises from God's Word which will equip you for avoiding worldly pollution. Take turns quoting verses which come to mind. This is the first step in this phase of true religion.

JUNE 10

*Don't show favoritism...If you really keep the
royal law found in Scripture, "Love your neighbor
as yourself," you are doing right. But if you
show favoritism, you sin* (James 2:1,8,9).

Do you know what is going to happen today? You will probably have an opportunity to live out this passage from James in your interaction with people. These verses highlight a common disease prevalent in our society and in all of our lives at one time or another. It's called prejudice. You know what that means: making an unfair or preferential judgment against another person.

Favoritism and prejudice can even pollute a couple's relationship with others. Have you and your spouse made comments like these: "We don't want to invite them. They just wouldn't fit in"; "They didn't go to college and I'm sure they wouldn't feel comfortable in our Sunday School class. Everyone else is a college graduate"; "It's better not to spend time with them. We're pro-life, and they're for abortion."

We are tempted to exclude people because they dress, talk, live, or socialize differently from us. And anyone who is different from us is a problem. Perhaps now is a good time to read James 2:1-13 aloud in its entirety.

Jesus told His disciples, "As I have loved you, so you must love one another" (John 13:34). This is the principle that sets us free from partiality and favoritism in our relationships with others. Jesus did not say, "I will accept you if..." He placed no prejudicial conditions of acceptance on anyone who came to Him. There must be no "if" clauses in our relationships with others, no conditions attached to becoming involved with them. There is one love which breaks down all social, economic, racial, ethnic, and religious barriers—and that's the love of Jesus Christ.

Can you think of someone you have avoided as a couple because of a prejudicial attitude? If so, what can you do today which will begin to dissolve that attitude and improve your relationship with them?

JUNE 11

No man can tame the tongue. It is a restless evil, full of deadly poison....Out of the same mouth come praise and cursing. My brothers, this should not be (James 3:8,10).

We have all seen the devastation a raging forest fire can produce in a lovely forest. It's hard to imagine that such devastation begins with a seemingly insignificant little spark. But the wounds produced by that spark will be visible on the land for several decades.

Your tongue has the same potential for destruction as a spark of fire. Some individuals and couples need a damage control engineer with them at all times because they constantly misuse their gift of speech. There are many ways to misuse the tongue. Here are three: gossip, rationalized hurtful comments, and insensitive comments.

Malicious gossip is a deliberate attempt to hurt another person by telling untrue or exaggerated stories about him or her. Not too many marriage partners use this hurtful device against each other, but unfortunately many use it against their in-laws!

Sometimes you will rationalize yourself into making hurtful comments you ordinarily wouldn't make about someone. But you wrongly convince yourself that what you have to say, as hurtful as it is, is necessary "for his (or her) own good." But the only comments which are for someone's good are those which build up.

A third way a tongue is misused is through comments which are spoken with insensitivity to another's feelings. Tragically, this is all too common in marriage! Ask yourself, does it need to be said? Can my partner handle emotionally what I'm going to say at this time? Is it really true, or is it just one person's perception or opinion? Is Jesus Christ in control of my tongue as I make this comment?

If you want to measure your maturity as an individual or a couple, start by evaluating whether what you say is a blessing or a curse. Does it create a warm, inviting campfire or a raging, destructive forest fire?

JUNE 12

The blind man said, "Rabbi, I want to see" (Mark 10:51).

Ophthalmologists do wonders today to correct vision problems. It is possible to have not only bifocals but trifocals—and blended ones at that! It is also possible to get one contact lens to correct a distance problem in one eye and another lens to correct a difficulty with nearsightedness in the other eye. And the brain is able to tell each eye how to function correctly. These new breakthroughs have enabled many people with very poor vision to enjoy almost perfect eyesight.

Some blind people are blind from birth, while others become blind through accident or illness. Some can be helped, but others remain in a sightless condition permanently. Have you ever wondered what it would be like to be blind? Put on a blindfold for an hour and attempt to function in your home as you normally do. You will probably end up with a few bruises and perhaps a broken vase or two. But when it's over you will have a deeper sense of compassion for those who are blind.

Most blind people want to gain the use of their eyes, as did the man who spoke to Jesus in today's verse. But can you imagine someone who can see but chooses not to? Perhaps in some ways we are all blind by choice. We look around us but fail to see the needs of others in our own neighborhood. We are often blind to our partner's needs which are right in front of our face. And we sometimes fail to see our need for spiritual growth and change, or we are blind to the sin in our life.

Where are you blinded by choice today? If you were to ask Jesus to heal your selective blindness, what would He need to touch? What would He need to do to cause you to see? What would He want you to see in the life of your partner? Jesus Christ was and is the sight-giver. He still restores eyesight today, and often the most needed restoration is spiritual eyesight.

JUNE 13

Do not repay anyone evil for evil (Romans 12:17).

Criticism. It stings. It hurts. It can ruin your entire day. No one likes to be criticized, especially if the criticism is false. As one person said, "Show me a man who likes to be criticized, and I'll show you a masochist!"

The closer the person who criticizes you is to you, the more it hurts. Spouses are often critical of one another in marriage. Sometimes our criticism of each other is valid, but often it's not because it springs from a wrong appraisal of our spouse or his or her behavior. You may not be able to control the fact that unjust criticism will come your way, but you do have control over how you handle it!

We can learn how to respond to criticism from people in the Bible who were criticized. Moses was criticized by the nation God called him to serve and by his subordinates. But the real pain came when he was criticized by his own family. Moses' own brother and sister spoke against him because he married a Cushite woman (Numbers 12:1). Aaron and Miriam were jealous of Moses and questioned whether God had really spoken through him (12:2). They even made their accusations public. That is when criticism really hurts! That is why when a problem occurs between you and your partner, it's best not to bring parents and other relatives into it. You may get over the problem, but your relatives may hang onto it for years.

Take a clue from Moses about handling criticism. First, he did not defend himself against the criticism of his family. He knew that the truth would eventually exonerate him, and it did. Second, he did not retaliate against his brother and sister. That's usually the first response to criticism. But when you retaliate you don't solve the problem, you compound it by becoming like the ones who have hurt you.

When did you last feel unjustly criticized by your partner? Talk about it together, and be sure to include words of forgiveness.[6]

JUNE 14

Some trust in chariots and some in horses, but we trust
in the name of the Lord our God (Psalm 20:7).

A newscaster polled people on a busy intersection in downtown New York. The question asked was, "What gives you security today? What do you place your trust in?" How would you answer that question? Have you ever thought about it? What can you live without at this time in your life and still feel secure? What would your life be like if you didn't have an adequate medical plan? a retirement plan? the hope of Social Security when you retire? Do you find security in the government? the stock market? Do you have confidence in your own ability to handle the various problems that you face each day? How would you handle life if your partner were no longer present? Could you function and feel secure if he or she were to die tomorrow?

Some of these questions are not pleasant, but they reveal the realities of life. And the elements of worldly security in these questions reflect many of the answers given to the newscaster in response to his question. These are the kinds of things people trust in today, but none of them are trustworthy. Many people trust in these earthly structures, but they are all so shaky that they could crumble overnight. That fact doesn't make me feel very secure! How about you?

David gave some serious thought to these questions. He knew the importance of the war machines of his day, but he knew human strength and ingenuity wasn't enough. Trusting in the name of God and what He has done for us through Jesus Christ is the greatest source of security. No matter what happens around us, we have His peace and stability. Can you think of a better option? Share together what tends to give you comfort and security. How could the presence of Jesus give you a greater sense of security?

JUNE 15

When I was in distress, I sought the Lord; at
night I stretched out untiring hands and my
soul refused to be comforted....I remembered
my songs in the night (Psalm 77:2,6).

When do life's troubles seem worse to you: during the day or at
night? Some nights you find yourself tossing and turning, unable
to sleep, and your mind runs wild. You go over the problem again and
again. But the more you think about it, the more the problem seems
to grow. Solutions don't come; you begin to feel all alone.

Asaph, the author of Psalm 77, talks about being tormented by his
troubles at night. He felt abandoned by God in the midst of his deep
personal pain. But he did the right thing by venting his feelings to
God. Often when you despair you discover how to wait patiently for
the Lord. He does answer, and being honest with your thoughts and
feelings is the first step to receiving God's solution to your problem.[7]

The following words from Don Wyrtzen's song "Then I Remembered" may be an encouragement to you:

> Troubled, I couldn't speak
> Worried, I couldn't sleep;
> Rejected, unloved, my longings were unfulfilled.
> I prayed to God for help,
> "O Lord, don't you hear me?"
> Distressed, I reached out my hands to Him,
> His voice said, "Peace, be still!"
> Then I remembered how He touched me
> And He made me His heir,
> How He's led me like a Shepherd
> I'm a wonder of His care;
> When I remembered all He had done for me,
> I was lifted from despair—
> He heard me, He touched me
> And He answered my prayer.[8]

JUNE 16

When I consider your heavens, the work of your
fingers, the moon and the stars, which you have set in
place, what is man that you are mindful of him, the
son of man that you care for him? (Psalm 8:3,4).

The psalmist raised an interesting question: "What is man?" You could be asking that question today. Usually the question "Who am I?" arises during adolescence. We begin to discover a little about ourselves at that time. During our 30s and 40s men and women tend to ponder the question again. The question of our identity is often a difficult one to answer.

Sometimes people are asked to describe who they are without reference to their work or family status. How would you answer the question, "Who are you?" If you're from Denver, you might say you're a Coloradan. But that's not who you are, that's where you live. You might say you're a Baptist or Presbyterian, but those are denominations. You might say you're a mother or a father, but what happens if your children are suddenly taken from you? Who are you then?

You might say you're a teacher or a clerk. That's not who you are, that's what you do. What happens to your identity when a recession hits and you're laid off? What happens when you retire? Do you retire your identity as well? You might say, "I'm a concert pianist." But what happens to your identity when an accident takes away three of your fingers? Who are you then?

When someone asks "Who are you?" there's one way to state your identity which is totally honest and which does not change with time or circumstances. You can say, "I am a sinner saved by the grace of God. I am God's workmanship created in Jesus Christ." You really can't get much more complete than that. It's the only identity that will survive the experiences of life which affect the job, family, and church.

Take a few minutes to talk together about your true identity as individuals and as a couple. Practice answering the question "Who are you?" with each other.[9]

JUNE 17

*Just as the living Father sent me and I live
because of the Father, so the one who feeds on
me will live because of me* (John 6:57).

How can you really live the Christian life? One way to illustrate the answer is with the story of the arctic tern. Each year this bird sets out on the longest migratory journey attempted by any bird. It flies thousands of miles from one pole to the other.

But there's another amazing fact about this bird. After an arctic tern's chicks are hatched and old enough to fend for themselves, the parents say goodbye and take off for the south pole. Weeks pass as the fledglings patiently grow and develop their wing muscles through play and practice flying. Then one day they leave the only home they have ever known to begin a journey over an unknown course to an unknown destination. And they make it to the South Pole!

Deep inside, the young arctic terns know they cannot stay where they were born; they must move on. Instinct drives them to make the same journey that their parents made months before. But how do they know when to leave? Why do they wait so long to succumb to that drive? They wait until they have the strength for the journey.

When you received Jesus Christ as your Savior, He came to live within you. Because of His presence, there is a desire written in your heart to become an expression of His will. But how do you do this? By using the power which is available to you. Look back at today's verse. You have the same power which was available to Jesus Christ! Jesus also said, "As the Father has sent me, I am sending you" (John 20:21). You're already strong enough to live a successful Christian life. The power is within you in Christ. Tap into it and begin to soar. Perhaps the two of you may find it helpful to talk about the direction God's power is to be used in your lives. How can your marriage reflect this power so others are drawn to Christ?[10]

JUNE 18

Be of the same (agreeable) mind one with another.
Live in peace (2 Corinthians 13:11, AMP).

When you watch the news at night, one of the main features is the weather report. It lets you know the current weather conditions as well as what to expect for the next few days. And the meteorologist usually goes into elaborate detail to describe the conditions: heat, cold, snow, rain, sunshine, hurricanes.

If you were to evaluate the current conditions of your marriage in meteorological terms, what would your weather report say? Just like the weather, some conditions in your marriage change daily or weekly. But what is the prevailing weather pattern in your marriage? Some people might describe their marriage as, "Plenty of sunshine and warmth with light gentle winds." Others might say, "Light rain squalls which give way to a calm serene atmosphere." Still others would describe their marriage as one major storm front after another with either blizzard-, hurricane-, or tornado-like conditions.

Some marital storms blow over in time leaving behind refreshing, brisk breezes and newly gained insights. Other storms, if they continue, leave a path of devastation and marital destruction. The marriage is gradually leveled as if relentless, pounding waves consistently beat against it and eroded it.

As you reflect upon the current status of your marriage, what is the forecast for the future? Is the outlook bright and encouraging, or is there a consistent storm pattern swirling around? Remember: You have an advantage over the weather forecaster. You can influence the weather pattern in your marriage. You can interrupt the presence of storm clouds. You can even change drought conditions by turning on a flow of love, acceptance, and encouragement to your partner.

Paul's words of counsel in today's verse can stabilize a marriage. Through talking and listening, differences with your spouse can be resolved and one-mindedness and peace can be achieved. How can this verse be reflected in your marriage today?

JUNE 19

*Be kind and compassionate to one another, forgiving each
other, just as in Christ God forgave you* (Ephesians 4:32).

The call to forgive is sometimes a difficult one, especially in marriage.
You may not always want to forgive your partner because harboring
the hurt seems to dull the pain you feel from being rejected or offended.
And yet forgiveness is the bonding material that keeps a marriage alive
and moving ahead for a lifetime. The call to be married is also the call
to forgive your partner hundreds of times over the years.

Forgiveness is not always fair or equitable. That's reality. Sometimes
you may feel like trying to make your partner pay for what he or she
has done. "It just isn't fair," we complain. "I want my spouse to feel
my scorn. After all, I was stung by what he (or she) did!" But who is
the loser when you don't forgive? You are. You end up with a videotape
running inside your memory that plays the hurt over and over again.
When you don't forgive you are allowing the other person to dictate or
control you. But when you forgive you are allowing God to dictate or
control your life. Is there any real comparison? Think about it!

Forgiveness is not forgetting. Whatever happened to you remains
in your memory banks. Forgiveness is remembering, forgiving, and
moving ahead in life. Eventually you move from painful remembering
to historical remembering: "Yes, that happened, but it no longer
impacts my life. Let's move ahead."

Forgiveness is not pretending or living in denial. You face the
offense and the ensuing hurt and talk about it so it doesn't become a
repetitive pattern of life.

And when you truly forgive, you can no longer bring up past inci-
dents and throw them at your partner either verbally or in your mind.
Remember the words of Proverbs 17:9 (NASB): "He who covers a transgression seeks love, but he who repeats a matter separates intimate
friends."

What do you need to discuss about forgiveness today?

JUNE 20

The people were amazed at his teaching (Mark 1:22).

"Amazing! Incredible!"

When was the last time you used these words to express your feelings or responses? What created this sense of amazement within you? Or has life become so mechanized, so full of logical explanations and reasons that you have difficulty responding to it with wonder, awe, or amazement?

Unfortunately many people lose their childlike quality of being surprised, impressed, or amazed at life. There are people who are so threatened by the unexplainable in life that they snuff out the wonder of it for themselves and others. That's sad—especially when it happens in our relationship with Christ.

When you read the Gospels or hear accounts of what God is doing in the lives of His people today, do you respond as the people of Jesus' day did? "Everyone who heard him was amazed at his understanding and his answers" (Luke 2:47); "And when Jesus finished saying these things, the crowds were amazed at his teaching" (Matthew 7:28). Have you ever felt amazed at the fact that Jesus Christ lives within you? Do you stand in awe of the power of God which is alive and active in you today? Are you open to being amazed and astonished by God? Think about it.

> It takes grace in our time to keep our minds open to wonder, to be ready for the tug from God, the push from the Spirit, and the revelation of deep things from the hearts of ordinary people. It takes grace, but it is a great gift. If you have a place in your life where your eyes can still gape, your knees quiver, and your mind boggle, you are open for wonder. And, open to wonder, you are ready for God's surprises, even the greatest of all: that it can be all right when everything is wrong.[11]

Ask God to open your eyes and fill them with wonder today.

JUNE 21

Do you have eyes but fail to see…? (Mark 8:18).

Eyes—we use them to scan the room, to focus so intently on someone that everything else begins to blur. Our eyes tell us stories. They invite people into our lives. Your eyes were an important instrument in bringing you to marriage. In his book *The Mystery of Marriage,* Mike Mason says:

> Marriage is, before it is anything else, an act of contemplation. It is a divine pondering, an exercise in amazement. This is evident from the very start, from the moment a man and a woman first lay eyes on one another and realize they are in love. The whole thing begins with a wondrous looking, a helpless staring, an irresistible compulsion simply to behold. For suddenly there is so much to see! So much is revealed when two people dare to stand in the radiance of one another's love. And so there is a divine paralysis of adoration; everything else stops, or at least fades into the background, and love itself takes center stage.[12]

When you first saw your partner, what did you see? The answer to your dreams? Undeveloped potential? Were you looking at him or her through rose-colored lenses?

Sometimes we see what we want to see and ignore reality. We look with a critical eye and discover all the imperfections. Or we look with an accepting eye and see the potential and value that God sees in a person. We can watch the soft skin of our partner slowly turn to wrinkles. But instead of turning away, we can choose instead to see the love that resides within him or her. These choices are available to each of us.

Ask God to open your eyes to see the hidden beauty that comes from within your partner. See him or her with the eyes that God uses. You may see something you've never seen before.

JUNE 22

*Trust in the Lord with all your heart, and do not lean
on your own understanding* (Proverbs 3:5, NASB).

Athletes do not always appreciate their coaches. Oh, a coach may
give excellent instruction, but he also must push his players to work
hard and excel. One athlete said, "The coach pushed me to limits that
I felt were beyond me. At times I felt I was going to drown." But this
athlete didn't drown. Instead he became an Olympic gold medalist.

Many athletes in training soon discover that their commitment
requires more discipline than they bargained for. Isn't marriage the
same? Mike Mason describes it this way:

> To put it simply, marriage is a relationship far more
> engrossing than we want it to be. It always turns out to be
> more than we bargained for. It is disturbingly intense, disrup-
> tively involving, and that is exactly the way it was designed
> to be. It is supposed to be more, almost, than we can handle.
> It was meant to be a lifelong encounter that would be much
> more rigorous and demanding than anything human beings
> ever could have chosen, dreamed of, desired, or invented on
> their own. After all, we do not even choose to undergo such
> far-reaching encounters with our closest and dearest friends.
> Only marriage urges us into these deep and unknown waters.
> For that is its very purpose: to get us out beyond our depth,
> out of the shadows of our own secure egocentricity and into
> the dangerous and unpredictable depths of a real interper-
> sonal encounter.[13]

Have you discovered marriage to be just that? That's why you can't
live it on your own. Let God join you in those depths which at times
may threaten to overwhelm you. In Him the depths of your marriage
relationship can be handled. You and your partner can grow more than
you ever imagined!

JUNE 23

The Lord gave and the Lord has taken away; may
the name of the Lord be praised (Job 1:21).

Isn't today's verse a strange one for a meditation for marriage? Perhaps, but perhaps not. Life involves both receiving and giving, and so does marriage. When you married you received the love of your spouse, but at the same time you gave away your freedom to think and act solely for yourself. There is great joy in receiving, but when you married you also entered into a relationship that entails the suffering of giving. Lewis Smedes boldly states: "Anybody's marriage is a harvest of suffering....Your marriage vow was a promise to suffer. You promised to suffer, only to suffer with, however, not from....A marriage is a life of shared pain."[14]

Think about it for a moment: In marriage you have the opportunity to experience a new world of hurts. The vulnerability which encompasses marriage opens your life up to this new, scary world. Your partner can fulfill your wildest dreams or disappoint you to the extent that your relationship becomes a nightmare. That's one type of suffering. But another type is sharing your partner's hurt and learning how to be a source of comfort to him or her.

Marriage is a call to share every aspect of your partner's life. Perhaps you are just discovering this truth about marriage. You both experienced suffering when you were single, but perhaps you're experiencing even more in marriage. Mike Mason says, "For it is not in the nature of love to deflect pain, but rather to absorb it, and to absorb greater and greater amounts of it. Marriage gives a face to suffering, just as it gives a face to joy."[15]

Think about it. Talk about it. How do you suffer with one another? How can you comfort one another? The suffering will inevitably be there. Be sure your support and comfort are there as well.

JUNE 24

In everything give thanks (1 Thessalonians 5:18, NASB).

Before you continue reading, find your wedding album and take out a photograph of the entire wedding party. As you sit and look at the photo (or if no photo is available, recall by name the people who were in your wedding party), reflect back on that special day. Can you remember...

> How you felt as you woke up on your wedding day and thought about the events of the day ahead?
>
> Who were the first people you talked to that morning?
>
> Did you call each other or talk to each other in person before the wedding? If so, what did you talk about?

It may be difficult to recall some of these events because of the years which have elapsed. Many people go into shock on their wedding day in order to survive the events! Can you remember...

> What your mother and/or father said to you that day?
>
> What the minister said to you before the ceremony?
>
> How the minister prayed for you during the ceremony? Would you have him pray the same prayer today for your marriage?
>
> Who were the people in your wedding party? Where are they today? Do you know how their marriages are today?

Can you also remember...

> What were three reasons you had for marrying your partner?
>
> What were several of the expectations you had for your marriage?

If you got married today, what would you do differently during the next six months than you did during the first six months of your marriage? In what way would Jesus Christ's place in your marriage be different today than at that time? Take time today to reflect, share your memories together, and give thanks to God for your marriage.

JUNE 25

*So they are no longer two, but one. Therefore what God
has joined together, let man not separate* (Matthew 19:6).

Remember that special day? You stood facing each other and recited your marriage vows. Do you remember what you said at that time? What do those vows mean to you at this point in your marriage?

In this day and age, how can a couple fulfill the commitment they made on their wedding day? Grace. God's grace is the only way a couple can survive all the pressures and temptations today.

There are no lasting marriages without the continuing secret touch of His grace, which comes to a couple in the form of the uncanny ability to keep a set of highly improbable promises to one another, promises involving such normally evanescent qualities as love, honor, trust, faithfulness.[16]

Did you use the words honor and faithfulness in your wedding vows? What do those words mean to you in your marriage? Very few couples ever sit down and explain to each other what they meant by their vows. We just assume that we understand what these sacred words mean. But do we really? Perhaps now would be a good time to explain to each other what you meant when you promised to honor, to be faithful, to respect, etc.

When you married, you pledged to keep your wedding vows. Jesus challenged you not to let anyone come between you and cause you to break your vows. How are marital vows kept? By your own strength? Not so. "The marriage vows give glory to God. While it is true that a man and a woman on their wedding day take a step toward a unique fulfillment of the commandment of love, it is even more true to say of matrimony that it is a sacramental outpouring of God's grace enabling such love to take place."[17]

Aren't you thankful that God's grace is a part of your marriage? Will you thank Him together right now?

JUNE 26

*Jesus looked at him and loved him. "One thing
you lack," he said. "Go, sell everything you have
and give to the poor, and you will have treasure in
heaven. Then come, follow me"* (Mark 10:21).

What did you give up in order to marry your partner? Have you
ever thought about it? Many individuals today simply try to
bring their single lifestyle into their marriage relationship. They think
a marriage partner is just one more addition to their already busy lives.
They believe they will somehow be able to fit a husband or wife in
around everything else.

But a rude awakening occurs when the truth of what marriage
really is penetrates these people: "A marriage is not a joining of two
worlds, but an abandoning of two worlds in order that one new one
might be formed. In this sense, the call to be married bears comparison
to Jesus' advice to the rich young man to sell all his possessions and to
follow Him. It is a vocation to total abandonment."[18]

When you married, no doubt you had to make some adjustments
and change a few habits. Perhaps you put some educational dreams on
hold for a while or even delayed buying a new car. But as Jesus' message
to the rich young ruler illustrates, true commitment to someone means
much more than that. When you married, you began to fulfill one of
Jesus' commands. Mike Mason relates: "For most people...marriage is
the single most wholehearted step they will ever take toward a fulfillment of Jesus' command to love one's neighbor, and often enough a
neighbor who has been left beaten and wounded on the road of love,
whom all the rest of the world has in a sense passed by."[19]

How can you be faithful in carrying out the commands of Jesus to
love your partner selflessly? It can't be imagined or carried out without
the grace and love of God. What a tragedy if His grace were not available. That's something to thank God for.

JUNE 27

Finally, brothers, whatever is true...noble...right...
pure...lovely...admirable—if anything is excellent or
praiseworthy—think about such things (Philippians 4:8).

Why did you marry your partner? Think about it. Why did you commit yourself for life to the person seated next to you? Furthermore, did you marry the person you thought you married? After an intense and disappointing disagreement with his wife, one husband expressed his frustration by saying, "Mary, you're not the woman I thought I married!" She looked at him with a slight smile and said, "I never was the woman you thought you married!"

Are any of us the people our spouses thought they married? Some individuals marry a phantom or a dream, and throughout their marriage they continue to chase that illusion. Many couples are surprised by marriage. Were you?

Regardless of why you married, the fact is that you are now married! Every couple is confronted by surprises and adjustments in marriage. We can allow these to totally throw us, or we can use them as opportunities for growth. Once you marry you are confronted with reality, but reality is not synonymous with trouble or disappointment! Reality carries the potential for making new discoveries and developing flexibility and protection against stagnation.

What makes the difference? Learning to live in the strength, comfort, and power of the grace of God; learning to direct your focus to the qualities Paul lists in Philippians 4:8; learning to take those discoveries about your partner which have the potential for disappointment and turn them into joy.

The issue is not so much who you married and why, but who you are and who you become in your marriage. As each of you develop and grow in Jesus Christ, you will discover that you have a better partner than the one you thought you married!

JUNE 28

Therefore, if anyone is in Christ, he is a new creation; the old has gone, the new has come! (2 Corinthians 5:17).

How long has it been since you received your mind transplant? "I've heard a lot about heart and liver transplants," you may be saying, "but what in the world is a mind transplant?" It happened when you invited Jesus Christ into your life. First Corinthians 2:16 states, "We have the mind of Christ." First Corinthians 1:30 (NASB) says, "By His doing you are in Christ Jesus, who became to us wisdom from God, and righteousness and sanctification, and redemption." Put these two verses together and what do you have? Not only do you have the mind of Christ, but you also have God's wisdom to apply in using the mind of Christ in your life. That's quite a transplant!

And it is so necessary! Most of the great battles of life occur in the mind. Most of the great battles and conflicts which occur in marriages originate in the mind. When you came into this life, you arrived with a mind affected by the Fall—original sin. It has a propensity toward negative thinking. Even now that you are a Christian, the residue of old thinking creeps in at times. Your mind is the source of the words you share with your partner. It is also the source of your behaviors and many of your emotional responses.

That's why we need a new mind and God's wisdom. Remind yourself daily that you have the mind of Christ, and be open to using it in your life. Paul certainly was clear about what we need: a spiritual mind (Romans 8:6); a renewed mind (Ephesians 4:23); a transformed mind (Romans 12:2); a Christlike mind (1 Corinthians 2:11); and a sound mind (2 Timothy 1:7).

What do you want in your marriage? Joy? Love? Harmony? Fulfillment? Intimacy? The reflection of the presence of Jesus Christ? There is a solution available that makes all of these qualities possible. It's called transformed thinking—a mind transplant. And it can happen to each of you.

JUNE 29

*The wisdom that comes from heaven is first of all
pure and full of quiet gentleness. Then it is peace-
loving and courteous* (James 3:17, TLB).

In order to prepare for a discussion on God's wisdom, read the following passage aloud together:

> The wisdom that comes from heaven is first of all pure and full of quiet gentleness. Then it is peace-loving and courteous. It allows discussion and is willing to yield to others; it is full of mercy and good deeds. It is wholehearted and straightforward and sincere. And those who are peacemakers will plant seeds of peace and reap a harvest of goodness (James 3:17,18, TLB).

Now talk through the following questions together:

1. What does wisdom mean to you?

2. How do you see yourself and your partner reflecting quiet gentleness?

3. Describe how the phrase "peace-loving" is compatible with resolving conflicts in marriage.

4. How does courtesy reflect a wisdom which comes from heaven?

5. What does it mean to you that wisdom from heaven allows discussion?

6. What might there be in your marriage at the present time that isn't being discussed but needs to be?

7. How can mercy be reflected in your relationship?

8. Which of your partner's good deeds do you most appreciate today?

9. Describe what the words "wholehearted" and "sincere" mean to you.

10. Put the phrase "seeds of peace and a harvest of goodness" into your own words.

JUNE 30

Let the peace of Christ rule in your hearts,
since as members of one body you were
called to peace (Colossians 3:15).

One of the most important people on the field during a baseball game is the umpire. He is there for one specific reason: to clarify and enforce the rules. His decisions are not always popular, but they are necessary.

In today's passage the verb *rule* implies umpiring. The peace of Jesus Christ is to be the ruler, the decision-maker, or the umpire in our lives. If you have the peace of Christ in your life, your attitude and perspective in life will change. When you think about concerns in your work and marriage in a way which reflects Christ, you will begin to see a difference.

For example, if you expect something to turn out in a positive way, you will probably approach it with a positive attitude and display more confidence. The way you speak and your posture will reflect your attitude. However, if you are fearful or negative it will show, and often that negativism will be instrumental in bringing about the negative results you fear. Saying to your partner, "You don't want to go out to dinner, do you?" is negative. Compare it with the positive approach, "Wouldn't it be great to go out to eat tonight?"

How do you become more positive, especially in approaching your partner? First, realize that you have the peace of Christ in your life. Second, change your negative thoughts into positive thoughts. Next, choose to believe that the peace of Christ can change your life. Let Him rule your life. Then, regardless of how you feel, act as though your new way of responding is going to be effective.

You see, you don't have to wait for your feelings to change first; you can act upon the knowledge you already have. And as you begin to change in your approach, you will discover a greater peace in your life. In time you may hear your partner say, "You seem so much more peaceful and calm. I've even noticed it in the way you approach me. And I appreciate it."

JULY

Consistency—that's what gives a marriage relationship stability and security. Consistency means being steady. You can count on it today and tomorrow. Consistency includes determination, patience, and strength....

JULY 1

Your beauty...should be that of your inner self, the
unfading beauty of a gentle and quiet spirit, which
is of great worth in God's sight (1 Peter 3:3,4).

Many husbands rejoice when they read the verse which calls wives
to express a quiet spirit. They equate this quality with not talking
or giving an opinion. But it has nothing to do with a woman becoming
a "nothing" or being a silent partner.

The Greek word for quiet really means a tranquility which comes
from within and causes no disturbance to other people. When a
woman possesses this inner peace and tranquility, she doesn't have
to prove herself to her husband or to anyone else. She is strong and
she knows it. She is strong and yet doesn't feel compelled to use her
strength to control or dominate others. There is an inner contentment
and satisfaction which is not based on accomplishments, position of
authority, ability to direct or control family members, or the recognition
of others.

A wife's inner peace, strength, confidence, and tranquility come
from relying and depending on God. She draws her strength and
wisdom from God. When this happens in a woman's life, the results
begin to be obvious to her husband, her children, her friends, and her
coworkers. She is free of anxious competitiveness and aggressiveness
to prove her worth and value. She knows what tranquility is because
of the affirmation given her by God. When she does speak, her family
can rest in the confidence that what she says is for their benefit.

The gentle and quiet spirit which springs from a godly woman's
heart is also seen in her willingness to follow scriptural guidelines for
her role as a wife and mother. Yes, this principle may be different from
what is usually taught in this day and age. But God's plan for wives in
Scripture has been around for almost 2000 years. That says something
about its value, doesn't it!

JULY 2

*Husbands, in the same way be considerate as
you live with your wives, and treat them with
respect as the weaker partner* (1 Peter 3:7).

Many of the packages we ship through the postal service and parcel delivery companies are stamped "Fragile! Handle with care!" A wife is not necessarily physically fragile, but she is to be handled with care in many ways. A husband is called by God to develop an attitude of respect in his heart for his wife. He is also called to give her a place of honor and to see his wife as having value. She needs to be convinced that her husband thinks she is special. And in most cases, a wife, with her sensitive intuition, will know if the response is genuine or not.

Some people overreact to Peter's statement that the wife is the weaker partner. This has nothing to do with her intelligence, work ability, or spiritual life. Most commentators interpret this weakness as referring to the obvious physical differences between men and women. The statement about weakness was intended to alert a husband to respect and be concerned about his wife's welfare.

Husbands, here are some suggestions for showing respect:

- Don't allow anyone to speak to your wife in a damaging or disrespectful way.
- Value her opinion and listen to her even when she disagrees with you.
- Walk into a room *with* her instead of *ahead* of her.
- Be careful to meet her needs in a group setting instead of leaving her alone while you talk with other men.
- Compliment her in public and in private.
- Be sensitive to her emotions and past hurts. Don't intrude in those areas, but support her instead.

Perhaps you could share together how respect can be expressed to an even greater degree in your marriage.

JULY 3

[You] are joint heirs of the grace (God's
unmerited favor) of life (1 Peter 3:7, AMP).

Joint heirs! What an exciting phrase. In 1 Peter 2:9 we are called "a chosen people." This is how God looks at each of us. We are chosen by Him and for Him. We are also considered children of the King. The titles that are given to the children of a king are prince and princess. And every believer enjoys this privilege.

Are you ready for two confrontational questions? Do you treat yourself as a co-heir? Do you treat your partner as a co-heir? You see, in Jesus Christ the two of you are spiritually equal. That's God's plan. A husband is called to treat his wife as a co-heir of the gracious gift of life. A wife is as spiritually endowed as a husband.

How can a husband reflect spiritual equality in his attitude toward his wife? By respecting and enabling her. Respect means to consider a person worthy of high regard. That's not always easy. Your partner works at different tasks than you do and sees life through different eyes than yours. It can be threatening to regard your partner's perspective with as much value as your own. And sometimes your spouse's behavior is a bit—shall we say—obnoxious, and your first inclination is definitely not to respect him or her. But God is saying, "Go ahead. Respect your spouse anyway."

A husband is an enabler to his wife. To enable actually means to make things possible or easy for another. A husband tries to assist his wife in achieving whatever it is that they are both working toward. He does his best to make it easy for her to grow and develop in the Christian life. And the blessings he receives in life, he wants for her also. Joint heirs! Take a few minutes and explore what that means to each of you and what it can mean in your marriage.

JULY 4

The Lord himself goes before you and will be with you; he will never leave you nor forsake you (Deuteronomy 31:8).

Before continuing with this meditation, read Deuteronomy 31:1-8 aloud together from your Bible.

Moses was a man God used in a mighty way. In this passage he is near the end of his life. The people of Israel are ready to enter the promised land. They have stopped at the river Jordan. Joshua has been chosen as Moses' successor. How do you think Joshua feels about his new assignment? An entire nation is behind him waiting for him to lead them. A new land is in front of him with unseen problems and hostile enemies. The challenges that Joshua faces at the Jordan are not unlike some of the challenges you face every day in the work you do.

Moses' words in today's passage can bring comfort to us as they did to Joshua. Each step you take today follows the path that God has laid out for you. When you are working around home or at your place of employment, remind yourself that God is for you and that He will not leave you! What might that truth do for your sense of confidence? Have you ever quoted today's verse to your partner before he or she leaves for the day? Look your spouse in the eye and share this blessing with him or her: "The Lord himself goes before you and will be with you; he will never leave you nor forsake you." The entire day will seem different with these words ringing in your partner's ears and heart.

Joshua was at a place of transition in his life. You will experience many transitions this year and throughout the journey of your marriage. How will you handle them? Some transitions are predictable and can be anticipated: the coming of children, their transition into adolescence, the empty nest, mid-life, retirement, etc. But there are many transitions which will surprise you and which cannot be anticipated. In each one the Lord is present and will be your source of comfort, strength, and guidance. As you move through today, remember whom you are following.

JULY 5

And Moses' father-in-law said to him, "The thing that you are doing is not good. You will surely wear out, both yourself and these people" (Exodus 18:17,18, NASB).

Apparently Moses was a workaholic. Are you? Is your spouse? If you tend to overwork, think about this:

> If I had my life to live over again, I'd try to make more mistakes next time. I would relax, I would limber up, I would be sillier than I have been this trip.
>
> I know of very few things I would take seriously. I would take more trips. I would be crazier. I would climb more mountains, swim more rivers and watch more sunsets. I would do more walking and looking. I would eat more ice cream and less beans. I would have more actual troubles, and fewer imaginary ones.
>
> You see, I'm one of those people who lives life prophylactically and sensibly hour after hour, day after day. Oh, I've had my moments, and if I had to do it over again I'd have more of them. In fact, I'd try to have nothing else, just moments, one after another, instead of living so many years ahead each day. I've been one of those people who never go anywhere without a thermometer, a hot-water bottle, a gargle, a raincoat, an aspirin, and a parachute.
>
> If I had to do it over again I would go places, do things, and travel lighter than I have. If I had my life to live over I would start barefooted earlier in the spring and stay that way later in the fall.
>
> I would play hooky more. I wouldn't make such good grades, except by accident. I would ride on more merry-go-rounds. I'd pick more daisies.[1]

Who tends to be the workaholic in your relationship? Who needs to learn to play more? When you do too much, soon there is nothing more to give and you lose the joy of life!

JULY 6

The heavens declare the glory of God; the skies
proclaim the work of his hands (Psalm 19:1).

Before continuing with this meditation, read the remainder of Psalm 19 aloud together from your Bible.

Noise. Confusion. Smog. Contamination. These are just a few of the negatives we live with each day. Where is God in all this mess and confusion? The psalmist assures us that God is here. He really is. He has made Himself known to everyone in the world through the works of nature. The dramatic imagery of the sunrise can make a difference each day of your life. Look for the sunrise each day and remind yourself, "There is an example of how God reveals Himself through His creation. He made the world and the heavens; man did not."

In verses 7-11 we see another way in which God has revealed Himself: through His Word. Notice two things about God's Word: what it is and what it does. His Word is perfect, as seen in terms from these verses like trustworthy, right, radiant, pure, sure, and altogether righteous. In other words, you can depend upon God's Word.

What does His Word do? What benefits do you receive from it? It revives your soul, makes you wise, gives you joy, and opens your eyes. Those benefits are awaiting you if you plunge into God's Word each day. And these benefits apply to your marriage, too.

The psalmist closes by talking about our sins and failures (vv. 11-14). How do you become aware of your faults or errors? The Word of God is one way. Your marriage partner is another, even though we don't always like to hear our spouse's perspective on our failures or weaknesses. Even when our partner is right, we resist what he or she has to say. When the psalmist asks for deliverance from willful sins he is talking about defiant acts. The more we give in to these, the more they begin to control our lives. Some of these can damage a marriage, too.

Share with each other how this psalm speaks to you. And above all, ask God for His strength and power.

JULY 7

I the Lord do not change (Malachi 3:6).

One of God's characteristics is His immutability: He doesn't change. He is consistent and constant. We need to pray in harmony with His character. Let's consider some of God's character traits and what they mean for our prayers:

> God is holy, so we must never pray for anything that would compromise His holiness or cause us to be unholy (Psalm 99:9; Isaiah 6:3; Revelation 15:4).

> God is love, and our prayers should both invoke the love of God for others and reflect the love of God in our own attitudes (Jeremiah 31:3; John 3:16; Romans 5:8).

> God is good, and the results of our prayers must bring goodness into the lives of all concerned (Psalm 25:8; 33:5; 34:8; Nahum 1:7; Matthew 19:17; Romans 2:4).

> God is merciful, and our prayers should reflect that we have received His mercy and are willing to be merciful ourselves (Psalm 108:4; Lamentations 3:22; Joel 2:13).

> God is jealous, and we dare not ask for something that would take first place in our hearts over God (Exodus 20:5; Deuteronomy 4:24; 1 Corinthians 10:22).

> God is just, and we cannot expect Him to grant a request that would be unjust or unfair to anyone (Psalm 103:6; Zephaniah 3:5; John 5:30; Romans 2:2).

> God is long-suffering, and neither our prayers nor our waiting for answers should show impatience toward Him who is so patient with us (Isaiah 48:9; Romans 9:22; 1 Peter 3:20).

> God is truth, and our prayers must never seek to change or disguise truth (Deuteronomy 32:4; Romans 3:4; Hebrews 6:18).[2]

Spend a few minutes discussing how these traits will affect your prayers together.

JULY 8

Blessed is the man who perseveres under trial,
because when he has stood the test, he will
receive the crown of life that God has promised
to those who love him (James 1:12).

Pressure! You know what it is—we all do. Recently, over-abundant rainfall in one section of the country caused the rivers and streams to pour water into a certain reservoir. The extra water exerted tremendous pressure on the earthen dam. In just two days, parts of the dam began to crumble and the entire structure weakened. Finally the dam collapsed under the pressure and many lives were lost.

Just like a weakened dam, sometimes we break under stress and pressure. James was aware of this. In chapter 1 he talks about the trials we face. He also tells us the result of standing firm. The person who does not crumble under trials, pressure, and ridicule is the person who shows that he or she has a deep relationship with Jesus Christ.

The trials we face today are different from those faced by believers in other countries over the centuries. Consider this: It is estimated that in the Dark Ages approximately five million Christians died for their faith. When the communists took over China over one million Christians died. Why didn't they renounce their faith in order to live? Because Jesus Christ was real to them.

Discuss the following issues together in the light of today's Scripture:

1. Describe how your life reflects the presence of Jesus Christ.

2. When is it most difficult to reflect your faith in Christ? What would help you reflect it more?

3. Who are the people who pressure you most to deny your faith?

4. Have you worked out what you can say to others who challenge your faith or your Christian stand? How could you tell another person about your love for God and your relationship with Christ?[3]

JULY 9

*God cannot be tempted by evil, nor does he tempt
anyone; but each one is tempted when, by his own evil
desire, he is dragged away and enticed* (James 1:13,14).

"The devil made me do it!"

We often laugh when somebody excuses his misbehavior with this old line. But deep inside we know that we all have a tendency to project the blame for our sin onto the devil, other people, or even God. Do you find it easy to say, "I'm wrong; I did it; I'm responsible." Probably not—especially to your partner! We seem to follow Adam's pattern of blaming. He probably blamed Eve first, then he blamed God (Genesis 3:12).

James speaks boldly to the issue of who's responsible for our sin. First, God isn't responsible. He can't be tempted by evil because He is holy and righteous. Isaiah referred to God as "the Holy One" 30 times. And God does not tempt us. He doesn't try to make you sin—not at all.

Second, the devil can't make you sin. It is true that Satan tempts you, but he cannot force you to commit an act of sin.

Third, no other human can make you sin. Other people can entice you, irritate you, and make the non-Christian lifestyle look more attractive. But you can't blame anyone else when you step over the line and disobey God.

The bottom line is this: Within each person is a tendency to respond to life with our old nature. We call this the sin nature; it's in every person. And sometimes we not only give in to it, we actually nourish it and give it life and power. The responsibility for our sinful response is ours alone. We have to shoulder that load. We have a choice.

Reflect on this: What temptations does your partner struggle with the most? How could you help him or her resist temptation? What is the greatest struggle with sin in your marriage? How can this be overcome?[4]

July 10

Then, after desire has conceived, it gives
birth to sin; and sin, when it is full-grown,
gives birth to death (James 1:15).

The vine begins to grow at the foot of the tree. It slowly creeps up the trunk, gradually killing the tree. When it reaches the top of the tree, a flower blooms from the stem of the vine as if to say, "I have conquered the tree."

The vine's name? The matador, meaning "the killer." This plant is a graphic example of what James is talking about in 1:15. Desire conceives sin, and sin brings death. Resentment in marriage brings death. Jealousy in marriage erodes trust and eventually creates a barrier between partners. You have two capacities within you: the old nature and the new. The results of living by each are very evident. Turn to Galatians 5:19-21 and discover the sins which come from evil desire. They are quite obvious in relationships where sin reigns. The new nature is seen in Galatians 5:22,23.

Many years ago a French preacher named Bourdaloue was trying to get through to the conscience of Louis XIV. He wanted to convey the truth of Paul's words in Romans 7:19: "For what I do is not the good I want to do; no, the evil I do not want to do—this I keep on doing." But before reading the verse, he started by saying, "I find two men in me." The king quickly interrupted him and said, "Ah, these two men, I know them well!" You probably know them well too. There is a battle which goes on within each of us.

How do you win the battle? First, don't blame God for the temptations. Second, accept the fact that you have two natures warring within you. Third, avoid those situations which fan the flames of evil desires. Fourth, use God's Word to resist temptation. Read 1 Corinthians 10:13. It's a powerful verse. Finally, realize that Jesus faced every temptation you face—and He overcame them successfully! Conclude today's reading by reading Hebrews 4:15,16 aloud. You're not alone in your temptations.[5]

JULY 11

Don't be deceived....Every good and perfect gift is from above, coming down from the Father of the heavenly lights, who does not change like shifting shadows (James 1:16,17).

Deception is a way of life for some. Spies in our government and other governments rely on deception to conduct their work. Sometimes we Christians are easily deceived. James' warning about not allowing ourselves to be deceived is linked to his words on the origin of temptation and sin (1:13-15). If we misunderstand his warning and blame God, the devil, or other people when we alone are responsible, we open the door to even greater distortion about God and who He is.

James goes on to tell us that every good and perfect gift is from God. Such simple things as food and sex are good gifts from God. Couples often thank God for their food at meal time, but not too many thank Him for sex at the time it is enjoyed!

Like anything that is good, the enjoyment of food and sex can be distorted. Some people actually live for food. Their entire day revolves around food. They use it to give them satisfaction. They wrongly believe that they can fill the emptiness in their life by filling their stomach with food. Sex is a wonderful gift as well. But it can also be polluted, even within the marital relationship. It's not uncommon to find sex used, not as a gift to a partner, but for self-satisfaction. The needs of the other person are considered second to personal needs.

Here is something for you and your partner to do together: Identify a number of the gifts God has allowed you to experience and enjoy as a couple. Think carefully about what they are. Often we take many of these gifts for granted. How do you think God wants you to use each gift? In what way could each gift be used to glorify God? This can be an exciting project for you, especially if you work hand in hand.

JULY 12

*Everyone should be quick to listen, slow
to speak* (James 1:19).

James' admonition in this verse can be illustrated by a poem by C.A.
Lufburrow:

The Echo

I shouted aloud and louder
While out on the plain one day;
The sound grew faint and fainter
Until it had died away.
My words had gone forever.
They left no trace or track,
But the hills nearby caught up the cry
And sent an echo back.

I spoke a word in anger
To one who was my friend,
Like a knife it cut him deeply,
A wound that was hard to mend.
That word, so thoughtlessly uttered,
I would we could both forget,
But its echo lives and memory gives
The recollection yet.

How many hearts are broken,
How many friends are lost
By some unkind word spoken
Before we count the cost!
But a word or deed of kindness
Will repay a hundredfold,
For it echoes again in the heart of men
And carries a joy untold.[6]

JULY 13

Therefore, get rid of all moral filth and the evil
that is so prevalent and humbly accept the word
planted in you, which can save you (James 1:21).

The terms moral filth and evil sound really strong don't they? The command to get rid of them comes directly after James' instructions regarding speech and anger (vv. 19, 20). There are many ways that a person can manifest moral filth and evil. One common way is by what we say through verbal anger, swearing, lying, and telling subtle off-color stories or blatant dirty jokes. As Christians, we are not to have any part in this or any other kind of moral filth or evil. Paul gave similar instructions in Ephesians 4:29: "Do not let any unwholesome talk come out of your mouths, but only what is helpful for building others up according to their needs."

Why do James and Paul make such radically confrontational statements to us? It's because our behavior and talk must be radically different from those who don't know Jesus Christ our Lord. We are called to stand out in the crowd, not in a proud or offensive manner, but with a simple, nonoffensive, loving spirit.

If you were to ask Jesus Christ, "Is there any kind of moral filth occurring in my life or in our marriage right now?" what would He say? That's an uncomfortable question to ask. But it is so easy for us to gradually slip into a pattern which doesn't reflect Christ in our lives. Sometimes one partner slips, the other finds it offensive, and conflict arises.

According to James, the antidote to moral filth and evil is the Word of God planted in you. This refers to two things. Jesus Christ dwells in you, and when you give your life over to Him, He enables you to live a life which reflects His presence. The written Word of God also dwells in you as you read it, memorize it, meditate on it, and follow its teachings. It is a two-fold process of receiving the living Word and the written Word. But if we follow this process faithfully we won't be so uncomfortable with the statement in James 1:21.[7]

JULY 14

Do not merely listen to the word, and so deceive yourselves.
Do what it says....The man who...continues to do
this...will be blessed in what he does (James 1:22,25).

Obedience. Parents spend great sums of money on books, tapes, conferences, and counseling sessions to learn how to develop this trait in their children. All branches of the armed forces demand unquestioned obedience of their recruits. Obedience is a quality that brings tremendous benefits to individuals, families, and society in general.

James tells us that we are to apply this quality to the Word of God. He says, "Don't just listen; do it!" That's quite direct. We are not to be people who are exposed to the Word of God and notice the things that need correcting in their lives, but then turn away and forget about the spiritual growth which needs to happen (vv. 23,24). Has that ever happened to you? to your partner?

A person who hears *and* responds to the Word receives two tremendous benefits: freedom and blessing (v. 25). Obeying God does not lead to bondage; disobeying God does. Being a servant of God actually leads to a greater enjoyment of life and freedom. Being a servant of sin is very restrictive with some rather negative consequences! But it's a choice each of us has to make.

Obedience to God and His Word brings blessings to our lives. Again and again Scripture states this (Joshua 1:7,8; Psalm 24:3-5; Proverbs 10:6). But just because we receive God's blessing doesn't mean we will be free from difficulties. God blesses us when we are obedient. But we can also experience His blessing during times of heartache and difficulty. Pain and joy go together. But perhaps you've already lived long enough to learn that!

JULY 15

Blessed are those who mourn, for they
will be comforted (Matthew 5:4).

Mourning —not a very popular word. It brings images of sorrow to mind. What does the word mean to you? It is often used synonymously with *grief*. Grief is intense emotional suffering or deep sadness caused by loss, disaster, misfortune, etc. The word grief comes from a Latin verb meaning "to burden." When you grieve, you bear a load of feelings over a tragic circumstance. Mourning is the experience of that burden of grief. Mourning involves remembering and thinking of a great loss of some kind.

Reflect back on your life. When was the last time you mourned over something or someone? What did you mourn over as a child? Have you shared with your partner the times in your life when you have mourned?

Jesus mourned. He wept over the sins of people and the consequences they experienced as a result. He wept over the city of Jerusalem which would not receive Him. The psalmist said to God, "Streams of tears flow from my eyes, for your law is not obeyed" (Psalm 119:136). Ezekiel heard God describe His faithful people as those "who grieve and lament over all the detestable things that are done" in Jerusalem (9:4).

Whom was Jesus talking about when He identified those who mourn? He was talking about those who grieve over the presence of sin in their lives. Grieving here does not mean carrying an excessive load of guilt, but rather a constructive sorrow.

The promise in this beatitude is comfort. When we grieve over the fact that we have sinned and fallen short of the glory of God (Romans 3:23), we are comforted by God through the free gift of forgiveness. Isaiah wrote that Jesus would bind up the brokenhearted (40:1; 61:1,2).

When you mourn over your sin, there is really only one person who can comfort you. Some people never find the Comforter, never meet Him. If you know Him, introduce Him to someone else who needs His comfort.

JULY 16

I am again in the pains of childbirth until
Christ is formed in you (Galatians 4:19).

Memories. Life is made up of them—some good and some bad. A marriage is made up of memories. Some of your memories you create together deliberately; others just seem to happen.

Sometimes the memories you bring with you into the marriage tend to haunt your marriage. They may be hurts you or your partner experienced early in life. When you came to marriage, some of these wounds were not healed; they were merely covered over by scabs. These unhealed emotional wounds tend to erupt when other difficulties in marriage rip off the scabs.

The way you remember what happened in the past is important. Often our memories become distorted as time passes. In one of his messages, Lloyd Ogilvie said, "We mortgage the future based upon what happened in the past. We have positive memories of the past which we can't imagine could ever be repeated, and we have negative memories which we know will be repeated. Often we become the image of what we remember instead of what we envision for the future!"

What about you and your partner? Do either of you have memories which interfere with your life or your marriage? Is the future of your marriage mortgaged on memories from the past?

To overcome a past hurt, you have to lower the walls you've built around the hurt and confront those concerns. Sometimes the change is immediate, but more often than not healing is a slow process. You can take down the walls of protection because of the presence of Christ in your life. Change is possible because our faith involves inner transformation, not just outer conformity. That's what the verse for today is all about. Your new life in Christ is put on from the inside.

Reflect on the ways that God's presence in your life has already changed your life. And for continual growth, give Him access to your painful memories. A slow process? Yes, but it's worth every bit of the time and energy you will invest.

JULY 17

*For we are God's workmanship, created in Christ
Jesus to do good works, which God prepared
in advance for us to do* (Ephesians 2:10).

Your partner is a work of art. So are you. Do you realize that? Think about the following words in light of today's verse:

> When a fanatic dealt several damaging blows to Michelangelo's Pieta, the world was horrified. It surprised no one when the world's best artists assembled to refashion the disfigured masterpiece.
>
> When sculptors arrived in Italy, they didn't begin repairing the marred face immediately. Rather they spent months looking at the Pieta, touching the flowing lines, appreciating the way each part expressed suffering yet ecstasy. Some spent months studying a single part such as the hand until finally the sculptors began to see more and more with the eyes of Michelangelo and to touch and feel as the master artist would have done. When the sculptors finally began repairing the face, the strokes belonged almost as much to Michelangelo as to themselves.
>
> Not Michelangelo's but rather God's sculpturing hand fashioned us from soil-dust into a masterpiece which surpassed even the Pieta (Genesis 2:7). It should not surprise us that God constantly refashions us—that as soon as we disfigure ourselves, He's already sculpturing the pieces back together....
>
> When we thank God for the gifts He gives us, we begin to see ourselves no longer from our own eyes but from His. If we know our giftedness, then we know how we require healing and thus we can become all that our Sculptor envisions.[8]

Jesus is your sculptor. He can remove those rough edges and lifelong cracks which hinder you today. Let Him renew you after His image.

July 18

Let everything that has breath praise the
Lord. Praise the Lord (Psalm 150:6).

Praise the Lord! Have you ever said that out loud? Praise is not only a response to God but a step in seeing change happen in your life. When you praise God for what He has done, for who He is, and for what He will do in your life, you are released to be more dependent upon Him and less dependent on yourself.

It's easy to praise God for what He has done because you can reflect back and identify something tangible. But what about the future? How difficult is it for you to praise God for what He is going to do? Such praise opens your life to some possibilities you may never have considered. By praising God, you not only become a risk-taker, but you become more aware of what He wants for you. This may be an uncomfortable idea for you. It may mean that you learn to praise God in an unpleasant job situation or during times of financial difficulty. It may mean praising God in spite of that taxing personal relationship in your marriage or family life. Perhaps you are troubled and perplexed about some situation in your life. This is exactly the time God wants you to praise Him.

Lloyd Ogilvie has an interesting thought along this line: "Consistent praise over a period of time conditions us to receive what the Lord has been waiting patiently to reveal to us or release for us."[9] Praising God is a response to His love, His goodness, His faithfulness, and His unbelievable concern for each one of us. When you praise God, you recognize His sovereignty. When you praise God, you transfer from trusting yourself to trusting Him.

What have you praised God for today? Take a few moments to reflect upon several things you have praised God for in the past and what you can praise Him for in the future. Share your praises with each other and then praise Him together.

July 19

Rejoice always;...for this is God's will for you in
Christ Jesus (1 Thessalonians 5:16,18, NASB).

When we rejoice in the Lord, we don't do so because we feel like it. Rejoicing is an act of the will, a commitment. When we rejoice in the Lord, we begin to see life from God's point of view. Praise is our means of gaining new perspective and guidance for our bogged-down lives.

You may think that you are too busy during the day to stop and praise God. That's just the time you should do it—when you are busy, fretful, and overwhelmed. Stop, clear your mind, and praise God. You will feel refreshed.

Praising God in advance of a solution is an act of faith, a way of saying, "I don't know the outcome, but I am willing to trust." Lloyd Ogilvie writes:

> Praising the Lord makes us willing and releases our imaginations to be used by Him to form the picture of what He is seeking to accomplish. A resistant will makes us very uncreative and lacking in adventuresome vision in the use of our capacity of imagination. God wants to use our imagination in the painting of the picture of what He is leading us to dare to hope for and expect. We become what we envision under the Spirit's guidance. That's why our own image of ourselves, other people, our goals, and our projects all need the inspiration of our imagination. However, until the Holy Spirit begins His work releasing it, our will keeps our imagination stunted and immature.[10]

Remember: Praise makes a difference in our lives because it's an act of relinquishment. Praise God for what He is going to do. After all, His perspective, plans, and solutions are the best that you can find anywhere. Praise the Lord!

JULY 20

My God shall supply all your needs according to His
riches in glory in Christ Jesus (Philippians 4:19, NASB).

Some businesses today operate from a deficit position rather than a surplus. Some individuals and some marriages operate the same way. These people feel empty, isolated, lonely, inadequate, and helpless. Many people go through life with important needs unmet. Some go through marriage in the same way.

Aside from your physical needs, do you know what your basic needs are? You need: security; love and belonging (being wanted, cared about, listened to, accepted, understood); self-esteem (receiving attention, respect, significance, value); and fulfillment of your potential of giftedness.

You and your spouse probably look to each other to meet some of these needs, and rightly so. But your partner cannot meet all your needs. God is the only one who can. He is the primary source for meeting your physical needs for food and shelter (Matthew 6:26,27). He meets your need for security and love (Romans 5:8; 8:35,38,39). God meets your need for significance or purpose (Ephesians 2:10; Philippians 1:21).

The more you believe these verses, the more you will be able to fulfill your potential and giftedness. In reality, you don't ever have to operate from a deficit. Because of what God has done for you and said about you, you can respond to yourself, your partner, others, and to life itself out of a sense of fullness. You are not deficient when you know Christ. Neither is your partner. Experience His resources. Use them. Enjoy them. Express your fullness to your partner and to the world![11]

JULY 21

Come to me, all who are weary and heavy-laden,
and I will give you rest (Matthew 11:28, NASB).

What do you do when you feel discouraged or depressed? How do you help your partner when he or she is discouraged or depressed? If you've never talked about this, now might be a good time to do just that.

Depression hits all of us at some time. Some people, however, seem to experience it more than just occasionally. Depression has been referred to as a wound of sadness. Jesus experienced depression when He was in the garden: "And taking with Him Peter and the two sons of Zebedee, He began to show grief and distress of mind and was deeply depressed" (Matthew 26:37, AMP). He was experiencing a sense of loss as He approached the cross.

It's not wrong to be depressed. Depression serves the purpose of alerting us that something is haywire in our lives. It is a warning system, and we need to listen to its message. When depression hits, instead of withdrawing from your partner, allow your spouse to give you comfort and encouragement. Deal with depression immediately before its darkness overwhelms you.

There are words of comfort in the Scriptures which can help us in times of depression. The Lord desires to lead us out of darkness. Isaiah 61:1 says that He brings glad tidings to the lowly, heals the brokenhearted, proclaims liberty to captives and release to those who are prisoners. In John 8:12 Jesus said, "I am the light of the world. Whoever follows me will never walk in darkness, but will have the light of life." The psalmist rejoices in God's healing, loving presence: "For You will light my lamp; the Lord my God will enlighten my darkness" (Psalm 18:28, NKJV).

Perhaps both of you can find comfort in those words of Jesus during times of discouragement or depression: "I came that they might have life, and might have it abundantly" (John 10:10, NASB).

JULY 22

A friendly discussion is as stimulating as the sparks
that fly when iron strikes iron (Proverbs 27:17, TLB).

Communication is a top priority for any relationship, especially marriage. Communication involves all the levels of talking, sharing, listening, and watching. Read the following helpful guidelines for marital communication from David and Vera Mace, and then communicate about them:

> A marriage can be likened to a large house with many rooms to which a couple fall heir on their wedding day. Their hope is to use and enjoy these rooms, as we do the rooms in a comfortable home, so that they will serve the many activities that make up their shared life. But in many marriages, doors are found to be locked—they represent areas in the relationship which the couple are unable to explore together. Attempts to open these doors lead to failure and frustration. The right key cannot be found. So the couple resign themselves to living together in only a few rooms that can be opened easily, leaving the rest of the house, with all its promising possibilities, unexplored and unused.
>
> There is, however, a master key that will open every door. It is not easy to find. Or, more correctly, it has to be forged by the couple together, and this can be very difficult. It is the great art of effective marital communication.[12]

Do you have friendly discussions? Are there any locked doors in your marriage? Perhaps today you can begin to forge the master key which will open up the locked doors in your relationship.

JULY 23

*If anyone can control his tongue, it proves
that he has perfect control over himself in
every other way* (James 3:2, TLB).

Words. What unbridled power they have. Remember the saying
you learned as a child: "Sticks and stones may break my bones,
but words will never hurt me"? That's a lie! You can rip someone to
pieces with what you say.

Notice what the Scriptures say about words and the importance of
controlling them:

> Anyone who says he is a Christian but doesn't control
> his sharp tongue is just fooling himself, and his religion isn't
> worth much (James 1:26, TLB).

> The tongue also is a fire, a world of evil among the parts of
> the body. It corrupts the whole person, sets the whole course
> of his life on fire, and is itself set on fire by hell. All kinds
> of animals, birds, reptiles and creatures of the sea are being
> tamed and have been tamed by man, but no man can tame
> the tongue. It is a restless evil, full of deadly poison. With the
> tongue we praise our Lord and Father, and with it we curse
> men, who have been made in God's likeness (James 3:6-9).

> For let him who wants to enjoy life and see good days
> (good whether apparent or not), keep [his] tongue free from
> evil, and his lips from guile (treachery, deceit) (1 Peter 3:10,
> AMP).

> Death and life are in the power of the tongue, and they
> who indulge it shall eat the fruit of it [for death or life] (Prov-
> erbs 18:21, AMP).

These are strong words, but they are true. Now, what do they mean
for your marriage relationship? How could any of these Scriptures
improve your marriage relationship? Think about it. Then talk about it.

JULY 24

*Gentle words cause life and health; griping brings
discouragement* (Proverbs 15:4, TLB); *How
wonderful it is to be able to say the right thing
at the right time* (Proverbs 15:23, TLB).

God is the model for our communication. He extended Himself to each of us and initiated contact with us. He wants us to initiate contact with Him and with others. He did not create us to be solitary but to interact. The Proverbs have good advice for us on this subject: "Some people like to make cutting remarks, but the words of the wise soothe and heal" (12:18); "A good man thinks before he speaks; the evil man pours out his evil words without a thought" (15:28, TLB); "A word aptly spoken is like apples of gold in settings of silver" (25:11).

What kinds of words does your partner share with you that are soothing and healing to you? How could they be improved? Share together for a moment.

Consider Dwight Small's comments about communication:

> No amount of communication can make marriage perfect, and therefore we should not expect it. God is perfect, the ideal of Christian marriage is perfect, and the means God puts at the disposal of Christian couples are perfect. Yet there is no perfect marriage, no perfect communication in marriage. The glory of Christian marriage is in accepting the lifelong task of making continual adjustments within the disorder of human existence, ever working to improve communication skills necessary to this task, and seeking God's enabling power in it all.[13]

You cannot *not* communicate. Silence communicates. Sometimes silence is louder than words. But our calling is to communicate with our partner outwardly. How is the sharing in your relationship? Talk about how your communication could be improved. Just talking about it is the first step.

JULY 25

*Love…is ever ready to believe the best of every
person* (1 Corinthians 13:7, AMP).

Assumptions—we all make them. Some people fill their lives with them. Others live by them, which can be a bit of a problem since assumptions contain a degree of speculation. Assumptions often undermine the stability of a marriage relationship. We think the worst of our partner instead of giving him or her the benefit of the doubt. Instead of believing our spouse to be innocent until proven guilty, you assume the opposite.

What do you tend to assume—the negative or the positive? When it comes to relationships, especially marriage, we are admonished to give the other person the benefit of the doubt. How do you do this? One way is to reinterpret what you tend to label as negative. Often what appears negative to you is simply an approach or characteristic that is different from yours. Here are some suggestions for changing your perspective:

- Don't assume that what he or she did which upset you was done on purpose.

- If your partner disturbs your sleep by rising a half hour earlier to exercise, be pleased about his or her concern to stay in shape.

- If your partner is quite verbal, you could see him or her as being friendly and giving thorough verbal descriptions.

- If your partner is quiet, he or she may be thinking something through before talking.

- A stubborn person could be viewed as persistent and determined.

When you label a behavior in a negative way, it doesn't eliminate the behavior; it reinforces it. Giving your partner the benefit of a doubt shows that you believe in his or her capability to become all he or she can be by the grace of God. This is how you turn your partner's liabilities into assets.

July 26

*So don't criticize each other any more. Try instead
to live in such a way that you will never make
your brother stumble by letting him see you doing
something he thinks is wrong* (Romans 14:13, TLB).

Contrary to popular belief, criticism is not a spiritual gift. It's not even a characteristic inherited from parental genes. But many people find it much easier to be critical than to be correct. The best thing to do with criticism is to find a cemetery lot and bury it! Criticism destroys. It divides. It separates. It creates distance between people. It's often used to ward off someone discovering our own defects. Jesus said: "Don't criticize, and then you won't be criticized" (Matthew 7:1, TLB).

Consider these thoughts: "Criticizing another rarely gives us a valid insight into life and living. Certainly criticism inspires feelings, but they're feelings of superiority, not sympathy. No, in most critical comments about people, there's more enmity than empathy."[14]

But when you do have to judge an action or person, what do you do? Do you let everything slide by? David Augsburger writes:

> Only when a man attempts to judge in honesty, in humility and in charity is his own eye clear. Only then is the plank of an unloving, malicious or vengeful spirit removed. Only then is the beam of his own sinful actions and attitudes withdrawn. Then he can see his way clear to remove the splinter in the other's eye. Not to label it and give his brother a sore eye. But to offer the hand of help. And healing.[15]

There is a substitute for criticism. It's called love. Love heals. Love protects. Love builds up. And more change occurs with love than with criticism.

JULY 27

We are being renewed day by day
(2 Corinthians 4:16); *Be made new in the*
attitude of your minds (Ephesians 4:23).

It comes in the mail—that little notice from the Department of Motor Vehicles. It's time to get into your car and head for the DMV office. Why? Your driver's license is about to expire, and you have the opportunity to renew it. Renewal is a part of our life. Whether we realize it or not, we are constantly in the process of renewing some element of our lives.

Do you know what renewal means? The dictionary says to renew is to make something like new, to give it new vigor, or to make it fresh. Something comes alive during renewal. Renewal signifies growth. The opposite is stagnation and decay.

Houses in a state of decay come alive through the process of renewal. So do businesses and ministries. But there are two other areas in which renewal sparks even greater excitement: our individual lives and our marriages. Perhaps such renewal has happened in your life. If not, it can!

Individual lives in a state of stagnation and decay come alive when we confront Jesus Christ. It is His presence which brings about renewal and makes our lives fresh. In his letter to the Ephesians, Paul states that we are able to put aside the old way of life and put on the new way of life (4:22-24). This is done through the process of being renewed in our minds.

Marriages, too, can come alive. I have seen stagnating, decaying marriages begin to blossom and come alive as they were renewed in Christ. They became fresh and alive. A new sense of love, romance, intimacy, commitment, trust, and hope appears.

What about your marriage? Where is renewal occurring? Where would you like it to occur? How would your partner like your marriage to be renewed? Hard questions? Perhaps. But they are necessary questions. Begin by asking God for guidance, and then talk about these hard questions as a couple. It may be the first step on the road to renewal.

JULY 28

Love never fails—never fades out or becomes obsolete
or comes to an end (1 Corinthians 13:8, AMP).

Being married is a mutual growing experience. The biblical principle which frees both partners in the marriage to be all they can be is the concept of mutual submission. Rather than suppressing each other, we are free to serve and help each other in love with the Holy Spirit present and active in our lives. When our marriage begins to move in that direction, the road may not always be smooth, but the journey becomes an extremely fulfilling one for both partners, as illustrated in this poem by Roy Croft:

> I love you not only for what you are,
> But for what I am when I am with you.
>
> I love you not only for what you have made of yourself,
> But for what you are making of me.
>
> I love you because you are helping me to make
> Of the lumber of my life
> Not a tavern, but a temple;
> Out of the words of my everyday
> Not a reproach, but a song.
>
> I love you for the part of me that you bring out;
> I love you for putting your hand into my heaped-up heart
> And passing over all the foolish, weak things
> That you can't help dimly seeing there,
> And for drawing out all the beautiful belongings
> That no one else had looked quite far enough to find.[16]

JULY 29

And let endurance have its perfect result, that
you may be perfect (James 1:4, NASB).

Recently a man purchased a large quantity of new carpet for his office. He wanted it installed as soon as possible. But the salesperson said, "Because you need such a large quantity, I will have to order more from the carpet mill. I can give you half of the order from what we have on hand, but I can't guarantee that what we receive from the mill will be the exact same color because our dye lots are inconsistent."

Have you ever been confronted with that problem: a lack of consistency? Is there a favorite restaurant you return to again and again because the quality of food is consistent?

Consistency—that's what builds a business. That's what gives a marriage relationship stability and security. Consistency means being steady. You can count on it today and tomorrow. Consistency includes determination, patience, and strength even when the world around you is falling apart. Some spouses are consistent in their sense of timing. Some are consistent in always remembering those special occasions.

The Word of God is our guide for this character quality: "Be prepared in season and out of season" (2 Timothy 4:2); "Let us not lose heart in doing good, for in due time we shall reap if we do not grow weary" (Galatians 6:9, NASB); "Jesus Christ is the same yesterday and today and forever" (Hebrews 13:8). Jesus is with us. He never changes, and His love for you is unchanging.

How's the level of consistency in your life? It might be helpful for each of you to identify areas in your own life in which these Scriptures could be applied. Before you discuss this, reflect on how your partner would like you to become a bit more consistent in your life.

One last thought: A consistent witness for Christ also goes a long way in drawing others to Him. Often that happens when a marriage relationship consistently reflects His presence. Hopefully yours will today.

JULY 30

Do not worry about your life, what you will eat or drink;
or about your body, what you will wear (Matthew 6:25).

Are you anxious? Concerned? Is there a difference between those two words? Yes, there is. Anxiety can immobilize us. Concern prompts action. In many marriages, one partner may have a tendency to be anxious, while the other may not. Which one of you tends to be more anxious or worrisome? How does this affect your relationship?

Why did Jesus tell us not to worry? Read Matthew 6:25-34 and look at the reasons He gives us.

Anxiety about material things affects our sense of proportion. If you are diverting the energy of your mind into worry about material items, there is little available to experience some of the unnoticed joys and delights of life.

Worry and anxiety can distort our spiritual perception. It keeps us from discovering the value God places on us. As Jesus said in verse 26, you are more valuable than a bird!

Think about this: Can you really change much of your life by worry? You can't prolong your life by worrying; however, you can shorten it. That's a fact. Do either of you have a physical problem which is caused by worry?

There's another reason to not worry. God will supply you with what you need. Worry is a pattern of unbelief. God is saying, "Trust Me. Believe in Me. Realize who I am."

Worry is trying to figure out life by ourselves and attempting to solve all our cares without God. Instead, we are to "seek first his kingdom and his righteousness" (Matthew 6:33). The Amplified Bible says, "Seek...His way of doing and being right." What's on your mind right now—the car payment, house repairs, physical problems, your relationship to your spouse or children? Whatever it is, God is saying, "Give Me your cares and anxieties. Trust Me." It sounds like a good offer, doesn't it? Take Him up on it.

JULY 31

*May the grace of the Lord Jesus Christ, and the
love of God, and the fellowship of the Holy Spirit
be with you all* (2 Corinthians 13:14).

Anyone who attends worship services, weddings, and funerals is
acquainted with benedictions—positive, uplifting words usually
spoken near the end of the service. Today's Scripture passage is often
recited as a benediction. Pay close attention to the benedictions you
hear in the next few months. They are more than just nice slogans
used to signal dismissal. What are they really saying? What promises
are mentioned?

Some ministers today create their own benedictions which are spon-
taneous, more personal expressions to their congregations. Here is one
which is often shared by Lloyd Ogilvie in his church, the First Presbyterian Church of Hollywood, California, and on his television program,
"Let God Love You":

> May the Lord go before you to light the path and give you
> direction. May He go behind you to guide your steps. May
> He go beside you to keep you from stumbling. May He go
> above you to protect you, and may He go within you to give
> you the power of the Holy Spirit.

What words of benediction and blessing do you need today? We all
need promises from the Word of God to strengthen us, encourage us,
lift our thoughts and feelings, and keep us moving ahead in our lives.
God's Word can do that for you. Search through His Word and write
down the promises you need. Also, write down the promises you think
your partner needs, and slip one in his or her purse or wallet where it
will be easily found.

As you conclude today's meditation, what benediction would you
like to give to your partner? Take a few minutes and think about it,
then talk about it. What promise from God's Word is most meaningful
to you today? Daily benedictions are not a bad idea. We all need to be
reminded daily of who God is and what He has done for each of us.

AUGUST

*What makes marriage an equal partnership is the manner
in which it is lived out, not the manner in which it is
structured. Husbands and wives mutually serve one
another in love; this is the vast difference Christ makes.*

AUGUST 1

Submit to one another out of reverence
to Christ (Ephesians 5:21).

What makes marriage an equal partnership is the manner in which it is lived out, not the manner in which it is structured. Husbands and wives mutually serve one another in love; this is the vast difference Christ makes. Perhaps it can be illustrated in this way.

Have you ever watched a ballet? In the ballet, one dancer leads, the other follows—not because one is better (he may or may not be), but because these are their roles. Charlie Shedd suggests that marriage under the biblical order is like a conductor leading a symphony rather than a potentate ruling over his realm. The husband's position of power and prestige is actually servanthood through committed love. A wife's position is not one of powerlessness but the creative power of servanthood.

Christian husbands and wives are called to beautiful complementary roles of loving service to each other. Dwight Small says, "The glory of the woman is the acknowledgment that man is incomplete without her. The humility of the woman is the acknowledgment that she was made for man; the humility of the man is the acknowledgment that he is incomplete without her. Both share an equal dignity, honor and worth."[1]

In his devotional book, James Bjorge sums up the relationship in this way: "Wise partners hang on to one another with open hands so that neither suffocates in submission."[2] What do you think about that statement? Share your thoughts and feelings with each other.

AUGUST 2

Bear with each other and forgive whatever grievances
you may have against one another. Forgive as
the Lord forgave you (Colossians 3:13).

What is forgiveness? Contrary to what many people think, forgiveness is not a feeling. It's a clear and logical choice on your part. But after you make the choice to forgive, it takes time for the emotional healing to occur. Often people differ in the amount of time they need. If you or your partner need more time, it doesn't mean that the early healer is more spiritual. Accept it as a personality difference.

Forgiveness is not demanding change from your partner before you forgive him or her. Your partner cannot guarantee that he or she will never make the same mistake again. Forgiveness means investing trust in your partner. You must give your partner the freedom to fail and grow in your relationship. Forgiveness is often difficult because there is a price to pay. It will cost you your love and your pride.

Forgiveness is not excusing or covering up behavior which is detrimental to the person committing the act or to the one against whom it is committed. Loving another person means confronting the person in love and saying, "I believe in you. I believe you have the capability through God's grace to change." Do you believe in your partner to that extent? Do you let your partner know this? Do you ever say to one another, "You know, I blew it. What I did was thoughtless and wrong. I am sorry for what I did. With God's help this is going to be evicted from my life. Will you forgive me?" Do you ever say to one another, "Thank you for asking for forgiveness. Yes, I forgive you"? Can you admit, "I am in the process of forgiving you. It may take a little time, but it will happen. And I will never use your offense against you again"?

These are hard words—difficult to say. But they are words that heal, words that can only come when your relationship is founded on Jesus Christ.

AUGUST 3

I lie awake; I have become like a bird
alone on a roof (Psalm 102:7).

Loneliness. Have you ever felt the pangs of isolation even though people were milling all around you? One woman said that her loneliness felt cold, like the loneliness the earth must feel in winter when the birds fly south and the flowers die. Her loneliness made her feel like she was the only person alive.

A song writer described the feeling of loneliness for us:

> If I were a cloud, I'd sit and cry,
> If I were the sun, I'd sit and sigh.
> But I'm not a cloud, nor am I the sun,
> I'm just sitting here, being no one.
>
> If I were the wind, I'd blow here and there,
> If I were the rain, I'd fall everywhere.
>
> But I'm not the wind, nor am I the rain,
> I'm just no one—feeling pain.
>
> If I were the snow, I'd fall oh so gently,
> If I were the sea, waves would roll o'er me.
> But I'm not the snow, nor am I the sea,
> I'm just no one—and lonely.[3]

Have you felt this way? When? What brought you out of your loneliness? It's easy to feel isolated and dehumanized in our world. You can even feel lonely when you're married. Marital loneliness often seems worse than if you had no one in your life at all. To overcome loneliness we often try to keep ourselves busy. But when we slow down, the loneliness is still there.

Jesus said that He would be with us always, that His arms of love would hold us. Loneliness can be lifted when we tell Him that we need His comfort. And it helps to let others know that we are lonely. After all, if you don't tell them, who will?

AUGUST 4

Blessed is he whose transgressions are forgiven,
whose sins are covered (Psalm 32:1).

Before continuing with this meditation, read the remainder of Psalm 32 aloud together from your Bible.

There is a price to pay for deception. David, the writer of this psalm, knew this very well. He tried to cover up his adultery and murder. His remorse and conflict of conscience described in this psalm may be something you've experienced. Most of us have as we've tried to hide some act which violated God's plan. The physical symptoms of unconfessed sin often reflect depression and even psychosomatic illness.

The psalmist uses three different terms for sin in this psalm: wrong-doing, sin, and iniquity. Wrong-doing is transgression, stepping over a known boundary. *Sin* is missing the mark. *Iniquity* is an inward moral perversity. Whatever it's called, sin must be confessed and forgiven, not hidden.

How would you explain forgiveness to someone? In this psalm forgiveness means to lift or remove a burden, to cover the ugliness of it, and to cancel a debt. When you forgive your partner for his or her offenses, your partner will feel as though a burden has been lifted. The ugliness of sin will be wiped away. He or she will feel like a tremendous debt has been canceled. We can forgive one another because we are forgiven by God for whatever we may have done. There is no limit to His forgiveness, and there should be no limit to ours with our partner.

This psalm not only tells us that God takes care of the past, but also that He will provide for our future. He will instruct us, teach us, and counsel us. But He wants us to be involved by using the mind He gave us. Participate actively in God's forgiveness. Confess your sins. Receive God's forgiveness. Extend forgiveness to your spouse. And rejoice that your life and your marriage will be free from the disastrous results of hidden sin.

AUGUST 5

Let each man of you (without exception) love his
wife as [being in a sense] his very own self; and
let the wife see that she respects and reverences
her husband (Ephesians 5:33, AMP).

If you were interviewed on a talk program and asked, "What is your definition of marriage?" how would you answer? Have you ever thought about it enough to give a clear and concise response? It's important to have a clear understanding of the meaning and purpose of marriage so you know what your marriage is supposed to reflect. Consider this definition for a moment:

> A Christian marriage is a total commitment of two people to the person of Jesus Christ and to one another. It is a commitment in which there is no holding back of anything. Marriage is a pledge of mutual fidelity; it is a partnership of mutual subordination.
>
> A Christian marriage is similar to a solvent, a freeing up of the man and woman to be themselves and become all that God intends for them to become. Marriage is a refining process that God will use to have us develop into the man or woman He wants us to become.

What do you think of this definition? There are certain key words which are important for you to discuss as a couple. What does commitment mean to you? What is a pledge? What does mutual subordination mean? How can marriage free you rather than restrict you? How has your marriage freed you to this point?

All of us experience numerous events which have the potential to refine us as individuals or as a couple. Some of these events are called upsets, crises, or tragedies. What has occurred during the lifetime of your marriage that God has used to shape you? These questions may take some time to reflect upon and discuss, but you will gain greater direction concerning your marriage through the process. Enjoy your discussion today.

AUGUST 6

*When a flimsy wall is built, they cover it with
whitewash, therefore tell those who cover it with
whitewash that it is going to fall* (Ezekiel 13:10,11).

In today's passage, Ezekiel the prophet uses vivid imagery to describe
the false prophets of Israel. Jerusalem was like a flimsy wall that was
covered with whitewash to make it look good. But the outward appearance didn't save it. It was eventually exposed, and it crumbled.

We understand the problem of false appearances. Sometimes
builders today use substandard materials in a home or office building.
They cover a cheap, shoddy construction job with an attractive facade to
attract buyers. Even though the defective materials and workmanship
are covered up, eventually they are discovered—often with disastrous
results. Similarly, when you purchase a used car, you often wonder
what is underneath that shiny new paint job and freshly steam-cleaned
engine. Then 700 miles later the rust begins to show and the transmission starts slipping! Cover-up seems all too common in our society.

Cover-up is a problem in marriage too. How many couples put on
a pretense that their Christian marriage is happy and fulfilled when
it's not? We smile to cover the gloom. We act happy to cover the pain.
We present an image of togetherness when socializing or attending
church, but in the confines of the home there is little depth to hold the
marriage together. Why are we so surprised when an apparently happy
couple announces plans to divorce? A cover-up was occurring. No one
reached out for help. No one said, "What you see is not the real story.
We are hurting. Help us. We've built our marriage on a flimsy base,
and we need a solid foundation."

Whitewashing a marital relationship isn't the answer. A recommitment to Jesus Christ, a willingness to make personal changes, a
desire to follow God's Word—all of these build a solid structure that
doesn't need whitewashing. Are there any flimsy walls in your marriage? Now is the time for some solid repairs. That's the way to build
for the future.

AUGUST 7

*And I will do whatever you ask in my name, so that
the Son may bring glory to the Father* (John 14:13).

Have you ever had the experience of having someone quote you,
but only quote one portion of what you said? Often when others
quote only a portion of your message it creates a distortion of what you
really said. How do you feel when others misquote you?

Perhaps our Lord feels the same way. So many times Christians
latch onto a portion of today's passage and ignore the context in which
it was spoken. We often claim the first phrase, "I will do whatever you
ask in my name," while ignoring that it is linked to the next, "so that
the Son may bring glory to the Father." The end result of our prayers
is not to get what we want but to bring glory to God.

Have you ever been glorified? Have you ever glorified another
person? The Greek word translated glory in John 14:13 is the word
from which we get our English word doxology. When you sing the doxology in church, you are paying homage to the divine presence or glory
of God. The word glory is translated as presence, weight, or substance.
In ancient Greece, when a prominent and important person would get
up to speak in the assembly, everyone sensed his "glory"—the importance of his presence.

When we pray, we should be aware of God's glory—the weight
of His importance and presence in our lives. Our prayers are for the
purpose of glorifying God and not simply fulfilling our own request.
Our lives and our marriages are to be dedicated to the glory of God.
Whenever you pray, it is important to ask the question, "Who will be
glorified by this prayer being answered?" We've been called to live for
the glory of God. Do your life and marriage demonstrate the presence
of God at work in your lives? That's something to consider. And when
you pray, do it so that in some way honor and glory are given to the
name of Christ.[4]

AUGUST 8

O God, please heal her! (Numbers 12:13).

You and Moses—yes, both of you have been criticized. Moses was criticized by his brother and sister (Numbers 12), but he did not defend himself or retaliate. By not taking action himself, Moses made room for God to act on his behalf. God responded to the self-centered behavior of Miriam and Aaron. He said to them, "Why then were you not afraid to speak against my servant Moses?" (v. 8). And because Miriam was the instigator, God struck her with leprosy. It's not likely that God will do the same thing to those who attack and criticize you unjustly. Perhaps you would like Him to, but He won't. You should be glad, because you would also end up on the receiving end of God's wrath for your criticism!

Consider what Moses did instead of attacking his sister and brother or holding a grudge against them. Imagine that you are Moses. You've been justified by God, cleared of the false accusation. You look at your sister and see her white as snow with leprosy (v. 10). You look at your brother and see him confessing his sin (v. 11). What is going through your mind? You might be tempted to gloat, "It serves them right. They got what was coming to them." But those weren't Moses' thoughts. He wasn't out for revenge, even though we are often tempted toward revenge when we are unjustly criticized. Moses' response can be summarized in the word *compassion*. Moses saw his sister, and in spite of the difficulty she had created for him, he cried out to the Lord, "O God, please heal her!" (v. 13).

When others wrong you, how do you pray for them? Do you ask God to pay them back by making their life miserable? Or do you ask Him to help them, comfort them, make their life better, bless them, and heal them? What people in your life—relatives, in-laws, neighbors, friends—need you to pray for them in that manner?[5]

AUGUST 9

Call to Me, and I will answer you, and show
you great and mighty things, which you
do not know (Jeremiah 33:3, NKJV).

Sometimes the future isn't clear. Sometimes it's clouded or hidden by a fog. Sometimes uncertainty about the future keeps us from moving ahead. The promise in Jeremiah is a great one for facing the unknowns in a marriage relationship. Perhaps the following poem from an anonymous author will stimulate your thinking about the future of your marriage.

No Marriage is Perfect

Marriage is a daily creation, not a packaged product.
Marriage is like a child who needs to be picked up and
    hugged, and given personal attention.
Marriage is not something simple to be weighed against
    expectations and rejected when found short.
Marriage needs delicate touch and patient treatment.
The handling of it cannot always be thought out ahead
    of time.
Often the way must be felt slowly, gently, in the dark.
The danger is not in the dark.
The danger is in losing hope or patience.

Take a few minutes to write your answers to the following questions:

1. How do you "hug" a marriage? List five ways.

2. How can you give your marriage a delicate touch?

3. What can your partner do or say to help you maintain your hope and patience?

Think a bit, write a lot, express yourself openly. Discuss your answers with each other tomorrow.

AUGUST 10

I loathe my very life; therefore I will give
free reign to my complaint and speak out in
the bitterness of my soul (Job 10:1).

You think you have problems; let me tell you some of mine! You wouldn't believe the day I had with your kids!"

Complaining. Griping. There is so much to complain about today: the traffic, weather, lines at the market, cost of food and housing, kids who won't behave, a spouse who won't listen, the off-key choir, and on and on. There is a time to voice our concerns and complaints. But some people never let up, not realizing that repetition does nothing to relieve, and only reinforces, the discomfort.

Job had plenty of complaints. He lost his possessions, all his children died, and his health went downhill. He didn't understand these circumstances, so he complained to God. Do you ever complain to God? Most of us do. It's after we've stopped complaining that we are able to hear Him answer us. Job learned to accept God's authority. After we complain perhaps we can see the issue more clearly and discover the blessings that we have been overlooking.

What *does* complaining accomplish? Is it possible to express complaints to our spouse in a way that brings about a change? Not usually. All too often a complaint against someone, especially a spouse, is launched as an attack rather than a helpful suggestion. It's not meant to change but to punish. If a wife complains to her husband, "You're never affectionate," he will likely respond, "I am too!" We tend to defend ourselves to our final breath. But if she voiced the same concern by saying, "I really appreciate it when you come home, give me a hug and a kiss, and ask how my day was," there is a greater likelihood that her husband will change. It's a simple process: Point to the behavior that you desire rather than to what you don't like.

When your partner doesn't do something you want or like, realize that he or she may be doing something positive which you are overlooking. Think about it.

AUGUST 11

*I...lead you along straight paths. When you
walk, your steps will not be hampered* (Proverbs
4:11,12); *What does the Lord require of you?...To
walk humbly with your God* (Micah 6:8).

You see them in the parks, on the highways, and at the beach. They
wear intense expressions on their faces. They often attach weights
to their rapidly pumping arms. They stride vigorously and purposefully
across the terrain. They are the walkers. They remind us that walking
is good for our health, even though we may prefer to stroll leisurely
through the countryside and enjoy the scenery and quietness.

Have you ever reflected on some of the paths and roads you've
traveled in your life? As we walk through life, we are constantly confronting many detours which can lead us away from our relationship
with the Lord. It's quite easy to stray, but sometimes we fail to find our
way back. Perhaps the way to stay on the straight path is by following
what the prophet Micah stated. Walking humbly before the Lord will
keep us focused upon Him rather than relying on our own abilities and
desires. The advice in 1 John 1:7 is also helpful: "If we walk in the light,
as he is in the light, we have fellowship with one another, and the blood
of Jesus, his Son, purifies us from all sin."

It's also helpful to think about Jesus and the path He trod on this
earth. Did you ever wonder what thoughts went through His mind as
He walked the road to Calvary? He knew what was waiting for Him
as He stumbled along under the weight of the cross. Yet He did not
detour; He stayed on the path the Father prepared for Him.

Is there a detour tempting you away from God's path for your life
or your marriage at the present time? Have you taken some errant steps
and realized, "This is risky!" Sometimes we rationalize and say, "This
won't hurt me or my marriage" or "It's no big deal; others are doing it."
But if you want the most out of life, you must continually walk humbly
on the lighted path God has shown you.[6]

AUGUST 12

My command is this: Love each other
as I have loved you (John 15:12).

Today's meditation centers on a wife's message about her husband. Wives, read it aloud to your husband. Then both of you reflect on its meaning for your marriage.

> I married a man I respect;
>> I have no need to bow and defer.
> I married a man I adore and admire;
>> I don't need to be handed a list entitled
>> "how to build his ego" or
>> "the male need for admiration."
> Love, worship, loyalty, trust—these are inside me;
>> They motivate my actions.
>> To reduce them to rules destroys my motivation.
> I choose to serve him, to enjoy him.
> We choose to live together and grow together,
>> to stretch our capacities for love
>> even when it hurts and looks like conflict.
> We choose to learn to know each other
>> as real people,
>> as two unique individuals unlike any other two.
> Our marriage is a commitment to love;
>> to belong to each other
>> to know and understand
>> to care
>> to share ourselves, our goals,
>> interests, desires, needs.
> Out of that commitment the actions follow.
> Love defines our behavior
>> and our ways of living together.
> And since we fail to meet not only the demands
>> of standards but also the simple requirements
>> of love
> We are forced to believe in forgiveness...and
>> grace.[7]

AUGUST 13

My command is this: Love each other
as I have loved you (John 15:12).

A husband wrote the following words to his wife as he struggled
with the pressures of time and over-involvement in his life. Do
these thoughts apply to your marriage right now? Husbands, read this
passage to your wife and then discuss it together. Let your partner
know how you feel about these words, especially if they reflect your
feelings at the present time.

The Nature of Love and Time

A rare delicacy touches her soft cheek; she's no common girl.
There is a gentle elegance in her step, that charming elegance that loses no warmth.
I often quietly observe her:
Charm is not alone in clothes or sophistication; it seems to
crown the simple things...a look, a touch, a smile
the conveyance of beauty through being.
The tragedy of our love is time...it takes time to capture the
reality of delicacy and elegant charm.

Yet...we may struggle with time or embrace him.
He may be our guard at the prison gate or our liberator into
each other.
As the hours seldom come to quietly observe you—my love
I shall liberate the moments and drink of your touch, your
smile, your look...
And consider great wealth those hours—even (God grant)
days when, alone at last, we shall be enfolded by the
warmth and beauty of our love.[8]

AUGUST 14

For this reason a man will leave his father and
mother and be united to his wife, and the two
will become one flesh (Ephesians 5:31).

Marriage is a relationship of partners. In marriage you belong to each other (1 Corinthians 7:4). Consider the following poetic definition of marriage. After you read it, share with each other which portion meant the most to you.

I Need You

I need you in my times of strength and in my weakness;
I need you when you hurt as much as when I hurt.
There is no longer the choice as to what we will share.
We will either share all of life or be fractured persons.
I didn't marry you out of need or to *be* needed.
We were not driven by instincts or emptiness;
We made a choice to love.
But I think something supernatural
    happens at the point of marriage commitment
(or maybe it's actually natural).
A husband comes into existence; a wife is born.
He is a whole man before and after, but at a point in time he
    becomes a man who also is a husband;
That is—a man who needs his wife.
She is a whole woman before and after.
But from now on she needs him.
She is herself but now also part of a new unit.
Maybe this is what is meant in saying,
"What God hath joined together."
Could it be He really does something special at "I do"?
Your despair is mine even if you don't tell me about it.
But when you do tell, the sharing is easier for me;
And you also can then share from my strength
    in that weakness.[9]

AUGUST 15

*We were under great pressure, far beyond our ability
to endure....But this happened that we might not rely
on ourselves but on God* (2 Corinthians 1:8,9).

It happens even in marriage where it should never occur. It's called
rejection. And whether it is intentional or unintentional, rejection
hurts. Ron Lee Davis shows us a good way to handle rejection:

> God is building a stable, proven character in our lives that
> is strong in both good times and bad. You will never know
> that kind of stability if you rely on people rather than God for
> the shaping of your attitude. People may elate you—or they
> may depress you. They may love you—or they may reject you.
> If your outlook is dependent on how people treat you rather
> than on God's unchanging, unconditional love, your life will
> be an emotional roller coaster ride—a wild journey in which
> the ups may not begin to compensate for the downs.
>
> Lloyd Ogilvie said, "One rejection can tip the scales
> weighted with hundreds of affirmations." It's true. The rebuff
> of one person can easily cancel out all the positive strokes we
> receive in our lives. That's why I keep a certain manila folder
> in my file cabinet. That folder is filed under "E" for "Encour-
> agement." It contains more than a hundred letters I have
> accumulated over the years. On those blue Mondays, when
> I feel pressured or accused by people, or when my self-image
> is sagging, I reach for my encouragement file and pull out a
> letter. Those letters comfort me, affirm me, and restore my
> perspective. Positive words from others enable me to endure
> rejection and persevere.[10]

As a married couple, each of you has been called to be a living
encouragement file for one another. Be sure you share encouragement
with your partner frequently—even daily!

AUGUST 16

When my life was ebbing away, I remembered
you, Lord, and my prayer rose to you, to
your holy temple (Jonah 2:7).

Did you ever want to start over—you know, have a new beginning?
It happens all the time. You're cooking a meal and thoughtlessly
add one ingredient twice. You're tempted to toss out the batch and start
over from scratch.

Some people wish they could have a fresh start in life. Did you ever
feel that way about your marriage? Did you ever wish you could turn
back the clock and have a new beginning? Perhaps you even have made
a list of what you would do differently.

Jonah was a man who needed a new beginning, prayed for it, and
received it from the Lord. Perhaps your selfish plan for your marriage
needs to be replaced by God's plan. Consider these words from Ron
Lee Davis and M. Scott Peck:

> God is at work for His good in our lives. This doesn't
> mean that everything that happens to us in life feels good.
> As M. Scott Peck says in *The Road Less Traveled:* "Life is dif-
> ficult. This is a great truth, one of the greatest truths. It is
> a great truth because once we truly see this truth, we tran-
> scend it. Once we truly know that life is difficult—once we
> truly understand and accept it—then life is no longer diffi-
> cult. Because once it is accepted, the fact that life is difficult
> no longer matters."
>
> Life is seldom more difficult than when our old dream
> dies and the new dream is not yet in view. At that moment
> we can only see the loss; we can't yet glimpse the opportunity.
> Our inclination is to seek the security of the familiar. The
> thought of relinquishing our cherished dreams and following
> God in a totally new direction frightens us.[11]

Let God give you a new dream for your marriage today.

AUGUST 17

Why are you downcast, O my soul? Why so disturbed within me? Put your hope in God, for I will yet praise him, my Savior and my God (Psalm 43:5).

The alarm rings and you're startled out of your sleep. The sun is up and the birds are singing. But you aren't. There's a cloud of gloom hovering over your head. You don't seem to have any energy. You rise, but your head is down and your eyes scan the ground. You feel a heaviness inside, like you're carrying the weight of the whole world. You don't know what to do, and your partner doesn't know what to do for you either. You go through the day in low gear, feeling exhausted. There doesn't seem to be any hope.

Ever felt that way? Probably. Will you feel that way again in your lifetime? Probably. When you are downcast or depressed you feel cut off from God and others. In fact, you probably tend to avoid God and sometimes your own spouse when you're depressed.

The psalmist knew the feeling of depression. It appears that he was talking to himself when he said, "Why are you downcast?" He then provided the solution for his own depression: "Put your hope in God." Look to God when you're feeling low. Ask Him for help. When you are discouraged or depressed, Jesus will come to you if you ask Him to. He knows the pressure of the world upon His shoulders.

It is still possible to praise God when you're downcast. You don't even have to feel like praising Him. In fact, that's a good place to begin—by telling the Lord that you don't feel like praising Him but that you are going to do it anyway. Our faith is not an either/or experience. We're not either full of faith and praise or full of discouragement and depression. Life is a combination of joy and pain, discouragement and praise, hope and struggle. Don't hesitate to praise God in one breath and tell Him what is bothering you in the next.

Ask your partner to help you praise God. Praise and worship just might turn that day around for you and your partner. And it helps when you do it together.

AUGUST 18

All things were created by him and for him. He
is before all things, and in him all things
hold together (Colossians 1:16,17).

You are asked the question, "Do you believe in God?"
You reply, "Yes, I do."

"Then, tell me about your God. Give me some specifics. What is He like? What are His characteristics?"

What specifics about God's character would you describe? Today's passage focuses on one primary characteristic. God is self-sufficient. He doesn't need anything or anyone. You need food, water, and air. But for God, nothing is necessary. All of life is in God, and life is a gift from God. God isn't interested in you because He is incomplete without you. He's involved with you because He loves you, not because He needs you.

Let's stretch our minds a bit more. Did you ever stop to think that God cannot be elevated? There is nothing above Him. No one can promote Him or demote Him like some executive in a company. God is completely independent of everyone else. We cannot make Him any more God than He already is. If every human became blind today, the stars would still shine. They exist in their own right and don't depend upon us. Similarly, if we as Christians did not exist, God would be no less than He is. Perhaps you've thought that God needs your support or that He needs you to defend Him before others. He doesn't need you, but He chooses to work through you and to call you to Himself.

Isn't it interesting that God who is all-sufficient wants to be involved with rebellious humanity? He certainly didn't need us to make His life more interesting or challenging. So if He didn't need to create us, He must have done it for some other reason. Perhaps that's what love is all about.[12]

AUGUST 19

I am he; I am the first and I am the last (Isaiah 48:12).

God doesn't change. He doesn't get better or worse. He is thoroughly and eternally holy. He neither improves nor deteriorates. The world around us changes, and people change. But God doesn't. This is one of the ways that God differs from us. We are so fickle and changeable even when we give our word.

There is no way in the world that you could persuade God to be different then He is. And He cannot be coaxed into fulfilling a selfish prayer! He is not here to bring His life into accord with our will. Instead we are here to bring our lives into line with His will.

What value does God's constancy and immutability have in a world where we cannot depend on others? Consider the words of A.W. Tozer:

> What peace it brings to the Christian's heart to realize that our Heavenly Father never differs from Himself. In coming to Him at any time we need not wonder whether we shall find Him in a receptive mood. He is always receptive to misery and need, as well as to love and faith. He does not keep office hours nor set aside periods when He will see no one. Neither does He change His mind about anything. Today, this moment, He feels toward His creatures, toward babies, toward the sick, the fallen, the sinful, exactly as He did when He sent His only-begotten Son into the world to die for mankind.
>
> God never changes moods or cools off in His affections or loses enthusiasm.[13]

God never changes; you can count on it! Talk about how God's unchanging nature benefits your relationship to each other.[14]

AUGUST 20

Whom did the Lord consult to enlighten him,
and who taught him the right way? Who was
it that taught him knowledge or showed him
the path of understanding? (Isaiah 40:14).

I sure have a lot to learn."

"About what?"

"About everything."

You have likely participated in this conversation at one time or another in your life. We all have so much to learn. As a married person, you'll be learning about marriage the rest of your life. If you are a parent, you'll be learning about parenting for the rest of your life. If you have a profession, hopefully you'll continue to learn and improve your skills.

There is only one person who has no need to learn and who has never learned at any time. That person is God. He has always possessed perfect knowledge. So what does this mean for us? He knows everything instantly. He doesn't have to wait for you to tell Him something before He knows it. And He knows everything perfectly. He knows you and your partner completely. He doesn't know one of you any better or worse than the other.

Is God ever surprised by anything? No. Does He ever discover anything? No. Does He ever wonder about anything? No. God knows you through and through. There is nothing that you can say, do, or think that He doesn't already know, even your secret sins: "You have set our iniquities before you, our secret sins in the light of your presence" (Psalm 90:8). There is no way you can ever hide from God: "Where can I flee from your presence? If I say, 'Surely the darkness will hide me and the light become night around me,' even the darkness will not be dark to you; the night will shine like the day, for darkness is as light to you" (Psalm 139:7,11,12).

God knew you before you even knew that He existed. He knows every thought and every feeling you have ever had—and ever will have—about your partner. He knows your inner tendencies and struggles. The good news is that in spite of all He knows about you, He loves you. That's reassuring.[15]

AUGUST 21

*Clouds and thick darkness surround him; righteousness
and justice are the foundation of his throne* (Psalm 97:2).

I want someone who is just and fair. But I also want someone who has
a good heart. Is it possible to find someone with both qualities?"

There are many kinds of people in whom we seek equally generous
amounts of justice and goodness: a judge, a counselor, a tax accountant,
a teacher. But often we find some people who are just and fair while
being cold and bad-natured. Or we may find goodness in a person who
is unfair in his judgments. Thankfully, God has no lack in either category. As you read through the Old Testament you discover that God
is completely just and fair, and He is thoroughly good and righteous.

God cannot be anything but fair. It is His nature. He must punish
the ungodly, but He does so justly. He provided the payment for sin
through the gift of His Son. He not only set the standard for righteousness, but provided a way for it to be fulfilled in everyone through
Christ. That's quite fair.

God is also good. It's because of His goodness that we benefit from
His compassion. He is kind, and He exercises good will toward us. And
because God does not change, the amount of His goodness is always
the same. Those who admit that they have sinned and need God will
discover the extent of His goodness. What we have done in the past
will not be held against us. That's how far His goodness extends.

What do these attributes mean to you and to your marriage?
Perhaps these thoughts cause you to feel that the God you follow and
worship is beyond comprehension for your limited mind. But that's all
right, for the vastness of His character prompts us to stand in awe of
Him and worship Him. And as a couple, if you faithfully follow Him
and reflect His justice and goodness toward each other, how can your
marriage possibly go wrong?[16]

AUGUST 22

*You have made my heart beat faster with a single
glance of your eyes* (Song of Songs 4:9, NASB).

Some wonderful thoughts on romantic love:
"Some sincere Christians consider romantic love the whipped
whipped cream on the sundae of marriage—decorative, but unnecessary. They see this as a lower form of love that husbands and wives
should disregard in their search for higher ground....

"In spite of all this, just about everyone inwardly longs for a thrilling
love relationship involving oneness, a deep intimacy with another person,
joy and optimism, spice and excitement, and that wonderful, euphoric,
almost indescribable sensation known as 'being in love.' Some people
say they are 'on cloud nine.' They mean that they feel energized, moti-
vated, confident to conquer because they know they are loved by their
beloved. There is a sense of awe in feeling chosen for this blessed state.
With it goes a thrill of anticipation in being together. Most important,
a fresh sense of purpose sweetens life because the two have found each
other and have, as the expression goes, 'fallen in love.'

"This is not overstating the case. Romantic love is good medicine for
fears and anxieties and a low self-image. Psychologists point out that
real romantic love has an organizing and constructive effect on our
personalities. It brings out the best in us, giving us the will to improve
ourselves and to reach for a greater maturity and responsibility. This
love enables us to begin to function at our highest level.

"Quite honestly, if you are not in love with your marriage partner in
this way, you are missing something wonderful, no matter how sincere
your commitment to that person may be. Even contentment can be
dull and drab in comparison with the joy God planned for you with
your marriage partner."[17]

AUGUST 23

*I belong to my lover, and his desire is
for me* (Song of Songs 7:10).

How was it with you when you first fell in love with the person
you married? Think about the qualities which attracted you to
him or her. Dr. Ed Wheat suggests the following pattern for renewing
your love.

> I am suggesting that both husband and wife must use
> their imagination to fall in love, renew romantic love, or keep
> alive the eros love they now have. Remember that love must
> grow or die. Imagination is perhaps the strongest natural
> power we possess. It furthers the emotions in the same way
> that illustrations enlarge the impact of a book. It's as if we
> have movie screens in our minds, and we own the ability to
> throw pictures on the screen—whatever sort of pictures we
> choose. We can visualize thrilling, beautiful situations with
> our mates whenever we want to.
>
> Try it. Select a moment of romantic feeling with your
> partner from the past, present, or hoped-for future. As you
> begin to think about that feeling, your imagination goes
> to work with visual pictures. Your imagination feeds your
> thoughts, strengthening them immeasurably; then your
> thoughts intensify your feelings. This is how it works. Imagi-
> nation is a gift from the Creator to be used for good, to help
> accomplish his will in a hundred different ways. So build
> romantic love on your side of the marriage by thinking about
> your partner, concentrating on positive experiences and plea-
> sure out of the past and then daydreaming, anticipating
> future pleasure with your mate. The frequency and intensity
> of these positive, warm, erotic, tender thoughts about your
> partner, strengthened by the imagination factor, will govern
> your success in falling in love.[18]

AUGUST 24

*Put on that nature which is merciful in
action* (Colossians 3:12, PHILLIPS).

Time is a precious commodity for all of us. Often we take the time
spent with our spouse for granted. Here is some good advice on
time and marriage from *The Marriage Collection*:

Are you using time in a way that blesses your marriage?
For example, do you thank God for His daily gift of time to
you as man and wife? Time is, after all, the invaluable raw
material of your marriage. You wake up in the morning and
it's always there—twenty-four precious hours to spend as you
choose. But do you live and love one another as if it were
the last day to enjoy your gift of time? What would you do
if you knew you were spending your final twenty-four hours
together? What would you say? How would you act toward
one another?

Do you regularly invite God into your precious slice of
time together? Have you gained His vision of what He wants
to do with your marriage?

Do you practice mutuality each day? That is, do you adapt,
accept, forgive, always making all things mutual in the spirit
of loving give and take?…

Do you value the ordinary days—even the dull routine—
of living together? Would you trade one ordinary day with
your partner for ten "exciting" ones without him or her? Be
careful how you answer. Perhaps you have already been doing
just that and calling it "working extra hard at the office" or
"pouring myself into the children."

Do you flee from the greatest sin of all—wasting your time
together on self-centeredness, self-justification, self-advance-
ment, self-pity, self-aggrandizement and self-righteousness?
Your time is far too precious for that.[19]

AUGUST 25

All Scripture is God-breathed and is useful for
teaching, rebuking, correcting and training
in righteousness (2 Timothy 3:16).

Charlie and Martha Shedd have a wise suggestion today:

"Isn't it sacrilegious to mark in a Bible?" Surprising how many times we are asked this question. For us the answer is a resounding No!

The Charlie-Martha Bible study method is based on three specific marks: candles, arrows, question marks. Each morning as we read our Bibles individually, we underline and mark.

When we come to an entirely new thought, a new insight, we underline and put a candle in the margin—a candle for new light.

When we read something we don't understand, have doubts about, something we can't believe, we underline and place a question mark in the margin.

Then there are the places that convict us. These make us realize we are not what we should be. Here we underline and use an arrow in the margin. (We do not place arrows for each other. We allow each the dignity of discovering his/her own sins.)...

Then once each week, sometimes more often, we sit together and share our marks. Straight out of God's Word comes the impetus for talk, talk, talk.

Where do we begin?

If one of us has a mark at the first verse in chapter 1, we begin there. "A candle? This is a new thought to me. What do you think?"

For us, Bible study together provides that caring friendship. In the interchange of arrows, we share quirks and foibles. With the tender touches of love and with God's help, we unbraid some tangled skeins. We help each other and He helps us to a new peace.[20]

AUGUST 26

Praise be to the God and Father of our Lord Jesus
Christ, who has blessed us in the heavenly realms with
every spiritual blessing in Christ (Ephesians 1:3).

Benefits—they're a major concern for most of us. We want to know what our benefits are when we take a new job, purchase a major item, or listen to a sales pitch. When you were first interested in marrying your partner, whether you realized it or not, you considered the benefits of spending the rest of your life with this individual. Part of the challenge of marriage is discovering those benefits and making sure that your expectations were realistic.

But your primary focus on benefits in marriage should be to make sure your partner is benefiting from your presence, not selfishly focusing on what you will get out of the relationship. Married life is a continuing process of seeking to be a benefit to your partner.

There is another area in which benefits are important: your faith in Jesus Christ. Imagine that someone came up to you and asked, "What's the big deal about being a Christian? What do you get out of it? What are the benefits? And don't hand me a bunch of clichés. What does your Bible say? Can you point me to a specific chapter and verse?"

Good question. There's also a good answer in Ephesians 1:4-6: "For he chose us in him before the creation of the world to be holy and blameless in his sight. In love he predestined us to be adopted as his sons through Jesus Christ, in accordance with his pleasure and will—to the praise of his glorious grace, which he has freely given us in the One he loves."

Paul began the passage by praising God and then describing how He has blessed you. What blessing? He chose you. Your salvation was not an afterthought. God didn't remember at the last minute, "Oh yes, I need to save..." You were in the heart and mind of God before He created the world. Can you grasp that and realize how significant you are?

How will you and your spouse be a blessing to God today?

AUGUST 27

Always keep on praying (1 Thessalonians 5:17, TLB).

How did your partner's family pray? Did they pray together as a family? privately as individuals? not at all? What was the pattern of prayer in your original family? Have you ever discussed these questions before? Perhaps right now would be a good time to talk about them. Take a minute to share, then continue reading.

If you grew up with a pattern of family prayer and devotions in your home, perhaps you expected a continuation of this pattern in your own marriage. You could be expecting your partner to take the lead. But what if family prayer is new to him or her? Your own personal devotional life will change as you enter and progress through the marital journey. Your prayer life is your own private communion with God, but it can be shared together. Consider what prayer does:

> Prayer is an awareness of the presence of a holy and loving God in one's life, and an awareness of God's relation to one's husband or wife. Prayer is listening to God, a valuable lesson in learning to listen to one another. Praying together shuts out the petty elements of daily conflict and anxiety, permitting a couple to gain a higher perspective upon their lives, allowing their spirits to be elevated to a consideration of eternal values and enduring relationships. Prayer helps a couple sort out unworthy objects of concern and helps them to concentrate on the nobler goals of life. All the threatening things that trouble a pair can find relief in the presence of God.[21]

Have you experienced the benefits family prayer can bring? They are yours. Let them be a consistent part of your life.

AUGUST 28

Since an overseer is entrusted with God's
work, he must be blameless (Titus 1:7).

Remember when you were younger and just beginning to date? Did your parents ever caution you not to go out with a certain person because of his or her "reputation"? A reputation is like a label. Once it's stamped on, it's difficult to remove. Often it precedes us wherever we go. Others may know all about us before they really know us!

How would you describe your personal reputation? Do people characterize you as blameless, the quality mentioned in today's verse? Does your marriage have the reputation of being blameless? Now there's a different thought—a blameless marriage, a marriage with a good reputation, one that draws people to Jesus Christ.

Have you ever thought about what gives a person a bad reputation? Let's consider several elements of bad reputation mentioned by Paul in Titus 1:7 in contrast to blamelessness.

The apostle talked about people with the reputation for being "overbearing...quick-tempered...violent." This kind of person flies off the handle and explodes quickly. Outbursts of temper do not draw others to Jesus Christ, and such behavior is often a hindrance to other Christians as well.

Paul cautioned believers about being "given to drunkenness." Many believers in Paul's day were tempted to revert to their old sinful lifestyle. Some of us may face the same temptation. But mature Christians exert control over anything that might harm their bodies.

Another characteristic of a bad reputation is "pursuing dishonest gain." The goal of these people was to get as much as they could for themselves no matter how they got it. People who live this way are selfish and lack integrity.

Spend a few minutes talking together about your reputation as individuals and as a couple. What kind of reputation do you want to have? What can you do to change your reputation?[22]

AUGUST 29

[An elder] must be hospitable, one who loves
what is good, who is self-controlled, upright,
holy and disciplined (Titus 1:8).

What are the characteristics of a good reputation? The qualities mentioned by Paul in today's verse don't apply only to church leaders. These five qualities will help all believers develop and maintain a good reputation.

Being "hospitable" is a mark of maturity in a Christian. It is the opposite of selfishness. Those who are known for reaching out to others and helping in times of need end up with a good reputation. How might you as a couple express hospitality to others?

Being "one who loves what is good" means that the direction of your life and marriage is the pursuit of what is good. Good works is the theme of Ephesians 2:10: "We are God's workmanship, created in Christ Jesus to do good works."

Paul refers to the characteristic of being "self-controlled" five times in his letter to Titus. He really wants to emphasize the importance of this quality in the lives of all of us. Every Christian, regardless of personality tendencies, is called to develop self-control. Do you know what this means biblically? It refers to a person who is in control of all his faculties—physical, psychological, and spiritual. When you're self-controlled you're not in bondage to your impulses.

Being "upright" and "holy" does a lot for a good reputation. How can this characteristic best be described? Simple. It's a life that is not dominated by sin. It means you have developed the ability to relate to others who don't know Christ while maintaining your Christian testimony.

The last quality is "self-discipline." The Christian life is a disciplined life. To be effective in work, school, and marriage takes self-discipline.

Now take a moment and talk together about how these five characteristics can be expressed through your marriage relationship so that it also has a good reputation.[23]

AUGUST 30

*[An elder] must be hospitable, one who loves
what is good, who is self-controlled, upright,
holy and disciplined* (Titus 1:8).

The following questions will help both of you evaluate your reputation in the light of God's Word:

1. Am I overbearing? Do I allow my old nature to take control of my relationships with others? For example, must I have the last word in every discussion? Do I find it difficult to agree with others? Do I force my opinions on other people?

2. Am I quick-tempered? That is, do I easily lose control of my temper? Do I speak before I think? Do I find it difficult to be objective about a situation when I am the object of criticism? Do I hurt people easily? Do people hesitate to ask me about sensitive issues?

3. Am I addicted to anything that affects my psychological and physical well-being? What about food? What about drink? What about any other oral habits?

4. Am I a pugnacious type of person? Do I strike out at others either physically or verbally? Do I ever resort to subtle ways of hurting people even though it may appear to be a gentle approach? Do I ever gossip about people under the guise of personal concern?

5. Do I ever pursue dishonest gain? Am I honest in all financial matters? Do I keep accurate records? If an employer, am I fair and honest with my employees? Am I aboveboard with the government?

6. Am I hospitable? Do I use my home as a means of ministering to others? Am I basically unselfish with my material possessions? Do I share my blessings with others?

7. Do I love what is good? What evidence do I have that I am overcoming evil with good? What about my lifestyle in general? Could I write "good" over what I read, what I see, what I listen to, and what I do?

8. Am I self-controlled? Can I classify myself as being sensible, sober, and having a sound mind?[24]

August 31

Therefore encourage each other (1 Thessalonians 4:18).

Consider this example of caring from a Chinese fable:

> A very old man knew that he was going to die very soon. Before he died, he wanted to know what heaven and hell were like, so he visited the wise man in his village.
>
> "Can you please tell me what heaven and hell are like?" he asked the wise man.
>
> "Come with me and I will show you," the wise man replied.
>
> The two men walked down a long path until they came to a large house. The wise man took the old man inside, and there they found a large dining room with an enormous table covered with every kind of food imaginable. Around the table were many people, all thin and hungry, who were holding twelve-foot chopsticks. Every time they tried to feed themselves, the food fell off the chopsticks.
>
> The old man said to the wise man, "Surely this must be hell. Will you now show me heaven?"
>
> The wise man said, "Yes, come with me."
>
> The two men left the house and walked farther down the path until they reached another large house. Again they found a large dining room and in it a table filled with all kinds of food. The people here were happy and appeared well fed, but they also held twelve-foot chopsticks.
>
> "How can this be?" said the old man. "These people have twelve-foot chopsticks and yet they are happy and well fed."
>
> The wise man replied, "In heaven the people feed each other."[25]

How can the two of you express care for someone else today?

SEPTEMBER

Forgiveness is not demanding change from your partner before you forgive him or her. Your partner cannot guarantee that he or she will never make the same mistake again. Forgiveness is an investment of trust.

SEPTEMBER 1

And whatever you do in word or deed, do all in
the name of the Lord Jesus, giving thanks through
Him to God the Father (Colossians 3:17, NASB).

We all have them; we just don't talk about them. They make up some of our darkest, deepest secrets. Or so we think. Our spouse usually knows about them. He or she ought to. Why? Because our spouse may be the person encouraging us to face them rather than ignore them. What are we talking about? Those little unpleasant tasks we just hate to do, the ones we give over to the power of procrastination. Yes, we think that if we put them off they will disappear, or better yet someone else will jump in and do them for us! Not likely!

Why do we procrastinate? Perhaps you had to do that task as you were growing up, and you just couldn't wait until adulthood and freedom. But guess what—it's still there! It could be a weekly chore like weeding or mowing the lawn. It could be cleaning that hall closet or the garage in which a car has never been able to fit. We avoid the task and give our reasons. We may even avoid work by procrastinating in our job as well. But consider this: The task or chore you avoid could be impacting your partner in a way that is damaging your marital relationship.

As a believer, you have both a calling and an opportunity to do everything in a way that will bring honor and glory to God. Think about that! Even cleaning the garage can bring you a sense of satisfaction, bring a smile to your partner's face, and serve as a testimony to the power of Jesus Christ to change a lifelong pattern! How is that for a benefit package?

God's Word says: "Let your light shine before men in such a way that they may see your good works, and glorify your Father who is in heaven" (Matthew 5:16, NASB); "Walk in a manner worthy of the calling with which you have been called" (Ephesians 4:1, NASB). Let the Word of God be reflected in you today. It's a great opportunity!

SEPTEMBER 2

What, then, shall we say in response
to this? (Romans 8:31).

Have you ever been at a loss for words? Perhaps your partner has a wisecrack to share in response to this question! But consider it seriously for a moment: Have you ever been so taken aback or overwhelmed by a gift, a surprise, or an honor that you weren't sure how to respond?

Paul raised an interesting question in today's verse regarding this concept. But to fully understand his question you need to read the previous two verses: "For those God foreknew he also predestined to be conformed to the likeness of his Son, that he might be the firstborn among many brothers. And those he predestined, he also called; those he called, he also justified; those he justified, he also glorified" (Romans 8:29,30).

In light of the good news that God called us and justified us, Paul seems to be speechless. Perhaps you are also speechless when you reflect on all you have received as a result of God's grace in choosing you. Whether you are the richest person in the country or the poorest streetperson in the ghetto, your earthly position has no bearing on what you are in Christ by God's choice. What you achieve or accumulate in life doesn't impress God in the least. He calls you, justifies you, and glorifies you solely because He chooses to do so in response to your faith.

Paul asks six more rhetorical questions in Romans 8:31-35 in the light of this great truth. Read them. Now notice how he summarizes his response to the knowledge of God's choice in verses 37-39. He states that we are more than conquerors and that nothing can separate us from the love of God in Christ.

Why did Paul state all of this? It's quite simple. He wants to give you a sense of security and hope. Whenever you become discouraged or depressed, look at God's promises to you. But when you read them, don't be totally speechless. Share them with your partner, because he or she needs encouragement also.

SEPTEMBER 3

I pray also that the eyes of your heart may be
enlightened in order that you may know the hope
to which he has called you (Ephesians 1:18).

Do you ever feel like a yo-yo?

Strange question? Perhaps. But some of you will probably answer in the affirmative anyway. Sometimes you feel like a yo-yo emotionally or spiritually; up one minute and down the next. Take a minute and ask your partner if he or she feels like a yo-yo in some area of life.

Many Christians have experienced the yo-yo phenomenon spiritually, even to the extent that they question their faith or their eternal destiny. Paul discovered that the believers at Ephesus were struggling with this problem. They weren't sure whether they would be with the Lord or not when they died. Paul took time to encourage them and build up their sense of security. He prayed that they would be settled and enlightened and really grasp the hope of eternal life.

The word *hope* is used in direct reference to eternal life. If someone were to ask you about your hope, what passages of Scripture would you share with them from God's Word? Consider these: "Let us be self-controlled, putting on...the hope of salvation as a helmet" (1 Thessalonians 5:8); "Paul, a servant of God and an apostle of Jesus Christ for the faith of God's elect and the knowledge of the truth that leads to godliness—a faith and knowledge resting on the hope of eternal life" (Titus 1:1,2); "We wait for the blessed hope—the glorious appearing of our great God and Savior, Jesus Christ" (Titus 2:13); "In his great mercy he has given us new birth into a living hope" (1 Peter 1:3).

When you understand the hope you have in Christ, you will experience the security, stability, and endurance you need in the yo-yo experiences of life (1 Thessalonians 1:3). Hope gives us something to hold onto (Hebrews 10:23). So when you and your partner find yourself bouncing around spiritually, hope will bring you back to an even keel. That's encouraging!

SEPTEMBER 4

*The voice of the Lord is powerful; the voice
of the Lord is majestic* (Psalm 29:4).

Before continuing with this meditation, read Psalm 29 aloud together in its entirety from your Bible.

Have you ever heard the voice of God speaking to you? The psalmist describes God's voice through the illustration of nature. Instead of being afraid of the crashing, rolling thunder, the writer saw it as a manifestation of the glory of God. Have you ever read this psalm aloud during a thunder and lightning storm? Try it next time the clouds roll in.

Seven times in the psalm the voice of the Lord is compared to a thunder clap. Look at the psalm again and notice the effect of the thunder. Does the word "awesome" come to mind? Sometimes we get the same effect when God penetrates our heart and speaks to us as individuals or as a couple.

What is the psalmist doing here? Is he merely giving a poetic description of the beauties of nature? No. He is calling us back to the sovereignty of God. Give God what is due Him. Verses 1 and 2 read, "Ascribe to the Lord, O mighty ones, ascribe to the Lord glory and strength, ascribe to the Lord the glory due his name." Our God is the God of glory. Psalm 89:6 and Job 1:6; 2:1 suggest that the mighty ones being addressed are angels who are to give God glory. But as redeemed ones, we can also join in praising the Sovereign Lord.

In Psalm 29:10 the psalmist turns from his reference to God appearing and speaking in the thunder to describe the power of God sitting enthroned forever. He is the God of power and might today as He was then and will be forever. And because of who He is, He can and will strengthen and bless you and your marriage with peace. And because He is the Sovereign Lord, He can equip you to bless your partner with peace. He can help you respond to your spouse in such a way that he or she feels more secure and restful in your presence. Since you have been given peace, let it flow out to those around you, especially your partner.

SEPTEMBER 5

I pray also that the eyes of your heart may be
enlightened in order that you may know the hope
to which he has called you, the riches of his glorious
inheritance in the saints (Ephesians 1:18,19).

You are a rich person."
  If you made that statement to your partner, how would he or she respond? How would you respond if your partner said it to you? From one perspective, it may not be the truth. If we're talking about money, very few of us are really rich. You may have accumulated a number of material possessions, but who actually owns much free and clear anymore?

But as today's verse states, there is a sense in which every believer is rich. Yes, you *are* a rich person. Paul spoke of your riches five times in the first three chapters of Ephesians as he described your blessings in Christ (1:18; 2:4,7; 3:8,16). What are those riches? Paul outlined them for you in Ephesians 1:3-14.

First, God the Father chose you in Christ before the foundation of the world (v. 4). He predestined you to be adopted as His own (v. 5).

Second, God the Son carried out God's plan of redemption by shedding His blood on the cross. He redeemed you through His blood and provided forgiveness for your sins (v. 7).

Third, God the Spirit has enabled you to respond in faith to God's love and has guaranteed your inheritance (vv. 13,14).

Now what do you say: Are you poor or rich? You have riches that no one can ever take away from you. These riches will bring you peace and security whether you are the poorest or the richest person on earth in terms of money and material possessions.

One last thought: What is usually expected of those who are rich? Yes—to share the wealth. Talk about how you as a couple can share your wealth in Christ with others.[1]

SEPTEMBER 6

The kingdom of heaven is like a merchant
looking for fine pearls. When he found one of
great value, he went away and sold everything
he had and bought it (Matthew 13:45,46).

How much is your partner worth? How much are you worth? You and your partner have inestimable value to God and to each other. That's a fact. But are you really aware of your worth? Do you really believe that you have value? What does your partner do or say that lets you know you are valued *by* him or her? How do you communicate your spouse's value *to* him or her? Take a moment to assure each other of your great value.

Jesus told a story about a pearl to communicate the value He places on you. Jesus Christ went into the slave market of sin and paid for your release. You were bought with a great price (1 Corinthians 6:20). Take a moment to read 1 Peter 1:18,19, and you will discover the great price God paid for you!

We usually give preferential treatment to the items of great value we possess. If you had a painting by a struggling amateur artist on your wall, you probably wouldn't install a burglar alarm to protect it or worry that it would be stolen when you went out. It's not that valuable. But if you happened to own a priceless Van Gogh or Monet, you probably wouldn't feel safe keeping it at home at all. These paintings are so valuable that they usually end up in carefully guarded private collections or museums. The value of an item usually determines the way it is treated.

Since God places such high value on you, you deserve to be treated with respect, care, and love. But wait! Before you admonish your partner to treat you with more respect, think about these questions: Do you treat yourself with respect, care, and love? Do you treat your partner with respect, care, and love? If you both focus on answering these two questions in the affirmative, you will be surprised at the respect, care, and love you will receive from each other.

SEPTEMBER 7

Lord, teach us to pray (Luke 11:1).

This is a surprise quiz. Do you know at least five elements which biblical prayer comprises? Confer with your partner for ten seconds, then read on.

During an average day, the number of prayers that God receives must be too great for us to comprehend. And a staggering number of these prayers would not contain the following five elements of prayer as taught by Jesus. Let's consider these five elements of prayer.

Worship is the first element. Jesus began His model prayer by saying, "When you pray, say: 'Father, hallowed be your name'" (Luke 11:2). This is worship. Prayer includes worshiping and praising God for what He has done and for who He is.

A second element of prayer is thanksgiving. Paul said, "I urge, then, first of all, that requests, prayers, intercession, and thanksgiving be made for everyone" (1 Timothy 2:1). What do you have to thank God for as a couple right at this moment? Think about it and discuss it together, and then thank Him.

The third element is confession: "If I regard iniquity in my heart, the Lord will not hear" (Psalm 66:18, NKJV). Prayer is a time of cleansing. This is the time to admit your sin and receive His forgiveness. You can only confess your own sin, not your partner's.

The fourth element is petition, asking God to meet your own personal needs. "Present your requests to God" (Philippians 4:6), Paul instructed. What need do you have at this moment which needs to be presented to God?

The last element is intercession: praying for others. Paul requested, "Pray for us" (2 Thessalonians 3:1). Do you as a couple have a list of names of people you pray for? If not, consider making one. Leave space on your list for writing in God's answer. Let others know you are praying for them. What a difference prayer can make in your life and in the lives of others.[2]

September 8

Love your neighbor as yourself (Leviticus 19:18).

You're selfish! You don't love anyone else except yourself! Don't you know that you're to love others first?"

Strong words! They were spoken in anger one day during a verbal exchange between a husband and wife. One partner accused the other of being self-centered rather than other-centered. Being totally self-centered is wrong, of course. But did you realize that we are called by God to love ourselves in a positive, biblical way? The Word of God is very clear about this. In addition to Leviticus 19:18, the instruction to love ourselves is also found four other places: Mark 12:31; Romans 13:9; Galatians 5:14; James 2:8. That's significant. Self-centeredness is wrong, but healthy self-love is very right!

Sometimes it is difficult to love others, even family members. And at times you may have to make extra effort to love your partner. The offensive behavior of others, distractions that take you away from them, physical or emotional exhaustion, drifting from the Lord—all of these can contribute to your waning love for others. But the Word of God says we are to love ourselves, and it's out of proper, biblical self-love that we are able to love others.

The type of love we are to have for others and ourselves is *agape*. You know the word. Agape love has nothing to do with selfish preoccupation or narcissistic focus. It's a love which focuses on a person's value and significance. That's what biblical self-love is all about. Do you have a high regard for yourself as a significant person? Do you place a high value on yourself as a child of God? God does, and it's all right for you to do so. God also calls you to value your partner in the same way, because he or she is significant also.

Talk together about your value to God and to each other. Don't be ashamed to admit to your partner that you are a person of value. But be sure to affirm his or her value too.

SEPTEMBER 9

That power is like the working of his mighty strength,
which he exerted in Christ when he raised him
from the dead and seated him at his right hand
in the heavenly realms (Ephesians 1:19,20).

Handle it carefully! Don't drop it! If you do, you may have an explosive encounter with a dangerous source of power. It's called dynamite. You probably aren't directly involved with dynamite in your daily life. But those who work with it respect its potentially dangerous power.

There is another kind of power that you have confronted, however. It is God's power. Paul wanted to make sure the Ephesians understood what God's power was like, so he used four Greek words to describe this power. He wrote, "I pray also that the eyes of your heart may be enlightened in order that you may know...his incomparably great power for us who believe. That power is like the working of his mighty strength" (Ephesians 1:18,19).

Power comes from the Greek word *dunamis*, from which we get our word dynamite. *Working* comes from *energeia*, the origin of our English word energy. Paul adds two more words to complete the picture: *mighty strength*. These four words have different shades of meaning. Power is the ability to accomplish what is planned, promised, or started. Working means inherent strength or brute power. Might is the power to resist and overcome obstacles. Strength is the actual exercise of power.

What was Paul trying to convey by using four words for power in one sentence? He wanted to graphically emphasize God's great power which was activated on our behalf to secure our salvation (Ephesians 2:1,4-6).

How can you benefit from the knowledge of God's power? Understanding the extent of God's power will help you feel secure in Jesus Christ (1 Peter 1:3-5). By knowing the extent of God's power, you can be assured of His guidance and protection in the midst of problems and pressures. And all of us will need this reassurance from time to time.[3]

SEPTEMBER 10

*He humbled Himself by becoming obedient to the
point of death, even death on a cross. Therefore also
God highly exalted Him* (Philippians 2:8,9, NASB).

Humility—what is it? If you want to try something interesting
today, ask several people for a definition of humility. They'll stop
to think, scratch their heads, and probably have difficulty stating a clear
definition. Can you define humility? Are you humble? If so, can you
explain why you think you are? Would your partner agree that you
are humble?

We are all called to be humble. In Philippians 2:3 (NASB) we read:
"Do nothing from selfishness or empty conceit, but with humility
of mind let each of you regard one another as more important than
himself." Jesus Christ is our example of humility. But as you read about
His life you will notice something interesting: Jesus was humble, but
He didn't put Himself down. His humility didn't have its root in a
sense of inferiority, weakness, or insecurity. That would have been
false humility. True humility comes out of a proper perspective of our
strength and value. Jesus knew His value to the Father. Knowing your
value to God is the first step in learning true humility.

When Paul tells us to esteem others better than ourselves he's not
saying that we are to consider ourselves worthless. Because of what
Jesus Christ has done for us, we can feel secure about ourselves and
develop a strong identity. And it's out of this strength that we are to
focus on the needs of others and discover how we can best minister
to them.

Dr. Bruce Narramore has summed up humility well. He says that
humility has three elements: Recognizing our need for God, realistically evaluating our capacities, and being willing to serve. That's
healthy. That's humility. What better place to reflect it than in your
marriage relationship.[4]

SEPTEMBER 11

*They show that the requirements of the law are
written on their hearts, their consciences also
bearing witness, and their thoughts now accusing,
now even defending them* (Romans 2:15).

"Give it up. Don't hang onto it anymore. Just give it up."
What in the world are we talking about? It's a simple, five-letter word: guilt. That's right, guilt. But shouldn't we feel guilty? you ask. No, not really. This may come as a shock to you since most people *do* feel guilty. Some people feel guilty much of the time. They don't really know what it's like to live without guilt. Yet guilt feelings can negatively interfere with relationships, especially marriage.

When you look at some of the Greek words dealing with guilt, you notice something interesting: The feeling of guilt is not there. According to the Word of God, you can be guilty of a crime and liable for judgment or punishment. And you can be guilty of a debt which must be paid. Judicial guilt is valid—it's in the Bible. But if you have feelings of guilt, they are your own. God is not the author of guilt feelings.

But what about being convicted for our sins? Isn't conviction biblical? Yes, but when the Bible talks about conviction, it's not referring to a feeling. The Greek word for conviction literally means to bring to light or to bring to awareness. Conviction is simply God's process of bringing our failures, weaknesses, and inadequacies to our attention. But it's not an emotional burden that God lays upon us.

When you feel guilt, you are saying that you have to do something to make up for your sin or at least to suffer for it. That's not God's plan. Constructive sorrow is a far healthier way of responding to your sins, inadequacies, and failures. You can regret and be sorrowful without running yourself into the ground. Guilt is self-depreciating. And if you tend toward self-depreciation, you may also depreciate others in attitude, speech, or behavior.

Are guilt feelings interfering with your relationship in some way? Talk about it together, then pray about it.[5]

SEPTEMBER 12

Let us throw off everything that hinders and the sin that
so easily entangles, and let us run with perseverance
the race marked out for us (Hebrews 12:1).

In most races there are more starters than finishers. Look at the
number of people who start swimming the English channel and
don't finish, who start the Iditarod dog sled race in Alaska and don't
finish, who start the Tour de France bicycle race and don't finish, or
who start the Boston Marathon and don't finish. In most endurance
races, there comes a time when the participant "hits the wall." The
"wall" is the point at which he or she is so tired that he or she groans, "I
can't go on. I've given all I can. I don't have any more to give." When
you hit the wall, you have to push yourself to continue. You have to go
against what your body and mind are telling you and continue on.

There is one word that distinguishes starters from finishers: perseverance. Anyone can start, but only those who persevere to the end
can finish.

There are more starters than finishers in marriage too. Of the
couples who start, only about half stay together "till death do us part."
All couples hit the wall and are tempted to quit from time to time.
There is the wall of finances and the wall of personality differences.
There is the wall of waking up one morning and finding you're in the
middle of a love recession. Your feelings of love aren't quite as intense
as they were when you first married. You need perseverance in marriage
or you will quit before reaching the finish line.

So what is a couple to do when they hit the wall? Persevere. Perseverance is the ability to hold up under the pressures which confront
every marriage. It is the ability to hang in there rather than just hang
on. When you hit that wall in your marriage, instead of recoiling and
giving up, stand there together, look at it, and then give each other a
boost over the wall. You can make it. Perhaps the first step is identifying any of the walls which you are currently facing. Then go for it![6]

September 13

*"Lord, how many times shall I forgive my brother
when he sins against me? Up to seven times?"
Jesus answered, "I tell you, not seven times, but
seventy-seven times"* (Matthew 18:21,22).

As a married couple, you can be involved in a creative act! No, I'm not talking about a new addition to your family. Each time you forgive your partner you are involved in creating a new beginning in your marriage. It's true that the hurts and offenses still exist, but when you forgive you refuse to let them become anchors which keep you from moving forward. David Augsburger describes forgiveness so well:

> Forgiveness takes place when love accepts—deliberately— the hurts and abrasions of life and drops all charges against the other person. Forgiveness is accepting the other when both of you know he or she has done something quite unacceptable.
>
> Forgiveness is smiling silent love to your partner when the justifications for keeping an insult or injury alive are on the tip of your tongue, yet you swallow them. Not because you have to, to keep peace, but because you want to, to make peace.
>
> Forgiveness is not acceptance given "on the condition" that the other become acceptable. Forgiveness is given freely. Out of the keen awareness that the forgiver also has a need of constant forgiveness, daily.
>
> Forgiveness exercises God's strength to love and receives the other person without any assurance of complete restitution and making of amends.
>
> Forgiveness is a relationship between equals who recognize their need of each other, share and share alike. Each needs the other's forgiveness. Each needs the other's acceptance. Each needs the other. And so, before God, each drops all charges, refutes all self-justification, and forgives. And forgives. "Seventy times seven," as Jesus said.[7]

SEPTEMBER 14

And just as we have borne the likeness of the
earthly man, so shall we bear the likeness of the
man from heaven (1 Corinthians 15:49).

Look at your partner. Note his or her physical characteristics. What do you see? Perhaps you are newly married, and you are still enjoying the excitement of physical attraction. Or maybe you've been married for a while, and your attraction to one another is more internal than external. Makeup, toupees, and padded clothes all help to hide our physical frailties.

You will never be a perfect physical specimen in this life. You can spend hours at the gym, but some bumps and blemishes will always be with you. It is for that reason that we must exercise a great deal of acceptance in marriage. None of us is the Greek god or goddess our spouse perceived us to be before marriage. But that's all right. We're all in the same boat. Our worth and value to each other is not based upon our appearance—or it shouldn't be. If it is, we're in danger. Not only are we at the mercy of others, but we will drive ourselves up a wall trying to perfect what was never perfect in the first place.

When it comes to our bodies, we can all relax. A day will come when they will be perfect. In eternity we will all have new bodies. We will be changed. And we won't be so concerned about how we look either. You're already a new person in Christ inwardly. The process of restoration has already begun on the inside. When you meet Jesus Christ face to face you will be complete.

Look at your body. Look at your partner's body. Tell each other, "It's all right to be incomplete physically now. Just wait. We were created in God's image and our physical bodies will be transformed when we die."

God's plan is for each of us to have a glorified body. It's just that His timing is a bit different than ours!

SEPTEMBER 15

*If you can find a truly good wife, she is worth more
than precious gems! Her husband can trust her, and she
will richly satisfy his needs* (Proverbs 31:10,11, TLB).

Many men turn to Proverbs 31 and hold it up for their wives to
read. They want a wife who is as industrious as this woman. She
shops, deals in real estate, prepares the food, and oversees the work of
the servants. Verse 17 (TLB) states, "She is energetic, a hard worker, and
watches for bargains. She works far into the night!" Husbands especially like the phrase, "She will richly satisfy his needs"!

Some husbands say, "I wish my wife were a Proverbs 31 woman.
Women like that are rare." But they don't have to be so rare. Not only
does Proverbs 31 describe the characteristics of this woman, it tells us
how she came to be this way.

The first ingredient is God. Look at verse 30 (TLB): "Charm can be
deceptive and beauty doesn't last, but a woman who fears and reverences God shall be greatly praised." A woman's positive response to
God in her life has much to do with the development of the qualities
listed in this chapter. Husband, one way to have a Proverbs 31 wife is
to encourage and help implement her spiritual development.

The second ingredient is her husband. He is the major catalyst in
her becoming all that she can be! Surprised? Verse 11 (AMP) reads,
"The heart of her husband trusts in her confidently." This husband
acknowledged his wife's abilities and did not take her for granted. He
appreciated her. Husband, when you invest trust in your wife and
believe in her, she will blossom.

Then in verse 28 (AMP) we read, "Her husband boasts of and praises
her." The husband in this chapter complimented his wife in front of
other men. Many husbands do that, but too many stop there. They
fail to share praise directly with their wife. Warm and genuine compliments will help release a wife to be all that she can be.

If a husband wants a quality wife he can surely have one—if he is
willing to play the role God has designed for him!

SEPTEMBER 16

*For God so loved the world that he gave his one
and only Son, that whoever believes in him shall
not perish but have eternal life* (John 3:16).

I feel awkward talking with my partner about God. I don't know what
to say, and I don't want to seem either pious or spiritually ignorant."

If you've ever felt that way, join the human race! It's not always easy
to discuss spiritual matters. What do you talk about? The following
exercises are given as guidelines for your spiritual discussions together.
These topics will probably require some additional time for reflection
and sharing. But it's worth the investment.

1. When did you first experience a closeness with God?
   Describe how and when this occurred.

2. Describe a time when you recognized that the Holy Spirit
   was definitely speaking to you.

3. When do you feel closest to God? When do you feel most
   distant from Him?

4. To whom do you usually pray: God the Father, Jesus the
   Son, or the Holy Spirit?

5. What are your mental images of God? Which images do
   you wish would fade away? Which ones would you like
   to be stronger?

6. Describe how God has helped you overcome guilt in the
   past. Describe any feelings of guilt you still have.

7. If you could ask Jesus Christ to touch your life and heal
   you from something right now, what would it be?

8. When you come face to face with Jesus Christ in heaven,
   what do you think He will say to you?

9. Which Scriptures have meant the most to you and why?

10. What was the first passage of Scripture you memorized?

Perhaps these thoughts and questions will trigger other topics so
your discussion can continue. Once you get started, you will become
much more comfortable with the process.[8]

SEPTEMBER 17

I urge you, brothers, in view of God's mercy, to offer your
bodies as living sacrifices, holy and pleasing to God—
this is your spiritual act of worship (Romans 12:1).

Can you imagine pulling a letter out of your mailbox, opening it, and reading, "Greetings. You have been selected to participate in a sacrifice—and you are the sacrifice. This is not simply a suggestion or a request. You are strongly urged to comply." How would you react?

That's the kind of letter Paul sent to the Christians in Rome. Paul's challenge carries a deep sense of urgency. He didn't say it would be nice if we presented our bodies to God as a living, holy sacrifice, he practically demanded it. He wrote with passion. Through the apostle, God is calling us to yield to Him something which is of vital importance to us—our lives.

God doesn't want a dead sacrifice, but one that is alive and active. He wants us to present our bodies to Him, then get off the altar and go live as husbands and wives who belong totally to Him. He is calling us to reflect His presence in our lives through our daily activity and morality.

How can we present our bodies to God as a living sacrifice? Perhaps this prayer penned by Chuck Swindoll will help:

> Lord, in this body there are certain drives and many desires. In my eyes, there are interests that are not from You. In these ears of mine and in these hands and in various parts of my body there are things that are attracted, like a magnet, to the world system. Therefore, I deliberately and willingly give You my eyes, my ears, my senses, my thought processes as an act of worship. I am Yours. Please take control of each one of these areas.[9]

Pray this prayer today and every day. Pray it together as a couple. Discover what God can do with a couple of living sacrifices.

SEPTEMBER 18

Do not be conformed to this world, but be transformed
by the renewing of your mind, that you may prove
what the will of God is, that which is good and
acceptable and perfect (Romans 12:2, NASB).

Have you ever felt pressured by others to do something you didn't want to do? You felt hemmed in, squeezed tight, and uncomfortably restricted by the pressure to conform. That's what Paul is talking about in today's verse. J.B. Phillips translates this verse, "Don't let the world around you squeeze you into its own mold." The Living Bible puts it, "Don't copy the behavior and customs of this world."

Conform—an interesting word. It means to assume an outward expression that does not come from within. To conform is to masquerade, to wear a mask. We are conforming to the world when Jesus Christ is within us but our actions don't reflect Him. We are not conforming when His inner presence is evident in our actions. Do you know one of the easiest places for conformity to occur? In marriage. We are sometimes so familiar with our partner that we get lax in our discipline, and our consistency of faith wanes.

The opposite of being conformed is to be transformed, to allow your outward expression to come from within. A caterpillar becomes a butterfly through transformation. You can be a transformed person. How? By the renewing of your mind. That's it, clear and simple. When your mind is renewed, then words, actions, and behaviors change.

First Corinthians 2:16 states that we have the mind of Christ. That's a tremendous possession. And possessions work best when they are used. In Colossians 3:1-3 we are told to set our minds on things above. You may want to read these verses aloud together and discuss them.

Two words—*conform* and *transform*. Which one is at work in your life? Think about it, talk about it, and let Jesus transform your life and your marriage.[10]

SEPTEMBER 19

Set your mind on the things above, not
on earthly things (Colossians 3:2).

You are part of the counterculture. As a Christian couple, your thinking and values are basically contrary to the values of society today. This contrast will be evident in many areas. Let's consider just a few of the world's attitudes and compare them to our Christian perspective.

The world says that the key to happiness is money. The more you acquire, the better your life. Look around you. This emphasis is evident in every facet of life. But you also discover that those who have wealth don't find happiness in it. The more you have, the more you spend. And greater pressures come with greater wealth. We only find true, lasting happiness in our relationship to Jesus Christ (John 10:10).

Society says the accumulation of money will meet our needs and make us significant people. Our self-worth is supposedly reflected in what and how much we have. This view necessitates that we sacrifice our relationships in order to work and accumulate as much as we can. But Scripture states that our worth is based upon who we are in Jesus Christ. Relationships last; wealth does not.

The world's ultimate goal is affluence and the easy life. Phrases like "I've arrived," "I've got it made," and "I'm going to retire at 50 and loaf the rest of my life" are heard more and more. But the easy life doesn't satisfy. The more you have, the more you want. Solomon wrote, "He who loves money will not be satisfied with money" (Ecclesiastes 5:10, NASB). The true goal in our life is to learn contentment regardless of how much or how little we have (Philippians 4:11,12).

What about you? Where do your thoughts about wealth fit into today's discussion? Perhaps it will be helpful to talk together about your goals and desires concerning money.[11]

SEPTEMBER 20

Because of his great love for us, God, who is rich
in mercy, made us alive with Christ even when
we were dead in transgressions—it is by grace
you have been saved (Ephesians 2:4,5).

Many people have a hard time understanding God's love. It is easy for us to love someone who loves us. But loving people at their worst, as God loves us, is hard for any of us!

The love of God described in this passage is a reflection of His grace. That's what grace is all about; it's God's love in action for every man and woman, none of whom deserve it. Perhaps it would be easier to understand God's grace-filled love by contrasting it to what God's love is *not*. For example, you never hear God say "I love you *because*…," "I will love you *if*…," or "I will love you *when*…" That's conditional love speaking, not God speaking!

Instead we hear God say "I love you *in spite of*…," "I love you *even when*…," "I will love you all the time *regardless of*…" That's unconditional love. God's love does not depend on who we are or what we do, but on who He is.

God calls you to love your partner in the same manner. Yes, it's easier for God to love unconditionally than it is for us because He is God. But because of His presence in our lives, we also can learn to love in this way.

Think about your partner for a moment. Does your love for him or her tend to be conditional? Have you spoken some of the conditional love statements above to your spouse? Perhaps at times you have; hopefully, not all the time.

Why don't you turn to your spouse right now and share the following statements of unconditional love. Complete each statement in a way which will assure your partner that your love does not depend on what he or she does or fails to do:

> *By God's grace and love, I love you in spite of…*
> *By God's grace and love, I love you even if…*
> *By God's grace and love, I will love you all the time regardless of…*

September 21

I am not saying this because I am in need, for
I have learned to be content whatever the
circumstances (Philippians 4:11).

Why do you attempt to live the Christian life? What do you hope to receive from all your efforts? Is there any reward? Many Christians believe their reward for following Christ and having faith in Him is financial blessing and material prosperity. Some ministers and televangelists preach this message.

But this doctrine is not taught in God's Word. Look at Paul and Abraham, for example. They were both godly men who were faithful and obedient. One was wealthy and the other had to rely upon others to survive. One had material blessings and the other didn't. Prosperity has nothing to do with faithfulness. If you view your financial success as the barometer of your spiritual health, trouble is on the horizon. You will eventually make some wrong assumptions about your spiritual condition. If you have a good month financially, you may think it is because you are having a good month spiritually, which may not be the case. If you have a bad month financially, you may become unfairly critical of your (or your spouse's) spiritual life or become angry at God. A marriage relationship can be affected by this kind of thinking.

Rewards from God do not always occur in the financial realm. And some of them may not even appear in our lifetime. Hebrews talks about the heroes of the faith who died "without receiving the promises, but having seen them and having welcomed them from a distance" (11:13, NASB). Oh, there are daily benefits to following God—salvation, wisdom, guidance, deliverance, peace, and a full life. Money can't buy what faithfulness can. But some of our rewards will come later, after we meet Jesus Christ face to face (1 Corinthians 3:10-15).

What have you already received as a result of faithful living? Talk about it for a few minutes. Sometimes it helps to appreciate God's blessings when we take inventory.[12]

SEPTEMBER 22

*For we brought nothing into the world, and we
can take nothing out of it* (1 Timothy 6:7).

How do/did your parents view money? What have you learned from them about earning, saving, and spending? How has their perspective on money shaped your views today? You may find it interesting to discuss these questions together as a couple. You may be surprised to discover how much you and your partner have been influenced in financial matters by your parents.

How does God view money? What is its purpose from His perspective? Ron Blue, a Christian financial consultant, uses three words to summarize how money is viewed by God.

First, money is a *tool*. God uses the abundance or scarcity of money in our lives to mold us and make us pleasing to Him. Paul learned contentment through the extremes of having much and having nothing (Philippians 4:11-13). It is possible in both situations to develop stewardship, build relationships, learn to use time effectively, etc. Perhaps it might be helpful to take a moment and imagine what your relationship with God would be like if you were just the opposite of what you are now financially.

Second, money can be a *test* in our life—a test of faithfulness. Read Luke 16:10-13. A key thought in this passage is that we cannot serve both God and money. That's an interesting thought. Many people would say they are not serving money, but their thoughts, attitudes, habits of accumulating possessions, and the amount of time they spend at work say just the opposite. The presence of money in life tests our determination to serve God.

Third, money is a *testimony*. Look at Matthew 5:13-16. Does your use of your money and possessions complement your commitment to be salt and light in the world? Whether you are poor, comfortable, or wealthy, the way you use your money can be a testimony for your Lord. How does your checkbook reflect that you are Christian? Can anyone else tell by looking at your checkbook, whom you are serving?[13]

You are responsible for the wrong I
am suffering (Genesis 16:5).

Rationalization—it's been with us since the beginning of time. It's a defense mechanism, a pattern of shifting the blame for our own irresponsible behavior onto someone else. It feels so good to see someone else squirm while we're wiggling off the hook.

Rationalization happens in marriage. Your partner says, "You left the door unlocked last night." Instead of owning up to your failure, you say, "Well, you forgot to fill the car with gas yesterday like you said you would. If you had done your part, maybe I would have remembered to do mine."

Adam and Eve were the first people to rationalize their behavior. Adam blamed God for giving him Eve, who gave him the forbidden fruit. Eve blamed the serpent for giving the fruit to her. Adam identified the real reason for his rationalism: fear (see Genesis 3).

Sarah blamed Abraham for the difficulty she was having with Hagar, the servant he took as a wife—at Sarah's suggestion—to bear him a son: "You are responsible for the wrong I am suffering. I put my servant in your arms, and now that she knows she is pregnant, she despises me" (16:5). When Moses accused Aaron of his part in making the golden calf, Aaron blamed the people, saying, "You know how prone these people are to evil. They said to me, 'Make us gods who will go before us'" (Exodus 32:22,23). And Pilate rationalized away his responsibility for the death of our Lord. He said to the angry crowd, "It is your responsibility!" (Matthew 27:24).

The reasons we rationalize are many: fear, jealousy, anger, a need for security, guilt, pride, lust. Perhaps this tendency is all the more reason we need to pray the prayer of David: "Search me, O God, and know my heart; test me and know my anxious thoughts. See if there is any offensive way in me, and lead me in the way everlasting" (Psalm 139:23,24).[14]

SEPTEMBER 24

O Lord, the God who saves me, day and
night I cry out before you (Psalm 88:1).

Depression—it hurts. Does it have a purpose? Think about these words from Dr. Archibald Hart:

> Depression is a symptom which warns us that we're getting into deep water. It is, I believe, designed by God as an emotional reaction to slow us down, to remove us from the race, to pull us back so we can take stock. I would even say that it is designed to drive us back to God in terms of trust and resources. It is a protective device which removes us from further stress and gives us time to recover.
>
> As humans, we have been designed to experience emotion, not just joy, but sadness as well. Perhaps the dark side of our emotions is to drive us to God. If we were happy all the time, maybe we wouldn't feel we needed God. With depression there is certainly a positive side. God has created us with the ability to experience depression for a very good reason, I believe.
>
> Depression is like pain. While pain is inconvenient, it is a warning system, essential for our survival. We wouldn't ask, "Why does God allow me to experience pain?" If I felt no pain, I'd be killed the first day I walked out my front door. God also has created me with the ability to experience depression so that I can have a very important warning system to tell me when things are wrong. But He doesn't allow me to be depressed in the sense of sending it my way as a form of punishment. He has taken all my punishment on the Cross. But He has given me a wonderful gift in depression which I should be able to use as an important warning system.[15]

When you're depressed, ask yourself, "What is my depression trying to tell me?" Then you can take action.

SEPTEMBER 25

Then Jesus went with them to a place called Gethsemane....
He began to show grief and distress of mind and
was deeply depressed (Matthew 26:36,37, AMP).

Does it surprise you to learn that our Lord experienced depression? In the garden, Jesus' humanity was burdened with the great pain and loss He was about to experience. Heavy burdens and personal losses are common causes for depression.

You have been or will be depressed at some time in your life. One struggle for many couples is, "How do I respond when my partner is depressed? How can I help? Should I talk to him, joke with him, tell him to snap out of it, ignore him, or what?"

Here are a few practical steps that you can take to minister to your partner when he or she gets depressed. The first step is to learn more about the causes and symptoms of depression before it strikes by reading a book or two on the subject. Gaining some information will help both of you prevent some depressions and successfully deal with others.

When your spouse gets depressed, insist that he or she have a complete physical examination to determine if there are any physiological causes of the depression. Throughout the process, give your partner your full support. When someone is depressed, faith and hope are at an all-time low. You may need to loan your spouse some of your faith and hope until his or hers returns. You must believe in your partner's abilities until he or she is able to believe in them again.

Remember that your depressed partner really hurts. Don't even hint that he or she needs to "snap out of it." Be empathetic, but not sympathetic. Pity won't help, but showing that you understand your partner's struggle may. Remind your spouse of the joy and accomplishments he or she has experienced in life. During depression it's difficult to remember those positive experiences.

Above all, follow Paul's words in dealing with your partner: "Be very patient with everybody" (1 Thessalonians 5:14, AMP).

SEPTEMBER 26

Brace up your minds (1 Peter 1:13, AMP).

Brace up your mind—that's an interesting thought. It literally means to get your mind prepared for action. As believers we are called to fill our minds with positive thoughts and to put out of our minds any thoughts which may hinder us, including focusing on our failures or the failures of others.

In his book *Bringing Out the Best in People,* Alan Loy McGinnis described his visit one Sunday to the church in New York which Dr. Norman Vincent Peale has pastored for over 50 years. As the aged minister stepped into the pulpit and began to speak, McGinnis realized why the congregation refused to let Dr. Peale retire, even at age 86. He preached a dynamic sermon on the subject of worry and doubt. He told story after story about people who, with the Lord's help, had overcome their difficulties.

After the service McGinnis complimented the pastor on his uplifting message and encouraging illustrations. Dr. Peale said that a number of people had criticized him over the years for telling so many positive stories. But he continued to use such illustrations, he said, because the Bible says nothing to us about rehearsing failure.

Isn't that an interesting concept—rehearsing failure! That's where many of us live: constantly mulling over our memories of failure instead of thinking about the instances of God's working in the past and how He will work in the future. Bracing up our minds involves refocusing our thoughts in the direction of what God is doing and will do, not what we have failed to do. If you are going to rehearse anything, rehearse God's capabilities and your victories. And as you look at your partner, don't think about how he or she has let you down. Such thoughts hold your spouse a captive of the past in your mind. Rather, rehearse good memories and positive expectations—they will set your partner free.[16]

SEPTEMBER 27

The Lord has sought out a man [David]
after His own heart (1 Samuel 13:14).

David was an interesting man. Just like each of us, he had strengths and weaknesses. As one author wrote, "He was a passionate man with lights and shadows in his character."[17] But in spite of his imperfections and failures, David was successful. Why? Is there anything we can learn from him to help us succeed? There really is.

First, David was totally available to God and His purposes. Unfortunately, too many of us are only partially or temporarily available to God. We tend to make our own choices in life rather than allow God to lead us.

Next, David was sensitive to God's Spirit. He was humble and had a contrite spirit. He also had a broken heart, but not in the sense we usually think of it. His heart and will were broken to God's will like a horse is broken to the saddle. Our usefulness to God is directly dependent on being disciplined in will and spirit to do His will no matter what the cost. Sometimes the cost is suffering. That's not a very comfortable thought, is it?

David was also successful because he had the capacity to repent and change direction when he was wrong. He was remorseful when he sinned. No excuses. No blaming. No justifications. Only, "I blew it; I have sinned. Forgive me, Father." Good words, important words, hard words to say.

Finally, David was a gifted person. He recognized his gifts and he used them—not just for himself, but for God.

No wonder David was successful. His pattern may help us consider the direction of our own life and our marriage.[18]

SEPTEMBER 28

*Jesus asked, "Do you see anything?" [The blind
man] looked up and said, "I see people; they look
like trees walking around"* (Mark 8:23,24).

Have you ever felt disquieted or ill at ease? There was something wrong spiritually, but you couldn't put your finger on it. Something wasn't clear to you, or perhaps you felt dissatisfied with yourself for some reason. If so, maybe you can identify with the blind man in Mark 8. Jesus had ministered to him, and he was in the process of being healed. His vision was starting to come back, but the clarity wasn't there.

Many Christians live their entire lives like this man at the halfway point of his healing: lacking clarity and direction. Some of us have felt Jesus' touch on our life, but the reality of what He has done for us is clouded over with a disquieting haze. If Jesus were to ask you today, "Do you see anything?" how would you answer? Would you be tempted to say, "Yes, I see everything clearly"? Or could you honestly say, "Lord, I have some serious questions; at times I even have doubts"?

God is not impressed if you say you're fine when you're not. He wants to hear you express exactly where you are spiritually. The blind man's honesty brought clarity to his life. Jesus touched his eyes again, and he really could see. If things are hazy in your life, don't try to bluff your way through. Tell Jesus about it. State it to Him. Let Him bring clarity to your life through His Word and His presence. He doesn't want any of us to remain the prisoner of doubts, misgivings, uncertainty, or unhappiness. But He can't really help us until we are willing to tell Him that we hurt.

Talk together about any areas where your life is clouded by doubt or uncertainty. Then pray together and receive a second touch.

SEPTEMBER 29

When their message came to him, Joseph
wept (Genesis 50:17).

When you read the account of Joseph's reunion with his father and brothers in one sitting, you may discover something about Joseph that you've never seen before (Genesis 42-50). You will probably notice that Joseph was a very sensitive man, as evidenced by the number of times he wept. During Joseph's first conversation with his brothers after being separated from them for years, "he turned away from them and began to weep" (42:24). When he saw his younger brother Benjamin, Joseph was deeply moved and "hurried out and looked for a place to weep. He went into his private room and wept there" (43:30).

The next time Joseph wept was when his older brother Judah volunteered to take Benjamin's place as a slave so their father wouldn't have to experience any more pain. On this occasion Joseph "wept so loudly that the Egyptians heard him" (45:2).

After Joseph revealed himself to his brothers, he wept over them and kissed them (45:14,15). When his father Jacob arrived in Egypt, Joseph "threw his arms around his father and wept for a long time" (46:29). And years later, when Jacob died, "Joseph threw himself upon his father and wept over him and kissed him" (50:1).

Why did Joseph weep? The reunion with his brothers brought back some painful memories, but Joseph was deeply touched at seeing his own flesh and blood again, so he wept. He also wept at the true repentance in his brothers, at his reconciliation with his family, and in grief over his father.

What about you? Have you wept with or for any of your family members? When was the last time you wept together as a couple? If you haven't, some day you will. Weeping is one of God's gifts to help us communicate the depth of our concern. If you have difficulty allowing yourself to weep, read the story of Joseph again—this time in one sitting.[19]

SEPTEMBER 30

It is good and proper for a man to eat and drink, and to find satisfaction in his toilsome labor under the sun during the few days of life God has given him (Ecclesiastes 5:18).

Do you ever wish you never had to work another day in your life? Do you dream about kicking back and enjoying yourself doing whatever you want to do?

Why do we work? Is it one of the results of the fall of man? There are several good reasons why we work. First, work is good. It is valued by God. The creation of the world was God's work, and He called it good. Work is not a result of the curse. The ground was cursed as a result of the Fall, but work was not part of that curse.

Also, Scripture commands us to work. Second Thessalonians 3:10 states, "If a man will not work, he shall not eat." If we don't work, we can't provide for the material needs of ourselves or our families. When we don't work we create an imbalance in our lives. For example, a marriage relationship will be out of balance when a wife must support her husband because he is too lazy to work.

Another reason we work is for fulfillment. The creative drive that God has given to us can be expressed through our work. This is true for both men and women. There are many wealthy individuals who continue to work, not for additional financial gain but for the joy and fulfillment that working brings them.

Work is also an opportunity for witnessing. As a Christian, your daily presence among non-Christian coworkers allows you to share Jesus Christ through your example of work and your words.

As you consider your work, remember: God is more concerned about your process of working than He is about the product of your work. Talk about that statement together. How does it apply to your job? Your partner's job?[20]

OCTOBER

Life is a combination of joy and pain, discouragement and praise, hope and struggle. Don't hesitate to praise God in one breath and tell Him what is bothering you in the next.

OCTOBER 1

I have loved you with an everlasting love; I have
drawn you with lovingkindness (Jeremiah 31:3).

Throughout our lives we have different feelings and thoughts about God. Sometimes we carry some negative thoughts about God with us into our marriage, and this could be a source of tension. Can you relate to any of these beliefs about God?

> God doesn't love me—not really—because I'm not lovable.
> God is obviously out to get me!
> God doesn't care about me as much as He cares about the "saints," the holy types, the talented, the good-looking, the smooth-talkers, the brilliant, shiny, squeaky clean, the unblemished.
> If only I could get God to answer my prayers, then I'd know He truly loves me.
> I can't trust God not to hurt me.[1]

Here are some responses to these statements, not from man, but from God Himself. Read each of the Scripture verses below aloud from your own Bible:

> God is the One who loves you nonstop (Jeremiah 31:3).
>
> God loves you even when you don't love or serve Him—even when you're sinning (Romans 5:8).
>
> God is for you, not against you; your Ally, not your Enemy; your Helper, not your Destroyer (Romans 8:31).
>
> God always does right by us; He never does wrong by us (Psalm 48:10).
>
> God's deeds in our lives are right, fair, and just—never wrong, never mistaken, never unfair or unjust (Psalm 65:5).[2]

Rejoice together in God's love today!

OCTOBER 2

Taste and see that the Lord is good; blessed is the
man who takes refuge in him (Psalm 34:8).

Have you ever made a statement and had someone correct you? Often we need the correction if what we said wasn't exactly accurate. Sometimes we attribute to God certain characteristics or responsibilities which are not correct. Consider the following:

> When we say, "God made me lose my job," or "made my child ill," or "made me marry a loser," or "made me fail in business"—God answers that He does only good, not evil: "Taste and see that the Lord is good; blessed is the man who takes refuge in him" (Psalm 34:8); "The Lord our God is righteous in everything he does" (Daniel 9:14).

> When we say, "Maybe God loves some people, but He doesn't love me"—God says He loves you specifically, even if you have become separated from Him by a rift: "The Son of Man came to seek and to save what was lost" (Luke 19:10); "God so loved the world that He gave His only Son" (John 3:16).

> When we say, "God has forgotten me"—God says He can't forget you because: "Can a mother forget the baby at her breast...? Though she may forget, I will not forget you! See, I have engraved you on the palms of my hands" (Isaiah 49:14-16).

> When we say, "God doesn't answer my prayers"—He says He will answer them. When the time is exactly right. And that time will be soon, even if it seems like a long delay: "Before they call I will answer; while they are still speaking I will hear" (Isaiah 65:24).[3]

What promise do you especially need to remember today?

OCTOBER 3

The pot he was shaping from the clay was marred in
his hands; so the potter formed it into another pot,
shaping it as seemed best to him (Jeremiah 18:4).

How would your partner describe God? What is your perception?
Have the two of you ever shared your belief of who God is and
what He is like? Sometimes we create God in our own image or in the
image of our parents. Often we see God as nonloving and noncaring.
Let these words clarify your perception:

> Developing and maintaining a more loving image of God
> won't protect you from the necessity of confronting your own
> personal hells on earth. It will make your problems easier
> to bear though. Just ask Job! He learned his lesson the hard
> way. After much suffering he finally found the sweet com-
> munion with his Loving Lord that turns the darkest hell into
> the brightest heaven. Had he found God's love sooner, he
> still would have suffered, but his outward suffering would
> have been met with inward peace. This is life's greatest chal-
> lenge: to maintain a genuine heartfelt faith in God's love in
> the midst of great difficulty.
>
> So the key for you is to get a glimpse of God as really
> being with you in your life struggles. Depending upon what
> you're going through, you may need to see God in any of a
> number of the ways He reveals Himself: a gentle and tender
> Father,…a Good Shepherd to guide you, a trusted Friend, a
> Master who accepts you into His family, a Potter to mold you
> into something special, a Vinedresser to help you be more
> fruitful, a Gold Refiner to purify you, a Bridegroom to marry
> you, a Brother to walk alongside you, a Deliverer, a Healer.…
> The One True God is far bigger than and different from any
> picture you may have of what He is like.[4]

OCTOBER 4

*I will bless the Lord at all times; His praise shall
continually be in my mouth* (Psalm 34:1, NASB).

Before continuing with this meditation, read the remainder of Psalm
34 aloud together from your Bible.

How do you handle a crisis in your life individually and as a couple?
When David wrote this psalm he had just escaped from the Philistines (1 Samuel 21:10-15). He pretended to be a madman, knowing his
captors would release him in that condition instead of kill him. Then
he hid in a cave with 400 men who were in distress, discontented, and
in debt. It was in the midst of these trying circumstances that David
wrote a psalm about praising God.

Notice that he didn't say that he would praise the Lord *sometimes*;
he said *all the time!* This must have been a time of fear for David and
his men because the Philistines were still trying to find him and kill
him. But notice what he says in verse four, "I sought the Lord, and He
answered me, and delivered me from all my fears" (NASB).

But did God take away his problems? No. He was still a hunted
man in the cave with 400 desperate men. Don't wait to praise God
until all your problems are solved. It will never happen! But when you
learn to praise Him in the midst of your problems, He will give you
the peace you are seeking.

David is essentially saying we don't have to be controlled by our
situation or circumstances. Have you discovered the truth of this psalm
in your work? in your personal life? in your marriage? Can you think
of a time when you experienced God's peace by praising Him in the
midst of your troubles? Have you shared this experience with your
partner? If not, do so now.

When you are under pressure and feel like everything is collapsing
around you, share your feelings with your partner. Pray about your trial
specifically, expecting God to lift the burden and the fear. But begin
the way David did—by praising the Lord. Take refuge in God, seek
Him, and receive His peace.

OCTOBER 5

Cast all your anxiety on him because
He cares for you (1 Peter 5:7).

"Don't worry!"

"Don't tell me not to worry! It doesn't help one bit. I know I shouldn't worry, but I don't know how to stop."

The advice not to worry is valid, but so is the response. A lot of people really don't know how to stop worrying, even though they know they should.

If you have ever been fishing, you know what it means to cast. You swing the pole back over your shoulder, then whip it forward. The lure and line go flying out into the water. I've had fishing friends say, "You really unloaded a cast that time!"

That's exactly the meaning of the word cast in 1 Peter 5:7. It means to give up or to unload. The most graphic example is that of a bulldozer with a large scoop. As it rumbles over to the waiting truck, the scoop is filled with dirt. But when the scoop is lifted over the truck bed and tilted downward, it unloads and drops everything with a thud.

When you as a couple find yourself burdened by anxiety, unload it onto God. The tense of the verb "cast" literally means a direct, once-and-for-all committal to God of all anxiety or worry. Sometimes it helps to say out loud, "God, we are giving You this burden; we will no longer dwell upon it." It may also help to write a note card reminding yourself that you have given your burden to God; it is no longer yours. Post the card where you will both see it often. You may want to try these tips with your burdens concerning work, the house, a problem child, or anything dominating your life at this time.

You can cast your worry on God with confidence. Why? Because He cares for you. He knows just how much you can stand. Isaiah 42:3 reads, "A bruised reed he will not break, and a smoldering wick he will not snuff out." He wants to strengthen you and help you stand firm.[5]

OCTOBER 6

*My son, if you accept my words and store up
my commands within you...then you will
understand the fear of the Lord and find the
knowledge of God* (Proverbs 2:1,5).

One of the conditions for safe, enjoyable boating and swimming
is water that is deep enough. If the water is shallow, you run the
risk of breaking through the bottom of the boat or scraping your body
raw from the sand or gravel. Shallowness is not a good condition for
boating or swimming. And it's not a good condition for our personal
lives either. But it happens.

Take a moment and read Proverbs 2:1-9. Now, do you know what
you've just read? You've just discovered the antidote for shallowness.
This passage gives us a way to develop depth in our personal lives. And
there are some practical benefits to following these guidelines. How
can we avoid shallowness? Consider four steps.

The first is to respond to the Word of God. Know it inside and out:
"My son, if you accept my words and store up my commands within
you..." (v. 1). Saturate your life with the Word.

Second, be open to what God is saying to you, and begin to desire
what He has for you: "...turning your ear to wisdom and applying your
heart to understanding" (v. 2).

The third step is to pray with feeling and desire: "If you call out
for insight and cry aloud for understanding..." (v. 3). The phrase, "get
serious," certainly applies to our prayer life.

The final step is consistency: "If you look for it as for silver and
search for it as for hidden treasure..." (v. 4). Prospectors spend years
searching. They are persistent and consistent. That's how we are to
approach God's Word.

The results of these four steps are found in verse 5: the fear and the
knowledge of God—that's depth! More benefits are found in verses
6-9. Identify them and share them with each other. If you want depth
in your life, here is your answer.[6]

OCTOBER 7

A champion named Goliath…came out of the Philistine
camp. He was over nine feet tall (1 Samuel 17:4).

Perhaps people in centuries past believed in and feared giants more than we do today. In those days, anyone who was taller than average ended up being labeled a giant. But in the era of seven-foot-plus basketball centers, giants have become an accepted commodity for us. The people of the Old Testament were terrified by the giants of their time. David didn't let Goliath's size get to him. David simply confronted the giant in the strength of the Lord and gave him a permanent headache.

Every marriage relationship confronts giants—those obstacles which seem too big to move. You've probably faced some of them already as a couple. Sometimes the giants are real. But at other times we seem to inject small, everyday problems with emotional steroids and make them into giants. Either way, the giants in marriage tend to stomp the daylights out of our relationship.

For example, there is the giant of marital boredom. The relationship settles into a pattern and becomes ho-hum and routine. No matter what you do, you can't seem to shake the boredom. How do you keep from letting the giant of boredom overwhelm you and your marriage? Simple. You employ the strength of the Lord and put forth the time and effort you once did to bring excitement back into the relationship.

Another giant is called "marital competition." Members of the opposite sex other than your spouse can sure appear enticing at times. But the giant of enticement is cut down by remembering that you are a child of the King, Jesus Christ. You've committed your life to Him, and your calling is to glorify Him in all ways. He wouldn't have called you to victory over this giant if it weren't possible.

Can you think of other giants which may be lurking around your marriage? Identify them, talk about them, then overcome them together in the strength of the Lord.

OCTOBER 8

Above all else, guard your heart, for it is the
wellspring of life (Proverbs 4:23).

It's small. It doesn't weigh much. It's basically muscle. It's divided into chambers. It has four valves. It is quite important. Without it, you don't exist. We've come so far medically that we are able to transplant one from one person to another. We even have some that are artificial. You know what it is, of course: your heart. Take your pulse. How many beats a minute do you feel? You can even hear your heart if you listen closely. Your physical heart is vital to your physical health.

Your spiritual heart is equally valuable to your spiritual health. Today's verse begins with a command, not a suggestion: "Above all else, guard your heart." To guard means to preserve or to keep. Isaiah 26:3 uses the same word as "keep": "You will keep in perfect peace him whose mind is steadfast, because he trusts in you."

To guard also means to weigh, as you would weigh a parcel or piece of luggage. In other words, weigh carefully anything that pertains to your heart. A paraphrase from the Hebrew is suggested by Charles Swindoll: "More than all else to be watched over and protected (as something in a confined place), it is imperative that you preserve and keep your heart sensitive; because from within it comes divine direction for your life."[7]

Your heart is the part of you that is capable of knowing God's will for your life. No wonder we need to guard it carefully! Read Proverbs 4, and you will discover how God directs you through your heart.

What about it: Is your spiritual heart in good shape? Is it open, sensitive, and available to God's leading? If so, you'll grow, and your marriage will be enriched as well. That's just one of the many benefits of a healthy heart.[8]

OCTOBER 9

*Now when he saw the crowds, he went up on a
mountainside and sat down. His disciples came to
him, and he began to teach them* (Matthew 5:1,2).

A re you a Christian?"
   "Yes, I am."
"Well, whom do you follow?"
"I follow Jesus Christ, the Son of God."
"If so, can you tell me ten ideas or concepts He taught?"

How would you handle that question? Could you answer it? Can
you identify Christ's most famous teaching? The Sermon on the Mount
(Matthew 5–7) is probably His best known but least understood and
probably least obeyed message. Yet these words are very relevant and
practical for today. Here is a brief overview for you to think about and
discuss:

If you want to know about the character qualities and conduct of
a Christian, look at the beatitudes in Matthew 5:3-12. If you want to
know how a Christian can influence the world around him, see the
metaphors of salt and light in Matthew 5:13-16. If you want to know
what your attitude should be concerning the law of God, Matthew
5:17-48 tells you about a new kind of righteousness. Jesus gives six illustrations which relate to murder, adultery, divorce, swearing, revenge,
and love.

Do you know what Christian piety is? What does the word mean?
How does piety differ from straight-laced legalism? Take a look at
Matthew 6:1-18. What is the place of ambition in the life of a Christian? What place do wealth and possessions have in our life? Or should
we even be concerned? Matthew 6:19-34 will give you plenty to think
about. And Matthew 7 will fill you in on such issues as judging, prayer,
and commitment to Christ's lordship.

Take some time this week to read the Sermon on the Mount aloud
together. It could make a difference in your life and marriage.

OCTOBER 10

Blessed are the poor in spirit, for theirs is the
kingdom of heaven (Matthew 5:3).

Have you ever thought of yourself as being poor? Probably not. Most of us prefer to avoid that condition. Poverty is not something to which we aspire in today's world. Too many images of street people come to mind.

But in today's verse Jesus isn't talking about being financially poor or materially destitute. To be poor in spirit is simply to acknowledge our spiritual poverty or bankruptcy before God. No individual, past or present, really deserves anything from God. There is nothing we can offer that will buy God's favor in any way. It's by His grace that we are saved.

This teaching isn't very popular today. We tend to be proud, but being poor in spirit calls for humility. We tend to be independent, but being poor in spirit calls for dependence on God and one another. We tend to believe we're not in such bad shape on our own, but being poor in spirit calls for us to recognize that we are sinners.

Isaiah the prophet wrote concerning humility: "For thus says the high and lofty One who inhabits eternity, whose name is Holy: 'I dwell in the high and holy place, with him also who is of a thoroughly penitent and humble spirit, to revive the spirit of the humble, and to revive the heart of the thoroughly penitent—bruised with sorrow for sin'" (57:15, AMP).

Here's a simple way of phrasing today's beatitude: Recognize your need of God, admit that He is the only One who can fulfill your life, and receive the kingdom of God with the humility of a little child. People who believe they can get ahead on their own ability, intelligence, looks, or cleverness are disqualified from this blessing of life. Too many people today have the gift of boasting and self-evaluation. The problem is that it's not a spiritual gift!

If you want God's blessings and rule in your life now and in the future, recognizing spiritual poverty is the way to go!

OCTOBER 11

Blessed are the meek, for they will
inherit the earth (Matthew 5:5).

The word meek is not a very popular word today. Some define it as being spineless or without much conviction. But meekness has nothing to do with a defect in character. People who display true meekness are usually those who have special character qualities. Whom do you know that you would characterize as meek?

Meekness means having an objective, humble view of yourself. The Greek word for meekness conveys the attitude, "There is a lot I need to learn from others, and I am a person who needs to be forgiven by God." Accordingly, William Barclay translates today's verse, "Blessed is the man who has the humility to know his own ignorance, his own weakness, and his own need."9

Why does the Bible describe Moses as meek (Numbers 12:3)? At one time he wasn't. But he came to the place where his life was under God's control. This is one of the ways that meekness and humility become a part of your life: You give your life to the Lord and allow Him to control you. If you have an ability, you give credit to God. Whatever you accomplish, you give credit to God. When you achieve something, you direct the accolades to God who is responsible for your achievement. Meekness also carries with it the attitude of amazement that God and others think of you and treat you as well as they do.

The meek find their satisfaction in living with a realistic perspective of themselves, confident in the fact that God loves and accepts them at all times. Meekness helps you disengage from the rat race of competition with others and stop playing the "look at how great I am" game. It's a different way to live.

How can the quality of meekness in each partner benefit a marriage? Are you seeing those benefits in your marriage? How can you help each other develop this quality? Talk about it.

OCTOBER 12

Blessed are those who hunger and thirst for
righteousness, for they will be filled (Matthew 5:6).

Have you ever been hungry? thirsty? Of course you have. But have you ever been starving? dying of thirst? Probably not. Perhaps if we had lived in Jesus' time this beatitude would impact us more. The people in Palestine lived constantly on the edge of hunger and thirst. They were fortunate to eat meat once a week. Those who got caught in a vicious desert sandstorm in Palestine experienced life-threatening thirst. They wrapped their heads in cloth, turned their backs to the wind, and waited it out for hours. The sand would fill their mouth and nostrils until they almost suffocated.

The hunger described in this beatitude is that of a Palestine native who was starving for food, and the thirst pictures those parched by a desert sandstorm who will die unless they drink. The intensity of these terms is foreign to us today. This beatitude actually poses some very serious questions to us: How much do you want righteousness in your life? Do you want it as much as a starving person wants food? As much as someone dying of thirst wants water? Do you have the same kind of intensity to see righteousness in your life?

What does righteousness mean to you? In the Bible there are three kinds of righteousness, but only two of them concern us here. There is moral righteousness, which reflects a character and behavior pattern that pleases God. How strong is your desire for this in your life? Biblical righteousness, however, is more than just an individual affair; it includes a social righteousness as well. It involves helping others around you who are being mistreated or taken advantage of, changing laws so they are more just, speaking out against problems in your city, neighborhood, or local school, and exercising integrity in your business dealings and family relationships.

Talk about it together: How can this beatitude be reflected in a marriage relationship?

OCTOBER 13

Blessed are the merciful, for they will
be shown mercy (Matthew 5:7).

A man stands in front of a judge. His face is lined with pain as he cries out, "Have mercy on me, your honor!"

"Why should I?" the judge responds. "You didn't show mercy to the person you harmed."

Mercy is more than a response we seek when we are in trouble. It's a quality we are to show as a way of life. What is mercy? Mercy is simply compassion for people in need. It responds actively to the pain, misery, and the distress of others. It doesn't mean just feeling sorry for someone. The word used in the Old Testament for mercy means the ability to get inside another's skin so you can see things with his eyes and feel with his feelings. It's genuine identification with another person. It means to experience or even suffer with another. We have a word for that today. Do you know what it is? *Empathy.*

Mercy means helping another person carry a load, often at our own expense! It may involve sitting with your partner and holding hands when he or she is upset. It may mean saying, "I feel your hurt, and I wish there was something more I could do."

It means weeping with a friend who just lost a family member. It means opening your life so you can feel the hurt of someone else. It means being kind in a way that another person needs you to be kind. It involves thinking of what the other person needs rather than what you want to do.

Mercy involves a sensitivity to discover what would help another person the most. It also involves forgiving another person when he or she doesn't deserve it. That's what forgiveness is all about, isn't it!

If you care, others will care. If you listen, others will listen to you. If you are merciful, others will show you mercy. It's contagious. And a great place to begin is in your marriage.

OCTOBER 14

*Blessed are the pure in heart, for they
will see God* (Matthew 5:8).

Why do you do what you do? What are your motives? That's a difficult question to answer because we don't always know our motives. For example, do we give to the church because of our love for God and desire to see His work continue? Would we give as much if we couldn't deduct our gifts from our income tax? Perhaps we do things for a variety of reasons.

The phrase "pure in heart" in today's beatitude speaks about motives. The word pure was originally used to describe corn which had been sifted and cleansed of all chaff. It was also used to describe an army which had been purged of all discontented, unwilling, and inefficient soldiers. When something was pure it was free of all impurities.

To be pure in heart means to be utterly sincere in your relationships with people and God. There is no phoniness or pretense. Your entire life is transparent before God and others. You don't play a role or put on a mask when you are with different people. You are who you are all the time. You are honest and open, which leads to a reputation of consistency. And your outward purity reflects what is going on inside. You allow God access to your heart and mind so He can do the necessary housecleaning. And when this happens, your relationship with Him deepens.

How would you relate this beatitude to your marriage? What does sincerity and purity have to do with the trust level in your marriage? Sometimes it's difficult to run the risk of being pure in heart in marriage. Fear arises to keep us from being transparent and open. Has this ever happened to you? Think about it and then discuss it. Sometimes spouses wear masks in their marriage to each other. Is there any way in which your relationship needs to change so there is greater sincerity in what you present to each other and other people? This is a hard question which may lead to a hard discussion. But it is important.

OCTOBER 15

*Blessed are the peacemakers, for they will
be called sons of God* (Matthew 5:9).

Many marriages are characterized by intense, heated conflict, and times of peace are rare. Yet we have been called to be peacemakers, to live peaceably with all people. In the old west a cowboy's revolver was sometimes referred to as a "peacemaker," because it was a quick way to settle disputes. That's not what today's beatitude is referring to, however! To be a peacemaker means to not be responsible for creating or perpetuating conflict.

God gave us His Son so that we could have peace with Him. Our peace cost Him dearly. It will also cost you to be a peacemaker. When you are involved in a quarrel, it is painful to apologize or honestly, lovingly confront the other person. Suppose two of your family members have an ongoing war with each other, and you attempt to bring about a reconciliation. Pain is involved. You run the risk of being misunderstood. You face the tension of attempting to listen objectively to each one and discover the truth. And you run the risk of failing, for your best attempts may be rejected. The same thing can happen at church when there is tension between members and you try to become the peacemaker. You could be slandered by some of them and your reputation stained.

Do you know why you are called a "son of God" when you engage in peacemaking? Because you are carrying on the very work that God started through the gift of His Son. God loved people, and we are called to do the same. And this means all people.

Take a minute and talk about the people you find difficult to love. Who are they? What will it cost you to become the peacemaker in those relationships? Are you willing to pay the price? How can you work on these relationships together?

OCTOBER 16

Blessed are those who are persecuted
because of righteousness, for theirs is the
kingdom of heaven (Matthew 5:10).

"They laughed at me and made fun of me because I wouldn't participate in what they were doing."

"I lost the promotion at work because I refused to take my clients
to that sleazy nightclub."

"I lost several 'friends' because I didn't go along with their gossiping
when we got together."

Modern day persecution because of our faith? Perhaps. It hurts to
be misunderstood and not accepted. Believers in China and other parts
of the world still face intense persecution. They lose their homes, some
end up in prison, and many are killed because of their faith.

Most of us have never really felt the piercing sting of persecution. It could happen to us as it does in other countries like China. It
could happen in ways hard to imagine if our democratic society were
overturned. You never know. But whatever type of persecution you
experience, do you know how Jesus wants you to respond? It's quite
simple. Rejoice and be glad. That's all. Be glad. Don't retaliate. Don't
sulk. Don't complain. Don't just grin and bear it. Rejoice and actually
"leap for joy" (Luke 6:23).

Matthew 5:11,12 tells us to rejoice and be glad when we are persecuted because of Christ. Read these two verses for yourself. Expect
opposition to your Christian stance. That's normal. If you are persecuted because of your stance for Jesus Christ, it means you are really
committed to Him and your commitment is evident to others. You are
having an impact in the world around you. Isn't it strange that living
for Him brings discomfort? But why not? Living for Christ means
confronting a world that is living contrary to the way God intended.
Your Christian life bothers them. It's convicting. So they will react to
you. But I guess Jesus understands that pretty well, doesn't He? Look
at what it cost Him.

OCTOBER 17

*You are the salt of the earth. But if the salt loses
its saltiness, how can it be made salty again? It is
no longer good for anything* (Matthew 5:13).

What an influence he was two years ago. The whole community felt his love and his impact for Jesus Christ. He brought others to Christ, and there was an honesty in the way he dealt with others. I don't know what happened to him. He still goes to church, but something is missing. He sort of blends in with others around him in the community. He's no longer distinct."

Today's beatitude talks about being different, being distinct, not being contaminated by the world around you or assimilated by non-Christians. When you are different you will attract people to your Lord. When you show that Jesus Christ makes a difference in how you face the daily pressures and challenges of life, people will be attracted to Him. When your marriage shows that Jesus Christ makes a dramatic impact, others will be attracted to Him. That's when you are salt.

Jesus' reference to salt struck a familiar chord with His followers. Salt was essential at that time as a food preservative. Similarly, our presence in the world should be a deterrent to the corruption of sin. Salt also gives flavor to food. Being a Christian adds a distinct flavor to your life—or it's supposed to! The ancient Romans stated that salt was the purest of all things. We are also called to be pure. Standards are lowered all around us in business, government, personal morals, and sometimes in the interpretation of the Scriptures. We are called to be the people whose standards are not lowered but elevated to the level of God's Word. James urges us to keep ourselves unspotted from the world (1:27). If we are contaminated, our witness is worthless.

How different and distinct are you? How different and distinct is your marriage? How's the salt content in your life and your marriage?

You are the light of the world....Let your light shine
before men, that they may see your good deeds and
praise your Father in heaven (Matthew 5:14,16).

Jesus referred to Himself as the light of the world (John 9:5). But He said we are the light of the world as well. He is asking that each of us be nothing less than what He claimed to be! We have been asked to reflect His light, but what does that mean in everyday life?

A light is meant to be seen. It has a purpose; it's useful. Your faith is meant to be seen by others. There is no such thing as a secret Christian. We are not undercover agents. How many of your acquaintances don't even know that you have faith in Jesus Christ? Think about it. How could they tell that you are a Christian? Your faith is to be visible in every phase of your life. It should permeate the way you respond to the abrupt telephone operator, the short-tempered salesperson, the driver who cut you off, and your partner who forgot to complete an important task for you.

A light is also a guide. It clears the way for other people. Your Christian convictions and strength may enable a weaker Christian to take a stand. Your support may make all the difference in the world to another person. Your light is to shine so that others see your good deeds. Your responses and lifestyle (individually and maritally) should have a goodness of quality which attracts others. Why? To draw attention to ourselves? Not at all. Your goodness is to draw attention to the presence of God in your life so that others will praise Him.

Do you want one last, difficult question? Could anyone in your life say, "There is a quality in you that's different. I want to know why you are different"? Could anyone say that about your marriage?

OCTOBER 19

Train yourself toward godliness (piety)—keeping
yourself spiritually fit (1 Timothy 4:7, AMP).

Many of us talk about what's important to us, but the bottom line is what we do about it. Consider the words of a husband as he reflects on the importance he places on marriage:

> One thing the world will not do is to give your marriage a priority position in life. If your relationship is esteemed, it is because you have made it so. If it is prized, it is because you prize it. If you and your mate have had the desperately needed time to interact with one another in a meaningful manner, it is not because our culture decided to give it to you. It is because you took it. Prioritizing is a way of life....If not, then we are constantly at work determining what is important to us and what is not. And the product of our decision making is evidenced by what, or whom, we invest our time and energies into.
>
> Couples who place their relationship in a high-priority position have the greatest potential for achieving what they want out of the marriage. Those who do not, have a lesser potential. It's as simple as that. High priority offers no guarantees...but the odds certainly do get better. Once again, if your marriage is truly valued, it is because you have decided to value it. Its priority is recognized by what you give it in time and energy. Your genuine investment will tell the story! Those of you who do not place your marriage in a place of high priority will drift.[10]

Your marriage does not have to drift. You have the ability to keep your marriage afloat and on course. Here are some questions to consider: Where do you want your marriage to go? Who is at the helm steering the course?

OCTOBER 20

An anxious heart weighs a man down (Proverbs 12:25);
A wise man's heart guides his mouth (Proverbs 16:23).

Y ou have heart trouble."
These are words a patient dreads to hear from his doctor. Our worst fear is that it's serious or even terminal. Heart defects or heart failure usually occur in men and women past the age of 50, but people of all ages can be affected by heart disease.

There is another malady which can hit us at any age. It's called a troubled heart. It's common. Perhaps you or your partner has one. It comes in many forms. The writer of Proverbs describes six of them.

First is the deceitful heart: "There is deceit in the hearts of those who plot evil, but joy for those who promise peace" (12:20).

Second is the heavy heart: "An anxious heart weighs a man down, but a kind word cheers him up" (12:25).

Third is the sorrowful heart: "Even in laughter the heart may ache, and joy may end in grief" (14:13).

Fourth is the backsliding or carnal heart: "The backslider in heart will have his fill of his own ways, but a good man will be satisfied with his" (14:14, NASB).

Fifth is the proud heart: "The Lord detests all the proud of heart. Be sure of this: They will not go unpunished" (16:5).

Last is the angry heart: "A man's own folly ruins his life, yet his heart rages against the Lord" (19:3).

Now that's real heart trouble! Perhaps your partner is troubled in heart in some way. Listen with sensitivity so you will be able to understand your spouse's troubles. How can you help? "A wise man's heart guides his mouth, and his lips promote instruction. Pleasant words are a honeycomb, sweet to the soul and healing to the bones" (16:23,24). Let God instruct you in what to say to the person with a troubled heart.[11]

OCTOBER 21

The Lord is my light and my salvation—
whom shall I fear (Psalm 27:1).

Before continuing with this meditation, read the remainder of Psalm 27 aloud together from your Bible.

When David wrote this psalm he was being pursued by his enemies. He begins by expressing his confidence in God as the source of his strength. Is that your first response when you are in a difficulty? Discuss this question with your partner.

All of us as God's people can rely on the promises in verses 1-6. Who guides you? The Lord, for He is your light. Who will deliver you? The Lord, for He is your salvation. In whom can you take refuge? The Lord, for He is the stronghold of your life. And because of these three truths, whom do you need to be afraid of? No one. Look at the same truths expressed in Romans 8:35-39. Because of the Lord, we have so much to rely on in this life.

After praising God for His strength and comfort in the first six verses, David moves into a prayer. Why would David pray, "Do not hide your face from me" (v. 9)? He recognized that he deserved God's displeasure because of his sins. But he wasn't despondent. He had the assurance that God would not forsake him, but that He would receive him as an adopted child (v. 10).

Have you ever felt like hiding your face from God? There are times when we don't feel worthy to be in the presence of God. Perhaps sharing that feeling with Him and your spouse is the starting point of prayer. He wants us to come to Him, and He will not turn His face away from us.

God wants us to make the same request that David did: "Teach me your way, O Lord" (v. 11). God desires us to have a dependent and willing attitude. Perhaps your prayer today as a couple can be a personal expression of verse 13. Your own confidence will grow as you realize you will see God's goodness. Wait for it, and wait for Him.

OCTOBER 22

*Whoever listens to me will live in safety and be at
ease, without fear of harm* (Proverbs 1:33).

Have you ever been disobedient in your marriage—you know, done
something your partner asked you not to do? Sure, we all have.
How did you handle your spouse's correction or reproof? Only you
can answer that. Probably you were uncomfortable, but eventually you
may have thanked your spouse for his or her corrective wisdom. Take
a moment and read about wisdom and reproof. You'll find it in Proverbs 1:20-33.

God often reproves us. The word reproof means to correct or to
convince. Scripture is full of reproofs. None of us are complete yet in
our character qualities. If we don't listen to the reproofs of Scripture,
our friends, employer, or spouse, we could be in big trouble. But why
do we tend to ignore the corrective statements of others or even the
Word of God? Proverbs 1:24,25 gives us four reasons. See if you identify with any of them.

The first is stubbornness: "You rejected me when I called" (v. 24).
The word rejected means to directly refuse.

The next reason is insensitivity: "No one gave heed when I stretched
out my hand" (v. 24). Not giving heed means lacking awareness or
being dull of hearing. What is said just does not penetrate for some
reason.

The third reason is deadly for a relationship. It's indifference: "You
ignored all my advice" (v. 25). To ignore means to let go. A current-day
phrase to express this is "I couldn't care less. Don't bother me."

The final reason is defensiveness: "You...would not accept my
rebuke" (v. 25). Literally, this means to be unwilling, unyielding, or
one who won't consent.

What a way to keep wisdom out of our lives! Reflect on these four
reasons and then spend some time identifying where they might exist
in your marriage. It might be tough, but it's a step toward acquiring
wisdom.[12]

OCTOBER 23

*For God so loved the world, that He gave His only
begotten Son, that whoever believes in Him should
not perish, but have eternal life* (John 3:16, NASB).

Do you remember the story of the ugly duckling? It's the story
of an ugly baby swan who ends up in a family of ducks. Some
people feel ugly physically or emotionally. We all have times when we
don't feel too good about ourselves. We may feel worthless, as though
we don't have anything to offer the world. We feel like a loser in just
about everything we do.

Some people feel this way all the time. Their spouses may affirm
them constantly, but the good words fall on deaf ears. These people
have their own internal critic who is deaf to the positive comments of
others. Because of this critic, they feel unworthy in their own presence.
They begin to believe that God is just as critical of them as others are.

Well, do you remember the story of the prodigal son and his forgiving father? No matter how you perceive yourself, you're accepted by
God. Consider what one author said:

> If deep inside you sometimes feel inadequate and that you
> must satisfy your "Heavenly Critic" to feel better about your-
> self, then picture the Loving Father. He opens His arms wide
> and runs out to embrace you, just as He did for His dirty,
> drunken son who did everything wrong. Only the uncondi-
> tional love of our Heavenly Father can enable us to feel truly
> adequate. We can receive that love when we replace the con-
> demning false god that rules our lives with an image of the
> Accepting God who loves and cares for us unconditionally.
> The Real God doesn't treat us like worms! He doesn't demand
> that we earn His love; He doesn't expect us to make up for
> our inadequacies. Instead, He replaces our weaknesses with
> His strength and makes us truly adequate. He freely gives us
> His love and seeks to transform us into glorious new creatures
> in Christ.[13]

OCTOBER 24

*Finally, be strong in the Lord, and in the strength
of His might. Put on the full armor of God, that
you may be able to stand firm against the schemes
of the devil* (Ephesians 6:10,11, NASB).

Not too long ago in our country's history the armed services relied
heavily on the selective service system to fill its quota of military personnel. In those days when a young man received a letter from
Uncle Sam which opened with the word "Greetings," he was probably
being drafted into the army.

Perhaps you never received a draft notice from the armed forces. As
a believer, however, you have been drafted to fight in another war. A
constant battle rages between God's people and Satan and his influence
in this world. If you have a quality marriage which reflects God living
out His life through the way you treat one another, watch out. You're
a target for Satan's attacks. He hates quality Christian marriages. As a
couple believing in fidelity and the permanent state of marriage, you're
fighting against a society which believes otherwise. The question is,
what are you using for weapons? What's in your spiritual arsenal? The
passage in Ephesians 6:10-18 contains an inventory of the equipment
you need to win the spiritual battle. Read the passage aloud together
right now.

In your daily battle against Satan and a society which serves him,
use the resources discussed in Ephesians. Also do what King Jehoshaphat did when confronted by his enemy in 2 Chronicles 20:21,22:
"Jehoshaphat appointed men to sing to the Lord and to praise him for
the splendor of his holiness as they went out at the head of the army,
saying: 'Give thanks to the Lord, for his love endures forever.' As they
began to sing and praise, the Lord set ambushes against the men...who
were invading Judah, and they were defeated."

A choir marching in front of the troops as front line warriors? How
strange. Stranger yet is what they were singing: praise to God. But they
were victorious. When you confront your enemy, praise God. Praise is
the best weapon you have![14]

OCTOBER 25

Be still, and know that I am God (Psalm 46:10).

Stillness and quietness are rare. We don't always know how to handle them. But for the sake of your marriage, you need childless, televisionless, phoneless, and workless discussion time together. We all need solitude for our individual lives. We also need marital solitude for our marriage.

When was the last time you had marital solitude? It won't just happen by itself. You've got to make it happen. Just like your time alone with God, you must plan your time alone with each other. How much time alone with God would you like each day? How much time alone with yourself would you like each day? How much time alone together would you like each day? Before you allow excuses to rule out any of these possibilities, put your schedule in writing. Ask your spouse to help you evaluate your time and schedule and discover some new options. Think about these words on marital solitude from a pastor:

> Although the shell of a union may endure, the spirit of the marriage may disintegrate in time unless mates take periodic and shared reprieves from the pressures they live under.
>
> The pressures we must often escape are not those we create for ourselves, but those brought into our lives from the outside. Nonetheless, they can wear our relationships thin.
>
> The key to keeping a cherished friendship alive may be found in breaking away long enough and frequently enough to keep ourselves fresh and our love growing. And usually that involves childless weekends. Without such moments of focused attention, it's difficult to keep the kind of updated knowledge of one another that keeps two hearts in close proximity alive and growing together. A growing marriage needs refreshed inhabitants![15]

OCTOBER 26

Anxiety in a man's heart weighs it down, but an
encouraging word makes it glad (Proverbs 12:25, AMP).

Did you realize that you are an artist? Oh, you may not be skilled with a paint brush or pencil, but you are still an artist of another kind. Your canvas is your partner. Dr. David Viscott writes: "Relationships seldom die because they suddenly have no life in them. They wither slowly, either because people do not understand how much or what kind of upkeep, time, work, love and caring they require or because people are too lazy or afraid to try. A relationship is a living thing. It needs and benefits from the same attention to detail that an artist lavishes on his art."[16]

You and your spouse are artists bringing to the canvas of each other's life the potential that God has placed there. Your statements and beliefs about your partner will help to shape that person. One way we do this is through affirmation. Jan and Dave Congo have an interesting thought in this regard:

> Jesus Christ verbally affirms each person ahead of schedule. When Jesus first met Simon, He looked him straight in the eye and called him Peter. What is the difference, you ask? Simon meant "reed," someone easily tossed to and fro. Peter meant a "rock," a symbol of stability. The name was not withheld by Jesus until Peter proved himself. It was given in love so Peter could grow into it. Affirmers see people as they are and accept them. Affirmers also see people as they can become.[17]

What do you see your partner becoming? Consider how you can affirm your spouse during this next week. What will you say each day to draw out his or her potential? Such verbal artistry can be really encouraging for both of you.

OCTOBER 27

*Why is my pain unending and my wound
grievous and incurable?* (Jeremiah 15:18).

Jeremiah the prophet went through some difficult times in his life. His ministry did not always go well. He felt discouraged and even rejected because of what wasn't happening. He had to live with a lot of pain.

Pain comes in many forms. Some of us practically have an anxiety attack when we visit the dentist. Those who are shy or introverted feel tremendous pain when forced to talk in front of a group of people. There is pain when the doctor cuts into the festering wound so it can heal. There is the pain of a pulled muscle. Often physical pain is insignificant compared to the pain of rejection.

You may have days when the words of Jeremiah become your words. It's even more tragic when these words express the state of a marriage relationship! We look at pain and ask "why?" But Jesus tells us to look at pain and ask "why not?"

We were never promised a pain-free life. Lewis Smedes writes: "We need to suffer some of the cussed wrongness of life in order to find its deep rightness. We have to feel pain we do not want to feel, carry burdens we do not want to carry, put up with misery we do not want to put up with, cry tears we do not want to shed. If we feel no hurt now, we will, when all is done, be the most miserable of all people."[18]

Like it or not, there is a purpose in pain. Pain brings home the reality of life. For some people pain is not the exception in their life but a constant companion. Jesus Christ went through pain and suffering. He knows what it's all about, and He promises to be with us during our times of joy and pain. What is the pain in your life at this time? If there isn't any, what do you think will be the next painful experience you will encounter? It will come, you know.

OCTOBER 28

*O God, you are my God, earnestly I seek you; my soul
thirsts for you, my body longs for you, in a dry and
weary land where there is no water* (Psalm 63:1).

Your throat is raspy. It feels like sandpaper. You try to swallow, but
there's no moisture. Thirst! All of your energies are focused on
finding some liquid. Your body is dehydrated. Clear, cool water is the
only way to quench that thirst.

Have you ever found yourself alone for hours without water in some
remote place? Hikers usually carry a canteen of water to prevent serious
thirst on a hike. Sometimes they fill their canteen from a spring only
to discover later on that the water was contaminated. That's even more
frustrating than thirst—to have water you can't drink. You end up
being as thirsty as if there was no water at all.

Physical dehydration and thirst aren't much fun. But there are two
other types of dryness that are even worse. One is marital dryness,
when there is no refreshment or replenishment for the marital relationship. Your marriage feels empty, dry, and lacking. This is a thirst that
doesn't have to occur.

But there is another type of dryness that could create a thirst in
marriage. Its called spiritual dryness. Have you felt that way: empty,
dry, spiritually dull, and even isolated from God? Do you have a spiritual thirst for God? God has been called the "spring of living water"
(Jeremiah 2:13). Jesus Christ said that He was the living water. When
you're thirsty, you need and desire refreshment. That is what today's
verse is talking about. When you are dry spiritually, how do you
quench your thirst? Sometimes people are unaware of the fact they are
spiritually dry. Perhaps it's time to check the water supply. It's a shame
to suffer from thirst when refreshment and replenishment are only a
prayer away.[19]

OCTOBER 29

If you leave God's paths and go astray, you
will hear a Voice behind you say, "No, this is
the way; walk here" (Isaiah 30:21, TLB).

P aths are laid out for a purpose. By following them we are able to arrive at our destination. But sometimes we are tempted to take shortcuts, thinking we will save time. Often shortcuts create more problems than they solve. At other times we fail to pay attention to the path and stray off course.

It's also easy to get off course in a marriage relationship. Then, when we realize the marriage is in trouble, we take the path of ease by leaving the marriage. The work and commitment needed to get back on course seem too great. Some individuals stray off course mentally or emotionally but remain in relationship.

But there is a better option. It's called staying on the path and listening to God call us back. Consider the insight and then the prayer of Dr. David Hubbard:

> Marriages...are supposed to be earthly, tangible, concrete, specific demonstrations of God's eternal covenant with His people. God does not quit. He sticks with His church through thick and thin, just as He clung to His people Israel in her crooked and perverse wanderings, as well as in her days of righteousness and justice. God's pledge never to leave us or forsake us is the prototype of our marriage vows. The greatest challenge we face in life is to let our lives in loyalty and love reflect God's constancy....
>
> Heavenly Father, we are frightened by our own fickleness. This makes your love all the more amazing. Give us the tenderness to be open to those who need our love. Let us learn to love from the one who wrote love's textbook, namely Jesus Christ. His love was so loyal and so lasting that He did not shirk even a cross for the sake of His bride. In His name and strength we pray. Amen.[20]

OCTOBER 30

*Then God said, "Let us make man in
our image"* (Genesis 1:26).

Who are you? Who is your partner? These are basic questions which
we tend to take for granted. If you were asked to tell who you
are apart from any reference to your work or occupation, would you be
able to do so? It's a stressful exercise for many people!

Sometimes our identity is all wrapped up in what we produce. But
God has a different perspective. The psalmist said, "When I consider
your heavens, the work of your fingers, the moon and the stars, which
you have set in place, what is man that you are mindful of him…?
You made him a little lower than the heavenly beings and crowned
him with glory and honor. You made him ruler over the works of your
hands; you put everything under his feet" (Psalm 8:3-6).

Why is man so worthy? The answer is found in Genesis 1:26,27.
Read these verses aloud together. We have this glory and majesty
because of the way God created us. God gave us life, meaning, purpose,
and His presence to carry us through this life.

But what does all this have to do with marriage? Well, look at your
partner right now. You're not just living with a marital partner but with
a person that God created. He gave your partner the breath of life. Your
calling is to care deeply and practically for that person, and as you do
so your respect and your feelings for him or her will become more positive. And the changes you see coming from this positive response will
have a positive effect on both of your personalities.

Understand your partner and yourself through God's eyes. You
both bear His image. And if you have children, they bear His image
as well. Just realizing that fact can impact how we think about another
person and change our behavior. That's not a bad result![21]

OCTOBER 31

*Do not love the world or anything in the
world. If anyone loves the world, the love of
the Father is not in him* (1 John 2:15).

Survival—it's the first law that many people live by today, Christians as well as non-Christians. How can we survive in a world which seems so anti-Christian? John gives us an answer in today's verse. We must live in this world, but we need to live as God's chosen people. It's so easy to be captured by the lure of the world around us with the glitter of moving up the ladder materially and socially. Sometimes it's difficult to be different from others in the business world or even at church. Dr. Lloyd Ogilvie asks some penetrating questions about this concern:

> The only way I know that we can evaluate the kind of love we have for the world is to make an inventory of our dominant desires. What is our basic purpose? Can we write it out in thirty words or less? Are we able to support our definition by the way we live? Ask the people closest to us where we live, work, and spend time! We all swing between our love for God and the wrong kind of dependent love for the world.[22]

How can we tell we are in love with the world? Sometimes we choose to do what feels good rather than what is best for us. Sometimes we try to fill up our emptiness with things, people, and activities that only God can fill. Sometimes pride permeates our life, usually characterized by defensiveness, excessive competitiveness, and the need to draw attention to ourselves. Often pride creeps into a marriage, and the marriage reflects the standards of the world rather than God's pattern. Do you see any evidence that pride may have slipped into your life?

When we don't love the world we acknowledge that all we are and have is a result of God's blessing, and it has been entrusted to us to be used for God's glory. Is this your goal today?

November

When you are under pressure and feel like everything is collapsing around you, share your feelings with your partner. Pray about your trial specifically, expecting God to lift the burden and the fear. Take refuge in God, seek Him, and receive His peace.

November 1

Dear friends, now we are children of God, and what we will be has not yet been made known. But we know that when he appears, we shall be like him (1 John 3:2).

Imagination is a gift which can change your life. Imagination is important in living the Christian life. It's vital in making things happen in your life. It's one of the ways that God directs us.

How do you use your imagination? Do you use it to create negative, hindering mental images? Or do you use it to expand your life and the possibilities God has for you? Look at today's verse, and use your imagination for a minute. Can you imagine what it will be like to be like Christ? Is the thought overwhelming? Robert Hicks penned an interesting poem that reflects upon our imagination.

> Filled with a strange new hope they came, the blind, the leper, the sick, the lame. Frail of body and spent of soul…As many as touched Him were made whole. On every tongue was the Healer's name, through all the country they spread His fame. But Doubt clung tight to his wooden crutch saying, "We must not expect too much." Down through the ages a promise came, healing for sorrow and sin and shame, help for the helpless and sight for the blind, healing for body and soul and mind. The Christ we follow is still the same, with blessings that all who will may claim. But how often we miss Love's healing touch by thinking, "We must not expect too much."[1]

Does your imagination hinder you or your partner? Or does it open doors of opportunity for you and your marriage? Perhaps it's time to ask the Holy Spirit to direct this powerful gift. Just imagine what that would be like!

November 2

*For whatever is born of God overcomes the
world; and this is the victory that has overcome
the world—our faith* (1 John 5:4, NASB).

Christian couples face a struggle in today's world. It is so easy to
conform to worldly standards that we lose our identity as Christians without realizing it. How can we overcome the world and present
a positive image of Jesus Christ as individuals and couples?

Do you know what the word *overcome* actually means? To overcome as a Christian means to experience continuous victory in the
midst of an ongoing struggle. In order to overcome struggles you need
courage. But how do we get it? Our courage comes from the fact that
Jesus Christ overcame Satan, sin, and death all at once. The psalmist
said, "Be strong, and let your heart take courage" (Psalm 31:24, NASB).
The courage to stand out in the crowd comes from the strength of Jesus
Christ.

Why do we lack courage? Perhaps it's because we are not involved
in issues or concerns in which we rely upon Jesus Christ. Too many
times we rely upon our own resources. But when we tackle something
we know we cannot achieve, and when we must rely upon the Holy
Spirit, that's when life gets exciting.

What about you? Is there something you're facing which needs to be
overcome through the power of Jesus Christ? In what area of your life
do you need a dose of courage? Often couples need courage from God
to face the occasional unpleasantries in their relationship. But facing
them is far better than denying them or repressing them. Facing problems with Christ is the first step in solving them.

Do you need to pray for courage right at this moment? In what area?
Hearing your partner pray for you can also be a source of courage.[2]

NOVEMBER 3

Word from the Lord was rare in those days, visions
were infrequent (1 Samuel 3:1, NASB).

Throughout history traps have been used by man to capture unsuspecting animals and other humans. Have you ever been trapped in some way? There are also traps that keep us from hearing God speak to us. These hindrances create situations which make God's voice rare in our lives.

Read through 1 Samuel 3:1-10 and you will identify one of several traps we must beware of. Just as Samuel didn't recognize God's voice, sometimes we don't recognize Him speaking either. We find it hard to believe that God is really communicating with us.

A second trap which we all struggle with is busyness. There is so much to do and so little time that we are constantly flitting from one thing to another. It is as though God is waiting to speak until we pause in our activity long enough to hear Him.

There is also the trap of distractions. You know what they are—noise of all kinds: the television, the telephone, the stereo, other people. How can we be conscious of God speaking with so much external interference? Jesus offered a solution when He said, "But when you pray, go into your room, close the door and pray to your Father, who is unseen. Then your Father, who sees what is done in secret, will reward you" (Matthew 6:6).

There's another trap, one that is very subtle. It's the trap of our mind-set. We may be ready to hear God, but we believe that He can only speak to us in a certain way: through a favorite writer, our pastor, a Christian TV personality, etc. But God often speaks through persons and situations when we least expect it. In the Old Testament He once spoke through a donkey! If He can do that, don't be surprised at ways He chooses to speak to you now. Just be open to listen.

When was the last time God really spoke to you? Think about it. Then share your thoughts together.[3]

NOVEMBER 4

*Fret not....Trust in the Lord....Delight yourself
in the Lord....Commit your way to the Lord....
Rest in the Lord* (Psalm 37:1,3,4,5,7, NASB).

Before continuing with this meditation, read the remainder of Psalm 37 aloud together from your Bible.

What do you fret about? How do you show that you're fretting? The word fret means to eat away, gnaw at, worry, or wear away. Beavers gnaw at trees, and the results are quite visible. The tree is chewed away at its base until it eventually falls to the ground. Fretting can have the same destructive effect on you—eating at you until you fall apart physically, emotionally, or spiritually.

The psalmist gives us the solution to fretting in the words *trust, delight, commit,* and *rest.* Trusting and committing involve letting go completely and flinging of yourself upon God, dislodging the burden or releasing it to Him. Perhaps it means that you pray, "Lord, I'm really concerned about this problem, but I'm going to give it to You. I will rest in the confidence that You are working even though I don't know the outcome. I give my problem to You, and I anticipate Your peace in my life."

Delighting means that you can enjoy the Lord for who He is, not just for what He can do for you. When you pray and release your burden, spend the majority of your prayer time delighting in Him through praise and worship. This focus can bring your life and your problem into proper perspective.

Do you know what it means to rest in the Lord? It means to stop struggling, to be silent, and to submit to what He ordains. That's the tough one. God works differently than we do, and He has a different time schedule than we do. But He invites us, "Give your problem to Me and trust Me to take care of it. Don't let it gnaw away at your insides, and don't spend all your time negatively rehashing it with others. Give it to Me completely."

Following the instructions in this psalm has done wonders for many people and many couples. Why not join the ranks of those who have found a different way to live?

NOVEMBER 5

Be strong and courageous, do not be afraid
or discouraged (1 Chronicles 22:13).

Every now and then you will find an article in *Reader's Digest* describing a courageous act by some person. Often tremendous risk was involved in the experience. The Congressional Medal of Honor is given by our government to men and women in the armed forces who act above and beyond the call of duty in life-and-death situations. These heroic deeds are accomplished because of the courage and determination of the individual.

Courage is the ability to continue on in the face of adversity. And if there is an ingredient needed for marriage survival today, it's courage. Why? Think about it for a moment. It takes a lot of courage for a husband and wife to submit to one another. It takes courage to put your spouse's needs and best interests ahead of your own. It takes courage to stick with a relationship problem until it is resolved rather than run away from it. It takes courage to stand in the workplace and declare that you believe in fidelity and permanence in marriage. It takes courage to listen to the ridicule of those whose value system is opposite to the Word of God.

It takes courage to look at your partner and say, "You were right and I was wrong. You have a much better idea. Let's do it your way. Will you forgive me for my stubbornness?" It takes courage to say no to a promotion which will require you to spend more time away from your spouse. It takes courage to develop the qualities of intimacy and transparency in marriage. It takes courage to admit to one another that you need to grow spiritually, that you're afraid at times to pray out loud, or that you're not always consistent in your devotions.

Courage—we all need it because we all struggle with these issues. Isn't it wonderful that we know the source of the courage we need? Isn't it wonderful that He supplies the courage we lack—that is, if we ask Him for it?

November 6

*If we confess our sins, he is faithful and just
and will forgive us our sins and purify us
from all unrighteousness* (1 John 1:9).

I know I should forgive my spouse, but I just don't have it in me to do it."

Have you ever felt this way? Don't worry; other people have felt this way too. As humans we don't have the ability within ourselves to truly forgive; we are only able to forgive because God has forgiven us. When we realize how forgiven we are, only then are we free to let go of the accumulated hurts stored within our hearts and minds. God is the source of our ability to forgive our partner. God has taken the risk out of confession and forgiveness. Lewis Smedes describes it this way:

> What makes the difference? The difference is a wooden cross dug into a hill where a man once died in shared pain for the sins of the world. On the cross, Jesus gathered all the pain we made God feel, and he felt it there with God. He felt the same pain God feels when we turn our backs on him and chase after the silly tin cups of our own making. Shared pain, between Jesus and God; this was his way of confessing our sins for us....
>
> There is a cross of shared pain in the life of God. This is why he never shuts the door to us. You can bet on it; he will always forgive. He does not merely forget, he does not merely understand; he puts himself at our side and says, "Let's start over. I will be your father. I will be your friend. I will be your savior. So let's get going."[4]

If God has done all that for us, if you are truly a forgiven person, then you can become a forgiving person. You have received the ability to give to your partner what God has extended to you.

November 7

Whenever anyone turns to the Lord,
the veil is taken away (2 Corinthians 3:16).

For some people, pretending is a way of life. Consider these comments on the issue of hiding behind a veil:

> Don't be fooled by me. Don't be fooled by the face I wear. I wear a mask. I wear a thousand masks—masks that I am afraid to take off; and none of them are me.
>
> Pretending is an art that is second nature to me, but don't be fooled. For my sake, don't be fooled. I give the impression that I am secure, that all is sunny and unruffled within me as well as without; that confidence is my name and coolness my game, that the water is calm and I am in command; and that I need no one. But don't believe me, please. My surface may seem smooth, but my surface is my mask, my ever-varying and ever-concealing mask.
>
> Beneath lies no smugness, no complacence. Beneath dwells the real me in confusion, in fear, in aloneness. But I hide that....I panic at the thought of my weakness and fear being exposed. That's why I frantically create a mask to hide behind—a nonchalant, sophisticated facade—to help me pretend, to shield me from the glance that knows. But such a glance is precisely my salvation, my only salvation, and I know it. That is, if it's followed by acceptance; if it's followed by love.
>
> It's the only thing that can liberate me from myself, from my own self-built prison wall, from the barriers I so painstakingly erect....
>
> Who am I, you may wonder. I am someone you know very well. I am every man you meet. I am every woman you meet. I am every child you meet. I am right in front of you. Please...love me.[5]

Talk about the masks you wear and what you need to do to minimize the pretending in your life.

NOVEMBER 8

We take captive every thought to make it
obedient to Christ (2 Corinthians 10:5).

Where did that child go? I told him to stay put. He's wandered off again."

Have you ever said those words about your child? Were these words ever spoken about you when you were young? There are many ways to wander. Sometimes we do it physically, but perhaps as adults we are more likely to wander off mentally. Do you remember some of the classes you took in high school or college that were downright boring? Did your mind wander during some of those classes? It's really embarrassing to have a teacher call on you when you've wandered off! We're brought back to reality with a jolt.

Have you ever wandered off mentally when you were praying? You know, right in the middle of your prayer you begin thinking about work, the children, that new car, or the upcoming trip. A few minutes later you realize that your allotted time for prayer is up and you didn't get very far! Perhaps that's why today's passage about bringing every thought captive is so important to a solid prayer life.

In a 1985 issue, *Reader's Digest* suggested that we have been "untaught" to concentrate by television. TV has such short program segments and brief commercials that our attention span has become abbreviated. As a result, we wander mentally when our partner talks to us, when we talk with God, and even when we read His Word.

One of the ways to control your thoughts during devotions is to pray and read the Scriptures aloud. Try it for a week and note the difference. You will concentrate better, retain what you read longer, and begin to discover that your thoughts can be controlled. God asks us to concentrate on Him. He knows the struggles we have with that. Why else would He have instructed the writers of Scripture to say so much about controlling our thought life? Obeying these passages can help you round up your stray thoughts.[6]

NOVEMBER 9

Let us fix our eyes on Jesus, the author and
perfecter of our faith (Hebrews 12:2).

How can you control wandering thoughts? Here are the suggestions of two writers:

> It is difficult for many people to quiet their minds....Ideas start to come up that jar them out of the silence....For such people it is helpful to have a notebook at hand. If one quietly records the thought...one can let it go and return to stillness. If the thought keeps on returning, one can then push it aside and say to it: You are taken care of. Stop bothering me.... Leave me alone; I don't have to be tyrannized by you....There is a great difference between avoiding a thought or emotion and laying it aside after taking the trouble to look at it.[7]

> Do not become distressed because your mind has wandered away. Always guard yourself from being anxious because of your faults. First of all, such distress only stirs up the soul and distracts you to outward things.
> Secondly, your distress really springs from a secret root of pride. What you are experiencing is, in fact, a love of your own worth.
> How do you deal with those things that distract; how do you handle those things that draw you away from the inmost part of your being? If you should sin (or even if it is only a matter of being distracted by some circumstances around you), what should you do? You must instantly turn within to your own spirit.[8]

Wandering thoughts tend to recede the more you fix your thoughts upon Jesus Christ.

NOVEMBER 10

*Here I am! I stand at the door and knock. If anyone
hears my voice and opens the door, I will come in and
eat with him, and he with me* (Revelation 3:20).

A knock on the door—when you hear it you wonder, "Who could
that be?" Sometimes God knocks at our heart's door, but how do
you know when God is knocking? That's confusing for some people.
One thing is sure: He doesn't force Himself upon you. He knocks at
the door, but doesn't knock it down. Jesus knocks and then asks us
to respond to His invitation. He waits to be welcomed and invited in.
Perhaps that's the first step in hearing God: welcoming His voice.

One of the reasons that God speaks to us is because He wants fellowship with us. He wants to communicate with us. Some people are
afraid to listen to God's voice because they are afraid He wants to
punish them. But that's not what His Word says. Listen to His invitation to you: "Come to me, all who are weary and burdened, and I
will give you rest" (Matthew 11:28); "Ask and it will be given to you;
seek and you will find; knock and the door will be opened to you. For
everyone who asks receives; and he who seeks finds; and to him who
knocks, the door will be opened" (Matthew 7:7,8).

John 10:2-4 talks about Jesus as the shepherd and us as the
sheep. Jesus knows each of His sheep. His approach is personal because
His relationship with you is personal. Do you sense that? Do you
understand that? Jesus is the bridegroom who approaches you as His
bride, the friend who approaches you as His friend. Why? Because He
loves you. He wants fellowship with you. He knocks because you are
on His wanted list. Now do you feel a bit more special? Take a moment
to remind each other how special you are to God.[9]

November 11

God...gave himself for our sins to rescue us
from the present evil age (Galatians 1:4).

How well do you know your partner's voice? Can you pick it out in a crowd of people? Of course you can, because you're familiar with it. His or her voice affects you personally. It's the same way with God's voice. One of the best ways to recognize God's voice is the effect it has upon you. Consider several of these positive effects.

First, His words can bring you encouragement. He is the "God of all comfort" (2 Corinthians 1:3). He encourages us through His promises and His confidence in us. Perhaps that's the pattern for relating to one another in marriage. Do your voice and your words to one another bring encouragement?

Second, God's words bring us peace. Nothing that God says to you will bring worry or fear. He tells us that we will have peace by relying upon Him. When that sense of peace during difficulties comes into your life, you have heard God's voice. Do your words to one another bring a similar sense of peace and comfort?

Third, His words and His voice bring hope. Hope is the expectation of good. As one commentator put it, hope "is a favorable and sure expectation. It has to do with the unseen of the future. The happy anticipation of good. Hopelessness is having no expectation of good or success; despairing."[10]

What characterizes your life right now: hope or hopelessness? What about your partner? Where could each of you use more hope at this point?

Our God is a God of hope: "May the God of hope fill you with all joy and peace as you trust in him, so that you may overflow with hope by the power of the Holy Spirit" (Romans 15:13). Did you notice that? When you are filled with the hope which comes from God, joy and peace will be the result. That's something to think about. Something else to think about is this: How can you be a greater source of hope to your partner?

NOVEMBER 12

The righteous will live by faith (Romans 1:17).

Keep the faith, baby!"

That was a popular expression years ago, even though we didn't always know what it meant. We are told today in sermons that we need more faith. And it's true. Faith causes us to move ahead in life. You have faith in your partner. Sometimes you can't explain it. You just know that you can depend upon him or her.

Perhaps the best definition of faith comes from the Word of God itself. Hebrews 11:1 reads, "Now faith is being sure of what we hope for and certain of what we do not see." Nineteen times in Hebrews 11 the words "by faith" are used to describe the life and exploits of God's leaders in Old Testament times. Whom today can you point to as a man or woman of faith? Have you read Hebrews 11 recently? There's a great promise in the last verse of that chapter. Go ahead and read it.

Faith is not an option in the Christian life. God actually demands faith on your part (Romans 1:17). The only way to be righteous is through faith. Did you know that your faith is a delight to God? He actually takes pleasure in it: "Without faith it is impossible to please God" (Hebrews 11:6). Also, God is the one who gives the basis and reason for faith when He speaks to you: "Faith comes from hearing the message, and the message is heard through the word of Christ" (Romans 1:17).

Faith does not always correspond with reason; faith goes beyond reason. You must listen to the voice of God and His Word in the face of what others may say. No one said that faith is always easy. Sometimes you may struggle. But just consider the alternative—what would your life be like without any faith? Think of that as you read Hebrews 11 again.[11]

November 13

To my dear friend Gaius, whom I love in the truth....But Diotrephes, who loves to be first, will have nothing to do with us (3 John 1,9).

We live in a society which emphasizes self: "Think of yourself first"; "Do yourself a favor"; "You deserve a break"; "You're worth it." But putting yourself first is a reflection of insecurity manifested in selfishness. The other way to live is called being gracious. How do you live graciously for others? for your partner? What are the characteristics?

Perhaps today's passage will help clarify graciousness in relationships. Contrast the descriptions of Gaius and Diotrephes. Diotrephes lived for himself instead of thinking of others. But John referred to Gaius as a beloved friend. When you call someone beloved it usually communicates delight, appreciation, and admiration. That's graciousness.

Being gracious is usually manifested through words of concern, love, and serving. One way of expressing graciousness from a scriptural perspective is through hospitality. This is practical graciousness. It's an expression of love. Paul told the church at Rome to "practice hospitality" (Romans 12:13). Peter said, "Offer hospitality to one another without grumbling" (1 Peter 4:9). In Hebrews the words are even stronger: "Do not forget to entertain strangers, for by so doing some people have entertained angels without knowing it" (Hebrews 13:2). Being gracious means reaching out to meet the needs of others around you.

It's one thing to hear the phrase, "There's a gracious person." But have you ever heard the expression, "There's a gracious marriage relationship"? Practicing gracious hospitality must have two dimensions: being gracious at home toward your partner and then being gracious and hospitable toward others.

Think for a moment: How could you be more gracious toward your partner? How would he or she like you to be more gracious? And as a couple, what can you do to practice hospitality toward some who need it, even if they don't deserve it?[12]

NOVEMBER 14

*Nevertheless let each individual among you also love
his own wife even as himself; and let the wife see to it
that she respect her husband* (Ephesians 5:33, NASB).

Do you have a respectful marriage? This is part of our calling as
believers. Today's passage instructs both husbands and wives to
respond to one another with respect. But do you understand what
that means? Respect in marriage means ministering to your partner
through listening, a loving embrace, a flexible mind and attitude, and
a gracious spirit. It means looking past faults and differences and seeing
strengths and similarities. It means sharing concerns mutually instead
of attempting to carry the load yourself.

Consider the following questions as you evaluate your respect for
one another:

- In a tense situation, do I cut off my partner when he or she holds
  a view different from mine?

- When I think my partner is wrong, do I become offensive and
  harsh trying to put him or her in place?

- In trying to get a point across, am I gently persuasive or opinion-
  ated and demanding?

- Am I driven so much by the need to be right that I try to pressure my spouse into my position? Do I intimidate my partner?

Yes, these are questions which meddle. But answering them is a
good step toward building a respectful marriage. As one author said,
respect begins when we "learn to practice careful listening rather than
threatened opposition, honest expression rather than resentment, flexibility rather than rigidity, loving censure rather than harsh coercion,
encouragement rather than intimidation."[13]

How's the respect in your marriage relationship?[14]

NOVEMBER 15

Glorify the God and Father of our Lord
Jesus Christ (Romans 15:6).

When Jesus Christ is Lord of the husband, the wife, and their marriage, several good things happen to enhance and enrich their
marriage. Consider these possibilities:

> Jesus as Lord of your marriage relieves each of you of
> the burden of "lording it over" the other. It is part of our
> fallen nature to want to control each other rather than sac-
> rificially to serve one another. When we submit ourselves to
> the Lord Jesus Christ, however, competition turns into loving
> empathy.
>
> Enrolling ourselves under the lordship of Jesus Christ
> turns each of us into both the student and the teacher of the
> other. Jesus opens our hearts to each other and enables us to
> learn from each other.
>
> A husband and wife with Jesus as Lord have in Him a
> higher authority than themselves, and thus they do not insist
> on "playing God" in the lives of their children. When we
> feel we are the final authority over our children, we lose our
> capacity to learn from them.
>
> Husbands and wives with Jesus as Lord have in Him a
> leader in times of major decision-making. When we turn to
> the Lord Jesus Christ and open our consciences to His Spirit's
> leading, some new events, remembrances, and forgotten facts
> will come to us. A whole new pattern will emerge.
>
> When Jesus is Lord of our marriages, He keeps us from
> idolizing each other and expecting each other to be perfect.
> He enables us to affirm each other's humanness, and to bear
> the burdens of each other's faults, thus fulfilling the law of
> Christ.[15]

What do you have to say to your partner after reading this?

NOVEMBER 16

*I have told you this so that my joy may be in you
and that your joy may be complete* (John 15:11).

Happiness is basically a choice which is not dependent upon situations or conditions. Each of us is responsible for our own happiness. Happiness can be enhanced by what occurs around us or what our spouse does, but we are more likely to be happy if we center our activities on others instead of on ourselves.

Dr. Archibald Hart suggests writing the following affirmations on cards, keeping them with you, and reading them periodically.

> *Just for today* I will set my affection on things above, not on things on the earth.
>
> *Just for today* I will not worry about what will happen tomorrow, but will trust that God will go before me into the unknown.
>
> *Just for today* I will endure anything that hurts or depresses me because I believe God controls what happens to me.
>
> *Just for today* I will not dwell on my misfortunes. I will replace my negative thoughts with happy and hopeful thoughts.
>
> *Just for today* I will choose to do some things I do not like doing, and I will do them cheerfully and with a happy spirit.
>
> *Just for today* I will make a conscious effort to love those who don't show love to me and be kind to those who do not appreciate me.
>
> *Just for today* I will be patient with those who irritate me and longsuffering toward those who are selfish and inconsiderate.
>
> *Just for today* I will forgive all those who hurt me—even forgiving myself.
>
> *Just for today* I will choose to BE HAPPY![16]

NOVEMBER 17

What does the worker gain from his toil?...[God] has
made everything beautiful in its time (Ecclesiastes 3:9,11).

For many people life is meaningless, empty, boring drudgery. Read the book of Ecclesiastes to discover the futility of life. It is especially empty without God. Can you imagine what it must be like for those who don't know God? In his thought-provoking book on Ecclesiastes, *Living on the Ragged Edge*, Chuck Swindoll describes the problem:

> To put it bluntly, life on planet Earth without God is the pits. And if I may repeat my point (Solomon does numerous times), that's the way God designed it. He made it like that. He placed within us that God-shaped vacuum that only He can fill. Until He is there, nothing satisfies. There is no hell on earth like horizontal living without God.
>
> Can you imagine being raised in a country that teaches everyone that "there is no God"? Perhaps you remember the Soviet athlete who in following his coach's instruction to do a three and a half somersault, tucked position, cracked his head on the ten-meter platform. Today he's dead.
>
> That tragedy made me stop and think how I'd feel if I were a parent in the Soviet Union, sitting in a hospital room with my boy dying on the bed in front of me. Think about it. There I sit, helpless to do one thing to revive him. I have no God to talk to. I find no comfort coming from the Supreme Being, because I do not think He exists. And there is no one to put his arm around me and tell me there's an eternal purpose in it all.[17]

But the writer of this Old Testament book also states that God has made everything appropriate in its time. He makes everything work together for good (Romans 8:28). What difference will God make in your life today? in your partner's life?

I will praise you with an upright heart (Psalm 119:7).

For the next few days we will be sharing affirmations created by Kenneth Boa on the basis of Scripture. Read these passages aloud together today, and allow God's Word to affirm your heart and mind

Like Noah, I want to be a righteous man, blameless among the people of my time, and one who walks with God (Genesis 6:9).

I desire to be righteous before You in my generation (Genesis 7:1).

I will be careful not to forget the Lord, my God, by failing to observe His commandments, His ordinances, and His statutes (Deuteronomy 8:11).

Like Hezekiah, I want to do what is good and right and true before the Lord, my God, by seeking Him with all my heart (2 Chronicles 31:20,21).

Like Josiah, I desire to do what is right in the sight of the Lord, walking in the ways of David and not turning aside to the right or to the left (2 Chronicles 34:1,2).

Like Job, I want to be blameless and upright, fearing God and shunning evil (Job 1:1).

I will be careful to lead a blameless life. I will walk in the integrity of my heart in the midst of my house. I will set no wicked thing before my eyes. I hate the work of those who fall away; it will not cling to me. A perverse heart shall depart from me; I will not know evil. Whoever slanders his neighbor in secret, I will put to silence; I will not endure him who has haughty eyes and a proud heart. My eyes will be on the faithful in the land, that they may dwell with me; he whose walk is blameless will minister to me. No one who practices deceit will dwell in my house; no one who speaks falsely will stand in my presence (Psalm 101:2-7).[18]

NOVEMBER 19

*Hanani...was a man of integrity and feared God
more than most men do* (Nehemiah 7:2).

Read aloud these affirmations from Scripture, as prepared by
Kenneth Boa, and allow God's Word to affirm your heart and
mind.

I will not follow the crowd in doing wrong (Exodus 23:2).

I will not be dishonest in judgment, in measurement of weight or
quantity. I will be honest and just in my business affairs (Leviticus
19:35,36).

I will not show partiality in judgment; I will hear both small and
great alike. I will not be afraid of any man, for judgment belongs to
God (Deuteronomy 1:17).

I will not pervert justice or show partiality. I will not accept a bribe,
for a bribe blinds the eyes of the wise and perverts the words of the
righteous (Deuteronomy 16:19).

I know, my God, that you test the heart and are pleased with integrity (1 Chronicles 29:17).

I will let the fear of the Lord be upon me, and I will be careful in
what I do, for with the Lord, my God, there is no injustice or partiality
or bribery (2 Chronicles 19:7).

I will walk properly as in the daytime, not in revellings and drunkenness, not in promiscuity and debauchery, not in strife and jealousy.
Rather, I will put on the Lord Jesus Christ and make no provision to
gratify the lusts of the flesh (Romans 13:13,14).

I do not want even a hint of immorality, or any impurity, or greed,
in my life, as is proper for a saint. Nor will I give myself to obscenity,
foolish talk, or course joking, which are not fitting, but rather to giving
of thanks (Ephesians 5:3,4).[19]

November 20

Ezra had devoted himself to the study and
observance of the Law of the Lord, and to teaching
its decrees and laws in Israel (Ezra 7:10).

Here is another selection of affirmations from Kenneth Boa. Read these passages aloud together today, and allow God's Word to affirm your heart and mind.

I have hidden Your word in my heart that I might not sin against You (Psalm 119:11).

I have kept my feet from every evil path that I might keep Your word. I gain understanding from Your precepts; therefore I hate every false way (Psalm 119:101,104).

Your word is a lamp to my feet and a light to my path. I have inclined my heart to perform Your statutes to the very end (Psalm 119:105,112).

I will not be quickly provoked in my spirit, for anger rests in the bosom of fools (Ecclesiastes 7:9).

I will watch and pray so that I will not fall into temptation; the spirit is willing, but the flesh is weak (Matthew 26:41).

I will devote myself to prayer, being watchful in it with thanksgiving (Colossians 4:2).

I will make it my ambition to lead a quiet life, to mind my own business, and to work with my own hands, so that I may walk properly toward those who are outside and may lack nothing (1 Thessalonians 4:11,12).

Since I belong to the day, I will be self-controlled, putting on the breastplate of faith and love, and the hope of salvation as a helmet (1 Thessalonians 5:8).

I should rejoice always and pray without ceasing; in everything I will give thanks, for this is the will of God for me in Christ Jesus (1 Thessalonians 5:16-18).

I will be diligent to present myself approved to God, a workman who does not need to be ashamed and who correctly handles the word of truth (2 Timothy 2:15).[20]

November 21

O Lord, you have searched me and
you know me (Psalm 139:1).

Before continuing with this meditation, read the remainder of Psalm 139 together aloud from your Bible.

Where can you go to learn what God is like? Psalm 139. And the first thing you learn about is God's omniscience (vv. 1-6). God is all-knowing. He knows everything about you. He searches, perceives, discerns, and is familiar with everything about you. Whether you're in your car, at work, at home, or in the mountains, you cannot hide. In fact, God knows your thoughts. Every thought that has flashed across the screen of your mind is known to God. What does that mean to you?

Verses 7-12 teach about God's omnipresence. The verses here reflect David's amazement that God's hand is everywhere to guide him and to hold him. The psalmist gives several illustrations of the extent to which God is everywhere. How can this truth make a difference in your daily life? Have you ever explored this truth about God with your partner?

God's omnipotence is expressed in verses 13-18. He is the source of creative power. God can search you out not only because He knows you and is everywhere, but because He made you. You were not merely a thought in someone's mind. God is the one who brought you into being. That means you are significant. No wonder David spends verses 17,18 praising God!

What is the significance of God's omniscience, omnipresence, and omnipotence in your life as a couple today? How can your awareness of these qualities make a difference as you confront your work, your fears, your struggles, and your past and present hurts? How can your individual lives and your marriage be different because of God's omniscience, omnipresence, and omnipotence? These three big, meaningful words are used to help us understand the God who created us, who loved us enough to send His Son for us, and who wants us to love and worship Him. What a wonderful God we serve!

November 22

Always give thanks for everything to our
God and Father in the name of our Lord
Jesus Christ (Ephesians 5:20, TLB).

Do you remember a special Thanksgiving day as a child? You probably have a storehouse full of Thanksgiving memories from over the years. Thanksgiving day will be here again in a few days—a day for family fun, festivities, and feasting. It can be a day in which you as a couple help shape pleasant memories for each person you will be with. Here are some suggestions to help you make this a day of memories.

Put on a tape recorder during Thanksgiving dinner, and let it run, recording all the conversation. This will provide some enjoyable listening later in the day. During dinner, ask everyone to share their first memory of Thanksgiving Day. What were they most thankful for as a child? Ask what each one is most thankful for spiritually during the past year. If you as a group of families and friends were to write your own psalm of Thanksgiving, what would you say? (You may want to save this project for after the meal.)

Discuss the following questions and answers as you eat: What do you know about Thanksgiving Day? Is it celebrated only in our country or others also?

The first thanksgiving proclamation occurred three years after the pilgrims settled in Plymouth. Thanksgiving was established to thank God for His goodness and to remind people that they now had the freedom to worship as they pleased. What would our life be like if that were not the case today?

George Washington designated Thanksgiving Day to commemorate the first pilgrim celebration. Thomas Jefferson discontinued it, but Abraham Lincoln reestablished it. Finally, in 1942 the United States Congress confirmed the date: the fourth Thursday of November. Canada also has an official Thanksgiving Day: the second Monday of October. But for believers, every day is to be a day of thanksgiving for knowing Jesus Christ.

NOVEMBER 23

Dear brothers, don't ever forget that it is best
to listen much (James 1:19, TLB);
Be a ready listener (James 1:19, AMP).

Who in your life would say that you are "a ready listener"? That may be an uncomfortable question for you, but it is important. Whether we are relating to another person or to God, listening is the connecting mechanism. Ask your partner these hard questions: When do you see me as a ready listener? In what ways could I become a better listener? And as you talk together, remember this thought from God's Word: "If you profit from constructive criticism, you will be elected to the wise men's hall of fame. But to reject criticism is to harm yourself and your own interests" (Proverbs 15:31,32, TLB).

Now consider some thoughts about listening:

> Listening is a sharp attention to what is going on. Listening is an active openness toward the other fellow. Listening is putting your whole self in a position to respond to whatever he cares to say.[21]

> If you listen you adventure into the lives of other people. We soon notice the people who really take us seriously and listen to what we have to say. And with them we tend to open more of our lives than with the busy non-listener. We share what really matters. Thus, if you are such a listener, the chances are good that others will invite you as a guest into their lives. Because they know you will hear them, they will entrust you with things that mean very much to them. And this too is most rewarding![22]

> In some wonderful way that we can never fully understand, God too is a listener. In his listening, as in his speaking, he both loves and judges. He is both the Father and the Lord. Through our creative listening he acts in both ways. And where our listening is imperfect, he will find other ways of expressing his perfect love and judgment.[23]

NOVEMBER 24

Two are better than one, because they have a good
return for their work: If one falls down, his friend
can help him up. But pity the man who falls and
has no one to help him up! (Ecclesiastes 4:9,10).

You may think that today's passage relates only to married couples. But marriage is not even mentioned here. This is a passage for everyone. We learn that it is better to go through life with another person than to try to tough it out all alone. With another person alongside we gain perspective, objectivity, courage, and another's opinion. In the process of living and working with another person, our rough edges are often smoothed off. Marriage just happens to be the primary relationship where this verse can be fulfilled.

Why are two better than one? The following lines help us understand: "Oh, the comfort—the inexpressible comfort of feeling safe with a person, having neither to weigh thoughts, nor measure words—but pouring them all right out—just as they are—chaff and grain together—certain that a faithful hand will take and sift them—keep what is worth keeping and with the breath of kindness, blow the rest away."[24]

Why does Solomon say that two are better than one? Look at the reasons in Ecclesiastes 4:9-12. You gain mutual encouragement when you are weak. Marriage is a calling to a support-and-encourage, affirming relationship. You also gain mutual support when you are vulnerable. When you are exposed and unguarded, your partner can help you during that time of vulnerability. How can each of you do that for the other?

When there are two, there is mutual protection when you are attacked. If you want some illustrations from Scripture of friends defending and encouraging one another, read about Elijah and Elisha, Naomi and Ruth, and David and Jonathan. Then consider how each of you can become more of a support to the other.[25]

NOVEMBER 25

Those who wait on the Lord shall renew their
strength; they shall mount up with wings like
eagles, they shall run and not be weary, they shall
walk and not faint (Isaiah 40:31, NKJV).

The seasons of the year bring different kinds of weather. There are days of bright sunshine as well as the dark, dismal, rainy days where everything is gray. Sometimes our days seem gray regardless of the weather outside. Even during the brightest days we can experience nothing but darkness inside.

One thing is sure, however: Whatever your day is like, God is with you. He is alive and present whether you feel His presence or not. He never deserts us. He doesn't abandon His children. And He doesn't say, "Pull yourself out of it. Shape up. Get your life together." Instead He says "Wait on me." To wait seems to imply resting on Him, relying on Him, and looking to Him as your source of strength.

Have you ever seen eagles soar? An eagle takes off from its perch and slowly climbs into the sky. When it finds an updraft the eagle keeps its wings outstretched and floats effortlessly for miles. And since it doesn't need to flap its wings, the eagle doesn't become weary.

In the same way, when we have troubles and burdens, instead of carrying them around like a 100-pound backpack, we need to heed God's invitation in Isaiah 40:31. God says, "Give Me your burdens. Tell Me about them. Give Me your worries and concerns." And when we do so we are able to soar as His faithfulness carries us through our difficulties. Isaiah's promise that we will run without becoming weary graphically points us to the Lord for our strength.

As you face the grayness which may cloud your life today, remember: In any storm of life, there is that time when the clouds begin to break and the rays of sunlight begin to penetrate. Talk about the areas in your life where you need to apply Isaiah 40:31. How can each of you wait upon the Lord today and find His strength?

NOVEMBER 26

*Everyone who hears these words of mine and does
not put them into practice is like a foolish man
who built his house on sand* (Matthew 7:26).

Those of us who grew up near the ocean can remember spending hours at the beach building sand castles. But eventually the tide came in and our castles crumbled and washed away. As adults we build castles of dreams and plans, but we run into the same kinds of problems, as Phillip Keller notes:

> All of us build our sand castles on the sands of time. All of us dream our little dreams of what we shall do with our lives. We dig our deep moats around those very private ambitions. We carefully erect our walls of self-protection to surround our elaborate aspirations. We shape and mold our decisions and personal choices into castles of self-interest and self-gratification.
>
> Most of us do this happily, blithely in our youth. We behave as though there were only time, lots of time, and us. We forget so soon that God is even there; and though He is, He seems as remote as the moon that turns the beach to silver at night.
>
> Yes, not only do we plan and build and scheme and work to erect our sand castles, we also forget that the tides of time and the power of God's presence are as inexorable as the ocean tides rising in response to the gravitational pull of the moon.
>
> For in the full flood of high tide—under the rising surge of the incoming wave, beneath the sweeping course of the ocean currents the castle—the walls, the moats, the work of our dreams—will disappear...lost in oblivion.
>
> Such is the end of those aims and ambitions built in thoughtless, careless abandon without reckoning on the power of God. Beautiful but for a day, they are swept away into nothing. Lord, help me to build on the Rock![26]

November 27

*Our conscience testifies that we have conducted
ourselves in the world, and especially in our
relations with you, in the holiness and sincerity
that are from God* (2 Corinthians 1:12).

How's your conscience? Bad question? People don't always like to
think about their conscience. They see it as a killjoy—something
that keeps them from having any fun in life. Discuss together for a
moment what conscience means to you.

Your behavior is directed by your conscience, which has been programmed from your childhood to distinguish between acceptable and
unacceptable behavior. Unfortunately, however, your conscience may
not have been programmed in keeping with God's Word. For example,
in some societies stealing and sexual intercourse outside of marriage
are acceptable. In one part of Africa, the most noble, self-sacrificing
act a mother can perform is to bury her twin daughters alive. In these
settings the conscience has been wrongly programmed, and wrong is
accepted as right.

What struggles have you experienced between your conscience and
your Christian faith? In order to operate as God intended it to, our conscience needs to be reprogrammed by the Holy Spirit and the teaching
of the Word of God.

A healthy conscience is discussed in Scripture. Three words are used
to describe it: good, pure, or clear, depending on the translation. But
when the conscience is not functioning as it should, it is described as
evil, seared, or dead. A conscience can become seared when you repeatedly participate in sin.

Conscience is almost always discussed in the Scriptures together
with faith. Our faith is dependent upon and determined by the condition of our conscience (1 Timothy 1:5-19; Hebrews 9:12-15; 10:16-22)
The more time you spend with God, the more clearly you will understand Him. This will bring clarity to your conscience. Allow Him to
remold your conscience today. He can do it.[27]

NOVEMBER 28

Train yourself toward godliness (piety)—keeping
yourself spiritually fit (1 Timothy 4:7, AMP).

Physical fitness has become the rage during the past decade. Spiritual fitness is even more important. Perhaps the reason for this is best expressed in the thoughts of a husband as he reflects upon three themes in his life:

> There is the theme of *crisis*. These are the times of turmoil… at least, initial turmoil. They are the "unexpected" of life. They are the things for which I am not prepared…I am surprised. But they are a vehicle which draws me closer to God. After time, stability is regained and victory is reported.
>
> The second theme is one of *calmness*. These are the times in my life when everything is at peace. There are no major demands being made upon me…no rigid schedules…no excessive expectations. In these calm periods of my life, time is definitely within my control. The Lord is consciously in the center of my day. There is always ample time and opportunity for prayer, Bible reading, and meditation upon His goodness. Truly, these are my best days….
>
> The final theme in my life is one of *hecticness*. Unlike the periods of calm, there is very little peace during these times. Demands abound…schedules are full…expectations are high. There is never enough time to get everything done and what time there is seems to be beyond my control. I desire for the Lord to be at the center of my day, but after all is said and done, He seems to get lost in the shuffle….Whereas periods of crisis and calmness serve to draw me closer to God, hecticness pulls me away. It is my adversary. Little by little, it subtly robs me of the closeness of my relationship with the Lord.[28]

November 29

*I said to myself, "Come now, I will test you
with pleasure. So enjoy yourself." And behold, it
too was futility* (Ecclesiastes 2:1, NASB).

Sometimes people end up chasing very elusive goals and treasures.
We think our marriage would be better if we had this or that. And
we give chase to obtain something new, but it always seems to run just
a bit faster than we do. It's always just out of reach. It's like the child
chasing after a butterfly hour after hour. But it's elusive.

The problem of pursuing unrealistic or unobtainable goals is not
new. John Bunyon, the famous seventeenth-century preacher, described
the problem very well:

> Behold how eager our little boy
> Is for this butterfly, as if all joy,
> All profits, honors, and lasting pleasures,
> Were wrapped up in her—or the richest treasures
> Found in her—
> When her all is lighter than a feather...
> His running through the nettles, thorns and briars
> To gratify his boyish fond desires;
> His tumbling over molehills to attain
> His end, namely his butterfly to gain,
> Plainly shows what hazards some men run
> To get what will be lost as soon as won.
> Men seem, in choice, than children far more wise
> Because they run not after butterflies,
> When yet, alas, for what are empty toys
> They follow them, and act as beardless boys.[29]

What are you chasing after in your marriage? Is it obtainable? What
will it give you if you ever capture it? Chasing after something elusive
is futile. Following after Christ is rewarding. He always knows what's
best for us.

November 30

It is for freedom that Christ has set us free. Stand firm, then, and do not let yourselves be burdened again by a yoke of slavery (Galatians 5:1).

You're not a replica of your partner. If you were, you probably wouldn't have married. You're not a replica of any other Christian either. Sometimes churches and well-meaning Christians try to make us into revised editions of themselves or what they believe a Christian should be. If you fall prey to this you will probably end up "under the law" in some legalistic structure. It's a new kind of slavery. But today's verse states that we are not to allow that to happen.

The way to be really free as a person and a couple and to develop into all that God wants you to be is to look to Him and His Word instead of looking to other people. Yes, others can give you some guidance and insight. But our basic source of study is God. Other people, like us, are imperfect. When we focus on them we end up making wrong comparisons. The Bible is full of examples. Cain compared himself with Abel and ended up killing him. Esau compared himself with Jacob, cared nothing about his birthright, and ended up losing his inheritance. Saul compared himself with David and had a mental breakdown. Those results aren't too encouraging, are they? Why look at others? That's slavery. Think about these two questions for a moment: What do you want your marriage to reflect? If the characteristics which come to mind are not present in other couples you know, are you willing to stand alone and be different?

Even though we have been set free we can so easily put the chains and handcuffs back on all by ourselves. Watch out that you don't sell yourself out to some new slave master. The freedom you have was paid for, and it was costly. It cost God His Son. But in setting you free He was saying, "You are worth it. You are free. Follow Me alone."

DECEMBER

❧

*You and your spouse are artists bringing to the
canvas of each other's life the potential that God
has placed there. Your statements and beliefs about
your partner will help to shape that person.*

DECEMBER 1

I urge you, brothers, in view of God's mercy, to offer your
bodies as living sacrifices, holy and pleasing to God—
this is your spiritual act of worship (Romans 12:1).

Have you ever wished you were someone else? Here's something to think about for today:

> We are only instruments, implements, tools for the building of God's temple. Some people are like the tools fitted for the delicate and delightful work of carving or painting. They have the joy, by their very touch, of converting and beautifying souls. Some, who are able to start great schemes and engineer important movements, are like the powerful cranes that lift masses of masonry into their places. But others, and probably we amongst them, are to do spade work in digging foundations; or we are to be like...the humble hammer that patiently hits nail after nail, or the humble nail itself, firmly fixed in a sure place, invisible, but doing one little piece of work well....
>
> It is impossible for me to express to God what He wants from you. But His ideal is that I should give to Him perfectly what He wants from me. It will save us endless trouble if we grasp that clearly. It will save us from the feeling that it must be easier for so-and-so to please God than for me. If I only had his chances! If I only had his temperament, or upbringing, his surroundings, his friends, his religious privileges, his sphere of work; or his voice, or command of language, or appearance! He is so rich in natural gifts, and I seem to have almost none; I'm a most dreadfully ordinary person.
>
> All this, and many more of the doubts and grumbles that sometimes pass through our minds, come from forgetting the plain, obvious truth that if God had made you different from what you are, He would have wanted something different from you.[1]

December 2

They gave themselves first to the Lord and then to us
in keeping with God's will (2 Corinthians 8:5).

How are you doing with your gift shopping? Are you struggling with it again this year? Perhaps today's verse will help. What would happen if your family agreed to give themselves first to the Lord and then to each other? For example, what if you spent only half as much on each other's gifts and donated the rest to missions or to a family in need? You may discover more of the joy of Christmas as you do.

In his fascinating article, "The Gift of Giving," Calvin Miller offers some additional thoughts about Christmas gifts:

> The wise men started it all, some say. Still, I like the way the Magi gave their gifts, for they presumably returned "to the east" without expecting Mary and Joseph to give them anything in return. Their gifts were meant for the baby Jesus, but there seemed to be no...obligation in their giving....Often at Christmas, gifts become such a subtle power play, resulting in obligation. Such gifts may subtly say, "While my gift appears free, repay me in kind," or "Enjoy this, Joe, but you owe me one now..."
>
> Let me suggest two ways to give a grace gift. First, be sure it's impossible to measure the cost of your gift. My daughter's Italian mother-in-law has taught her to cook authentic Italian goods. So when my daughter wants to please me most, she fills a bowl with meatballs swimming in her marvelous marinara sauce, and I am content through long winters....Second, realize that non-material gifts are the best way to say, "Don't try to pay me back."...One friend promised to pray for me all through the Christmas season.[2]

Do you have some new ideas for gifts now?

DECEMBER 3

Be kind and compassionate to one another, forgiving each
other, just as in Christ God forgave you (Ephesians 4:32).

When you forgive someone, including your spouse, you find relief from the conflict within you. The pain you have felt for days, weeks, or years is healed. As Lewis Smedes puts it: "When you forgive someone for hurting you, you perform spiritual surgery inside your soul; you cut away the wrong that was done to you so that you can see your 'enemy' through the magic eyes that can heal your soul."[3]

A graphic illustration of forgiveness is seen in the life of a great artist.

> Leonardo da Vinci was one of the outstanding intellects of all time. We're told that just before he commenced work on his "Last Supper" he had a violent quarrel with a fellow painter. So enraged and bitter was Leonardo that he determined to paint the face of his enemy, the other artist, into the face of Judas. In this way, he could take his revenge and vent his spleen by handing the man down in infamy and scorn to succeeding generations. The face of Judas was therefore one of the first that he finished....
>
> But when Leonardo came to paint the face of Christ, he could make no progress. Something seemed to be baffling him, holding him back, frustrating his best efforts. At length he came to the conclusion that the thing which was checking and frustrating him was the fact that he had painted his enemy into the face of Judas. He therefore painted out the face of Judas and commenced anew on the face of Jesus, and this time with the success the ages have acclaimed.
>
> The lesson? You cannot at one and the same time be painting the features of Christ into your own life and painting another face with the colors of enmity and hatred.[4]

DECEMBER 4

He who dwells in the shelter of the Most High will
rest in the shadow of the Almighty (Psalm 91:1).

Before continuing with this meditation, read the remainder of Psalm 91 aloud together from your Bible.

What are you counting on for security? A CD account at the bank? An IRA for your retirement? An inheritance from a wealthy relative? These are all important, but none of them is really secure. The writer of Psalm 91 directs our thinking in a different direction. The first two verses tell us who God is and what we can expect by trusting in Him. There is no risk or danger of God not coming through. He will be there even when our other sources of security are not.

In verses 3-13 the psalmist expresses in detail the results of trusting in God. He uses imagery which would relate to the people living at that time. How would you express these thoughts in today's language and society? Reflect on that for a moment; share your thoughts with your partner.

Verse 5 talks about the terror of night. Many adults still fear the dark. And for many, darkness seems to threaten their sense of security. Do your fears increase at night? Do you worry more at night? Does your partner? If so, what do you ask of God at that time?

In the last three verses, the Lord Himself speaks, promising to rescue us, protect us, answer us, be with us, deliver us, honor us, satisfy us with long life, and show us His salvation. Why? Because we love Him. But be careful. God is not saying that He will get you out of every trouble. He may not make all your problems go away, even though you wish He would. But He is saying that He will be with you during your difficulties.

Are you and your spouse facing something today in which you need to be reminded of God's promises in Psalm 91? Talk about it, then express your trust in the Lord together.

DECEMBER 5

Never will I leave you (Hebrews 13:5).

"I know that I can trust my partner. When he gives me his word, I can count on it."

These words reflect security. Being able to count on the word of another person is comforting. And this is one of the ingredients which makes marriages last. When your mind is filled with doubts and uncertainty in any relationship, you feel at the mercy of that person. We want to have someone in our life whom we can count on. We want to be able to take him or her at his or her word. Often as children we heard the promises our friends made to us. We believed them. But when they broke their promises we soon learned not to trust others. We learned to be cautious, to protect ourselves from broken dreams.

Because we are human, there are times when we don't follow through on what we say. We attempt to, but we fail. Fortunately there is one person we can count on to do what He says. God comes through with the promises He makes. And what He offers is so much better than what anyone else can promise. Consider these verses:

- "Never will I leave you; never will I forsake you" (Hebrews 13:5). What a promise!
- "Surely I am with you always, to the very end of the age" (Matthew 28:20). He guarantees unending companionship.
- "You may ask me for anything in my name, and I will do it" (John 14:14). Did you notice what He said: "I will"?
- "Whoever comes to me I will never drive away" (John 6:37). That's a promise of acceptance.

If you want to count on someone, you know whom to go to. And because He is already part of your life, you can also become a dependable person, even more dependable than you are today.

DECEMBER 6

I want to know Christ and the power of his
resurrection and the fellowship of sharing
in his sufferings (Philippians 3:10).

How do you relate to God? Richard Exley has identified four different ways that believers tend to respond to God. As you consider these four ways, try to determine which of them best represents the way you relate to God.

First, there are some people who love God for self's sake. They use God for their own benefit and try to get out of Him all they can for themselves. Getting is their goal, and they know little about the real meaning of a relationship.

There are others who move past this level and want to be used by God "for His glory." They are involved in doing things for God, but they often lack wisdom and love. Perhaps this level is best represented in the prayer of Mozart's rival Salieri in the film *Amadeus*: "Lord, make me a great composer. Let me celebrate Your glory through music, and be celebrated myself. Make me famous through the world, dear God; make me immortal. After I die, let people speak my name forever with love for what I wrote." Many want to be used by God, but they also want to share the limelight with God.

The third level is the desire to be like Christ. This person longs "to be conformed to the likeness of [God's] Son" (Romans 8:29). His or her prayer is not so much "give me" as it is "make me" or "use me."

The last level focuses on spiritual intimacy. When you reach this level you simply hunger for the relationship of knowing God and being known by Him.[5]

Perhaps we all start out with demanding prayers. But as we grow we realize that there is more to any relationship—including marriage—than just getting. Remember that your relationship with Jesus Christ is more than something you get or do. It's an expression of who you are in Him. Where is your relationship today? Where would you like it to be tomorrow? On what level would you say your marriage relationship exists? On what level would you like it to be? Discuss this together.

DECEMBER 7

*Behold, as for the proud one, his soul is not
right within him; but the righteous will live
by his faith* (Habakkuk 2:4, NASB).

Habakkuk is a small book tucked near the end of the Old Testament. Perhaps you thought the prophet's words about faith came from the Book of Romans. Well, you're right. The theme of the righteous living by faith is found in Romans (1:17) and also in Galatians (3:11). The repetition of this theme alerts us to its importance in our lives.

Rev. Bob Kraning, a former director of Forest Home Christian Conference Grounds in Southern California, gave an inspiring message on Habakkuk 2:4. He cited three factors about faith which are important to every Christian.

First, faith gives us a special way of seeing the present and the future. We are able to believe in the potential and possibilities of others rather than see them remain the way they are for the rest of their lives. Faith frees us up to encourage others to be all they can become.

Second, faith enables us to endure under difficult circumstances. It's a way of living life in the face of unpleasantries. When you live by faith, you become a transcender. We're able to go beyond the limits, to step over the obstacles, to override the limitations around us, and to handle situations which seem to be totally overwhelming. Read Habakkuk 3:17-19 for an example of faith. The prophet's situation seems overwhelming. But look at his attitude! What would happen in your marriage if you responded to your problems in this manner? Perhaps reading verse 18 out loud each day would make a difference in your life.

Third, faith pleases our God. It's His plan that we learn to live in total trust upon Him no matter what the circumstances. Risky? Yes. Somewhat scary? Yes. But consider the alternative.

DECEMBER 8

*But just as he who called you is holy, so be
holy in all you do; for it is written: "Be holy,
because I am holy"* (1 Peter 1:15,16).

Do you want to know how to get the most out of your life? The
answer is clear in Scripture, but perhaps it's not the most popular
one for many people. Let's consider what the apostle Paul had to say
about it:

> Paul said that we are "created according to God, in true
> righteousness and holiness" (Ephesians 4:24).
>
> To be like (according to) God is a big order. What do we
> have to do to be like God? The key words are righteousness
> and holiness.
>
> To be righteous is to line up our lives with the claims and
> principles of a higher authority. It is to have a sense of moral
> integrity that reflects the very nature of God. It is to accept
> eagerly and joyfully the responsibilities God gives us through
> His Word as the essence of productive living.
>
> In the practical sense, righteousness completes assign-
> ments, keeps promises, pays bills, honors commitments, keeps
> appointments, strives to be on time, and establishes a reputa-
> tion of reliability.
>
> To be holy is to live out this righteousness in an observ-
> able way so that people will see our good works and glorify
> God (see 1 Peter 2:12). To be holy is to be set apart or conse-
> crated for service in the kingdom. It is a behavioral style that
> thinks like God, loves what God loves, hates what God hates,
> relates to other people as God has related to us, and acts like
> God acts.[6]

That's quite a lifestyle, isn't it? Have you ever wondered what that
means for your marriage? How can righteousness and holiness be
reflected in your marriage today?

DECEMBER 9

Therefore confess your sins to each other and pray for
each other so that you may be healed (James 5:16).

Bless this husband. Bless him as provider and protector. Sustain him in all the pressures that come with the task of stewarding a family. May his strength be his wife's boast and pride, and may he so live that his wife may find in him the haven for which the heart of a woman truly longs.

"Bless this wife. Give her a tenderness that makes her great, a deep sense of understanding, and a strong faith in You. Give her that inner beauty of soul that never fades, that eternal youth that is found in holding fast to the things that never age. May she so live that her husband may be pleased to reverence her in the shrine of his heart.

"Teach them that marriage is not living for each other. It is two people uniting and joining hands to serve You. Give them a great spiritual purpose in life.

"May they minimize each other's weaknesses and be swift to praise and magnify each other's strengths so that they might view each other through a lover's kind and patient eyes. Give them a little something to forgive each day, that their love might learn to be long-suffering.

"Bless them and develop their characters as they walk together with You. Give them enough hurts to keep them humane, enough failures to keep their hands clenched tightly in Yours, and enough of success to make them sure they walk with You throughout all of their life.

"May they travel together as friends and lovers, brother and sister, husband and wife, father and mother, and as servants of Christ until He shall return or until that day when one shall lay the other into the arms of God. This we ask through Jesus Christ, the great lover of our souls. Amen."[7]

DECEMBER 10

The Lord was with Joseph (Genesis 39:2).

Have you read the story of Joseph lately (Genesis 37, 39-50)? His experience is applicable to us today. Did you ever wonder if he tried to figure out what God was doing with his life? Sometimes we do. Consider the words of Richard Exley on this topic. They will give you something to think about.

> We, too, can endure any hardship, overcome any difficulty, as long as we can be assured that God is with us. What we cannot endure is the thought of facing life's vicissitudes alone. Yet it is at this very point that many of us lose heart. Somewhere we have picked up the notion that if we live a faithful and obedient life, we will be spared pain and sorrow that is so much a part of our fallen world. Such an idea is neither Christian nor scriptural and sets us up for some devastating disappointments. When we equate all suffering with the absence of God, or at least with His disapproval, we leave ourselves open to unspeakable temptations. At the very time we need most to be assured of God's love and faithfulness, our theology leaves us with nothing but tormenting questions....
>
> A common mistake, in times of difficulty and disappointment, is to try to figure out how God is working (that is, what good He is bringing out of all our suffering). It is a mistake, because, for the most part, His ways are far beyond anything we might imagine. In fact, trying to discover His ultimate purpose in such situations often leads either to absurd conclusions or to outright despair. For example, the way God worked in Joseph's life was obvious only in retrospect. Who could have imagined how He would weave slavery, false accusations and imprisonment into His grand design?[8]

DECEMBER 11

*Two are better than one, because they have a good
return for their work. If one falls down, his friend
can help him up. But pity the man who falls and
has no one to help him up!* (Ecclesiastes 4:9,10).

Jesus,
I've been thinking a lot about friends lately.
Everybody is talking about relationships,
    and really knowing each other,
      but no one seems to do much about it.
Or everyone wants to have the same friend
    —that person who's up in front of the crowd
    or the gal with the toothpaste smile
    and the winsome personality.
Hardly anyone seems willing
    to build relationships with ordinary people.
You know—the harried housewife with three preschoolers,
    the overweight, under-confident teenager,
    or the quiet guy on the edge of the crowd.
Who was Your friend, Lord?
I know you had a lot of acquaintances,
    and the twelve who shared the ministry,
    but who was Your friend?
I mean the person
    with whom You could let your hair down.
Where You didn't have to watch every word
    or meet someone's unending expectations.
You know, where did You go when You had to get away,
    but You couldn't bear to be alone again?
Was Lazarus that special friend for you, Lord?
I think maybe he was.
I started to pray, 'Give me a friend like that,'
    but I thought better of it.
Instead I pray,
'Let me be a friend like that.'"
Amen."[9]

DECEMBER 12

Darkness was over the surface of the deep, and the Spirit of God was hovering over the waters. And God said, "Let there be light," and there was light (Genesis 1:2,3).

Maybe you had this experience as a child or even as an adult. You enter a basement, an attic, or a room in a strange building at night. Before you can find the light switch the door behind you slams shut, sealing you in pitch darkness. You can't see your hand in front of your face, and you can feel the panic rising within you. You start to grope around the room for the light switch. Finally you locate it and flip it on, and immediately the room floods with light. Your panic flees instantly as your eyes welcome the security of the light.

We rely so much on electricity that we almost can't live without it. But there is another source of light which is even more important for us today. It's the Holy Spirit. The Spirit was actively involved in the work of creation. When God creates, He does so through the Holy Spirit. Both in the work of creation and redemption, the Holy Spirit functions as the divine illuminator. He illumines the Word of God to us as we read it so we can understand. He illumines our mind and guides us in how we are to pray. He illumines the direction for our life.

Being in a room without light is not the only struggle with darkness we encounter in daily life. Each of us struggles with the darkness of understanding life and marriage. Why did this or that happen? Why did our spouse do what he did or say what she said? And we often feel like we are in darkness when our understanding of God and His Word is clouded.

Where is the darkness in your life today? Where does your partner sense darkness in his or her life? Are you groping for spiritual insight or for God's will for your life? The illuminator is available. All you have to do is turn on the switch by inviting the Holy Spirit to flood your lives with His light. Allow Him to flood your path with light today. You always see better when the light is on.

DECEMBER 13

Get rid of all bitterness (Ephesians 4:31).

You've just finished a delicious meal at a gourmet restaurant. The waiter brings the dessert menu with numerous delectable choices. You select something you've never tried before; the foreign name leads you to believe it's rich and sweet. You cut into it with your fork, slip the first bite into your mouth, and begin to eat. But your mouth suddenly goes into shock! Your taste buds expected something tasty and sweet, but the expression on your face reflects a bitter taste which is curling your tongue. You try to wash the taste away with a gulp of coffee, but it lingers on your palate, completely obliterating the last hints of the main course you enjoyed so much.

Have you experienced a bitter taste in your mouth which overpowers other tastes? The same occurs in a marriage relationship. Often bitterness begins with the common hurts and disappointments of life. But if not dealt with, these feelings of bitterness erode positive attitudes and turn a joyful heart and marriage sour. Bitterness creates a negative disposition which leads to a person developing a tongue as sharp as a two-edged sword. And bitterness usually creates an overall feeling of ill will toward life, God, others, and ourselves. It's a source of marital pollution which in time destroys everything in its way.

Why are some people so bitter? Why are some husbands and wives so sour in their attitudes? Because they have been hurt, offended, taken advantage of, betrayed—perhaps not once but again and again. And the offenses snowball into one giant attitude of bitterness.

Regardless of the source of bitterness, today's verse is clear: Get rid of all bitterness. It doesn't say "Get rid of it if..." It doesn't say "Get rid of it when..." It says "Get rid of it"—period. Why? Because a life without bitterness is the best way to live—for you and for the others in your life.

DECEMBER 14

*Get rid of all bitterness....Be kind and compassionate
to one another, forgiving each other, just as in
Christ God forgave you* (Ephesians 4:31,32).

How do you find freedom from the bitterness which pollutes lives
and marriage relationships? One single word: *forgiveness.* What
is forgiveness? Forgiveness is

- no longer being chained to the hurt.
- no longer using the wonderful gift of memory as a weapon.
- no longer hurting others as we have been hurt.
- never mentioning the offense again.
- making yourself vulnerable and open to being hurt again.
- learning to live a life free from lingering pain.

In his helpful book *Forgive and Forget,* Lewis Smedes writes:

> Forgiving, then, is a new vision and a new feeling that
> is given to the person who forgives.... True forgivers do not
> pretend they don't suffer. They do not pretend the wrong does
> not matter much....
> You will know that forgiveness has begun when you recall
> those who hurt you and feel the power to wish them well.[10]

What about a future hurt? Yes, there will be some. How do you
tackle the fresh hurt? Face it; accept it. And as you learn to forgive,
learn to forget. We don't really forget anything we experience, but we
can head in that direction by disregarding hurts, overlooking them,
and ceasing to notice them. This will help change emotional remembering to historical remembering.

December 15

Do not love the world or anything in the world....
For everything in the world...comes not from the
Father but from the world (1 John 2:16,19).

Temptation—the lure to do something wrong. We all experience it. When he was in Egypt, Joseph was tempted. You can read about it in Genesis 39. Potiphar's wife kept after him day after day trying to get him into her bed. But he resisted. How did he have the strength to withstand her seduction? There are two reasons given in God's Word for Joseph's response.

First, he would not violate Potiphar's trust in him. Joseph told her, "No one is greater in this house than I am. My master has withheld nothing from me except you, because you are his wife" (v. 9). Potiphar left Joseph in charge in the house because he trusted him. And Joseph was not about to break that trust.

Your partner trusts you. You trust your partner. Any straying from a trust relationship, including the times you let your mind or emotions wander to other members of the opposite sex, is a direct violation of trust. Resisting sexual temptations is a sign of integrity.

Second, Joseph resisted temptation because he would not disobey God. He believed that his involvement in an illicit relationship would be an offense against God. Joseph said so to Potiphar's wife: "How then could I do such a wicked thing and sin against God?" (v. 9).

You would do well to memorize Joseph's statement and ask the Holy Spirit to bring it to your conscious mind whenever you are sexually tempted by another person. The temptations are real. They are there. But so is God. Let Him help you in your resistance to temptation.[11]

DECEMBER 16

God is faithful, who will not allow you to
be tempted beyond what you are able, but
with the temptation will provide the way of
escape also (1 Corinthians 10:13, NASB).

Joseph was faithful to God and resisted the temptation of Potiphar's wife. How was he rewarded for this? He was thrown into prison (Genesis 39:13-20)! Have you ever wondered how Joseph felt about that? He did the right thing and ended up in prison for his efforts. It doesn't seem fair, does it? Can we learn anything from Joseph's experience and from the Scriptures about resisting temptation? Yes.

First, it's often when you are successful that you are the most vulnerable to temptation. You need to be on guard because Satan will attack you when things are going well. Paul put it bluntly: "If you think you are standing firm, be careful that you don't fall!" (1 Corinthians 10:12).

Second, unless you have clear-cut, definite convictions about what is right, it will be difficult for you to handle temptation. Joseph had a commitment to his Heavenly Father and his earthly master. He would not violate the trust of his master or sin against God.

Third, you will have a difficult time resisting temptation if you constantly open yourself to sinful opportunities. Not only did Joseph refuse the woman's invitations to go to bed with her, he also refused even to be with her (Genesis 39:10). Are you consistently exposing your eyes or your mind to the kinds of things which will erode your resistance to sin? You can't avoid everything, of course, but the blatant and subtle messages in movies and television programs for multiple sexual relationships bombard us. If you saturate your thinking with these ideas, in time you may begin to accept the media's portrayal as truth. It may be a lifestyle for some people but not for God's people.

Like Joseph, your life may not always be trouble free just because you resist temptation. But God will honor you for your stand as He did Joseph.[12]

DECEMBER 17

When [Joseph's] brothers saw that their father loved
him more than any of them, they hated him and
could not speak a kind word to him (Genesis 37:4).

Jealousy and hatred can destroy family relationships. Joseph wasn't a perfect brother, of course, but the hatred Joseph felt from his brothers wasn't all his own doing. Their father Jacob clearly favored Joseph above his other sons. Preferential treatment like this usually sets the stage for unrest in a family. Think back to your family. Who was the favorite? Did he or she receive special treatment? If so, what? Have you ever been the favorite of someone (other than your partner!)? How did it feel? How did others respond to your being the favorite?

One of the factors which can interfere with a marriage is a poor relationship with one of your own family members: a parent, sibling, grandparent, aunt, uncle, or cousin. You may feel jealousy or hatred toward this relative because of something which happened in the past. It's difficult for you to like this person. You would rather avoid him or her because of the bitter feelings between you. And you may expect your partner to have the same feelings and side with you. But it's important to realize that your spouse doesn't have the same history to deal with that you do. Your partner can talk through your feelings with you and help you work through them, but he or she may not want to react to your relative in the same way as you do.

Some of these problem relationships may have the potential for reconciliation and some may not because of the other person's unwillingness. But there are some things you can do to keep jealousy and hatred from spreading in your family.

First, be sure not to favor any of your children above the others. Treat each of your children and your other relatives with respect and concern.

Second, pray together for the relatives with whom you have difficulty. When you pray, your feelings, your reactions, and some of your struggles will diminish.

DECEMBER 18

Elkanah her husband would say to her, "Hannah,
why are you weeping? Why don't you eat? Why
are you downhearted?" (1 Samuel 1:8).

The Word of God is our guideline for how to respond to one another in marriage. Yet there are very few examples of couples in the Bible to study. Samuel's parents, Hannah and Elkanah, provide a rare glimpse of such interaction. Read the entire account in 1 Samuel 1:2-20. It's quite interesting.

Hannah was very unhappy because she was childless. And according to the custom of those days, Elkanah, a wealthy man, was able to take another wife, Peninnah, to bear him children. Peninnah wasn't a very loving woman. She would antagonize Hannah by reminding her that she was barren. But Elkanah loved Hannah, listened patiently to her problems, and attempted to comfort her. He also treated Hannah very well. In fact, he seemed to favor Hannah over Peninnah (v. 5).

Elkanah is a positive model of a husband. He noticed that his wife was distressed. Not all husbands do. He went to his wife and tried to draw out her feelings and lift her discouragement. Not all husbands do. All too often they want to fix the problem instead of listen. Apparently Elkanah also tried to do a little fixing. He said, "Don't I mean more to you than ten sons?" (v. 8). Perhaps he was kidding, perhaps he was serious—we don't know. For all husbands, a good question at a time like this is, "How can I help you the most: by listening, being with you, or making suggestions?" Asking a direct question is a lot better than trying to be a mind reader.

Elkanah made another statement in verse 23 which reflects one more quality of a good husband. During a discussion with Hannah in which their opinions differed, Elkanah said, "Do what seems best to you." That shows respect, belief, and trust. And those qualities make healthy marriages today. How can each of you show a greater amount of respect, belief, and trust in one another's abilities? It helps to talk about it.

DECEMBER 19

*But let endurance and steadfastness and patience have
full play and do a thorough work* (James 1:4, AMP).

Work, effort, direction, steadfastness, time—words which are familiar to some people and foreign to others, especially when it comes to marriage. But they make the difference between a lifetime of being together or a brief time of struggle and a visit to court. Consider what occurs when these words are left out of marriage:

> Drifting is one of the most common forms of marital failure. In fact, I would venture to say that the majority of those couples found in our churches from Sunday to Sunday have marriages which are "adrift." Just think about that for a moment. Look across the pews. Would you guess that a majority of your friends have marriages that are in trouble? Probably not. Neither would they.
>
> Drifting. Not only is it the most common form of marital failure, it is also the most dangerous. It is subtle. It is quiet. It is non-offensive. It sounds no alarms. It just gradually creeps into our lives. And then it destroys.
>
> Step by step, the emotional deadness sneaks up on us as we move further and further away from our mates. The appearance of "all is well" is our placard. We fail to see the absence of real caring. Why should we see it? We have our pre-occupations to keep us busy. The absence of emotional pain is accepted as a sign that everything is okay. We are busy, we are content, and everything is "fine." We have grown accustomed to the way things are.[13]

Are there any drifting tendencies in your marriage? It might help to take a close look at them right now. Sometimes they are very subtle, but they are there.

DECEMBER 20

Godliness [spiritual training] is useful and of value in
everything and in every way (1 Timothy 4:8, AMP).

Success in marriage doesn't just happen. It requires planning and discipline. Consider one husband's thoughts on the subject:

> I do not deal with problems as they arise because it is easy or because it is comfortable. Most of the time it would be easier to avoid some of these conflicts and problems but I recognize the consequences of avoidance—the distancing, the coldness, the indifference. I do not want these saboteurs to creep into my marriage, progressively destroying that which I hold most dear....
>
> To counter this tendency requires planning. I have to work at placing my marriage in a priority position. I have to consciously contend with these pitfalls. I have had to develop my own personal method, something particularly suited to me, in order to move toward my goal...an intimate relationship. You will have to do the same.
>
> True success is never an easy achievement. Happy and fulfilling marriages are products of extreme effort. They are desired, sought after, fought for, and planned. They never just happen. Couples frequently complain how their marriage just fell apart. All of a sudden, they just fell out of love...just lost interest in a husband...just fell in love with another person or career. Nothing just happens...whether good or bad.
>
> Healthy marriages follow a road...a road that is planned. You do not have to plan to fail. That can be accomplished without planning...and usually is. But you DO have to plan to succeed.[14]

DECEMBER 21

Roll your works upon the Lord—commit and
trust them wholly to Him;...so shall your plans be
established and succeed (Proverbs 16:3, AMP).

What are you committed to right now in your life? Think about it for minute: What are your burning commitments? What has God called you to be committed to? Think about your commitment to marriage as you read these thoughts shared by a marriage counselor:

> The commitment to marriage as a relationship allows for the development of intimacy. Within the secure context established by the institution of marriage, the relational vows are fulfilled. By plan and design, mates can give to and receive from one another demonstrations of love. By so doing, they foster growth and closeness in all of the dimensions of love. At least, this is the ideal.
>
> Things do not always go according to plan, and not infrequently, there is no plan at all. Hectic schedules, selfish motives, the demands of daily living...these culprits and many like them combine to dim our memory of exactly what was said during the wedding ceremony. The once-spoken vows are forgotten. The once-demonstrated pledges of love become absent behaviors....
>
> Commitment is a characteristic of behaving in love....A prerequisite to marital stability and growth is a commitment to both marriage as an institution and marriage as a relationship. Commitment to marriage as an institution establishes a context in which growth can occur. Commitment to marriage as a relationship guarantees that the act by which a marriage is built will be demonstrated. Together, and only together, a marriage is made.[15]

Tell your partner which statement made the most sense to you and which one will most enhance your marriage today!

DECEMBER 22

And they were continually devoting
themselves...to prayer (Acts 2:42, NASB).

D o you want an intimate marriage? Of course you do. Deep intimacy comes from a pattern of praying for and with one another.
But is there a biblical mandate for this? Interesting question. We can
assume from today's verse that the early believers prayed aloud together
for one another. But there are many other instances in Scripture which
admonish us to pray for one another. As you read on, remember: Your
spouse is the primary "one another" in your life!

In the Book of Ephesians Paul gives us a model of intercessory
prayer. In 1:18 he prays that the believers might come to know God
better: "I pray...that the eyes of your heart may be enlightened." Have
you prayed that prayer for yourself recently? Have you prayed for your
partner in this way? Perhaps you could take a moment right now and
talk about how each of you would like to know God better. Identify
the areas in which you have questions. Perhaps there are questions
you continue to struggle with that you have never shared with another
person. God is not threatened by your doubts, and your spouse will
gladly pray about them with you.

Paul also prays that the believers will "know this love that surpasses
knowledge" (3:19). Perhaps this next question will surprise you, but
here it is anyway: Have you ever prayed that your partner will know
and experience Christ's love more than yours? Interesting thought?
Each of us has a need to love and be loved, but that need can never be
adequately filled by a person. Only God can completely fill our need
for love.

Paul also prays that the Ephesians will know the power of God in
their lives (1:19,20). Do you want to do something exciting for your
partner? Look at him or her and promise, "I'm going to pray that you
fully know the power of God in your life each day. You can count on
that." Wait and see what that prayer will do for your spouse, your marriage, and your own life![16]

DECEMBER 23

When [the shepherds] had seen him, they spread
the word…about this child.…[They] returned,
glorifying and praising God for all the things
they had heard and seen (Luke 2:17,20).

Christmas traditions—we all have them. They're sometimes a source of marital conflict. Perhaps you came from a home where gifts were opened Christmas eve, but your partner's family opened them on Christmas day. One of you always had roast duck for dinner, and the other had ham. We all have different ways of celebrating Christ's birth.

Is it possible for believers to celebrate Christmas in a way which reflects the pattern in today's passage? Consider the shepherds. They spread the word about Christ, and they glorified and praised God at the Savior's birth. Take a moment now and talk together. How will you glorify and praise God on Christmas day? Will just the two of you praise Him together, or will your spiritual celebration occur with one or both of your families?

Let's take the pattern one step further. The shepherds shared with others about the birth of the Christ-child. We live in a world that celebrates Christmas. But many people don't celebrate it for what it really is. They focus on Santa Claus, gifts, or parties instead of Jesus, "the reason for the season." As you talk with others at work, at the health club, or at the market, how will you let them know what Christmas means to you? How could you tell them about the significance of Jesus Christ?

One man tells other people, "On December 25th we celebrate the birth of Jesus Christ. That's an important date for the history of the world. But there are two other dates that are even more important." Most people ask him, "What dates are those?" His response is, "The day Jesus died on the cross for our sins and three days later when He rose from the dead. If He hadn't done that, we would be lost. What do you think about Christ's death and resurrection?"

That's a different way to celebrate Christmas, isn't it?[17]

DECEMBER 24

There was no room for them in the inn (Luke 2:7).

Crowds—masses of people milling about, pushing, shoving, and looking for bargains. Perhaps that's why many people dread the shopping mall around Christmastime, especially on the day before Christmas. Frenzied shoppers with glazed expressions cling to their lists and scurry from store to store. Sometimes you have to elbow your way through the aisles to get to the department you want. Often you can hear the cry of a small child who is momentarily separated from his parents in the teeming crowd. Some couples drive to the mall, take one look at the cars and hordes of people, shake their heads in dismay, and leave. There's no room for them in the parking lot.

Have you had that experience? If so, perhaps you have a slight hint of what it must have been like for Joseph and Mary as they arrived in Bethlehem on that first Christmas eve. They too were pushed out. They looked and looked, but there was no room for them at the inn. Before He was even born, our Lord was rejected and turned away. The words "no room for you" followed Him throughout His life. Herod didn't have any place for Him in Israel, and He fled with His parents to Egypt. His hometown of Nazareth didn't welcome Him during His ministry. He even had to die outside the city and be buried in someone else's tomb. There was just no room for Him anywhere.

In the lives of many people today, He's still being crowded out. With all of the Christmas festivities, He is an afterthought. Instead of a place of honor at Christmas, Jesus Christ is often shoved into a corner. Jesus died for that innkeeper, for Herod, for the soldiers at the cross, and for us. He isn't asking to live in a room in our home; He wants to live forever in our hearts. He welcomes us as His own. Let's welcome Him into our thoughts, our daily lives, and each activity as we celebrate His birthday.

December 25

His name will be called...Prince
of Peace (Isaiah 9:6, NKJV).

Peace in our lives. Peace in our marriages. Peace between races. Peace between nations. Jesus Christ is the Prince of Peace, and He came to bring peace to a disturbed world. How has the Prince of Peace brought His peace to your little world?

We all ache for peace. When we turn on the news (and perhaps today would be a good day to leave the newscast off!) we hear of the upset in our communities and around the world. We hear politicians making promises about peace and leaders of nations claiming they have the only foolproof plan for peace. Don't believe them. They've been saying that for years. Peace between people comes through Jesus Christ. Man cannot produce a lasting peace, but Jesus Christ can. It starts with that inner peace which comes when He is present within a life. It spreads as that peace changes a life and as family members begin responding to one another through the guidance of Jesus Christ.

The peace that Jesus brought and that can be celebrated today is the peace of forgiveness and reconciliation. That's what Christmas is all about. And since today is the day we celebrate Jesus' birthday, what are you doing as a couple to make this a special day for Him? How will He be given the attention which is due Him? What will you sing to Him today around the table? Perhaps you could ask each person during Christmas dinner, "When did Jesus become real to you?" Ask each one to share the fondest memory they have of a worship experience at Christmastime.

How will you share His peace today? Talk about something you could do today as a family which would bring the peace of Christ to someone's life: visit someone in the hospital or nursing home, phone an elderly relative who lives far away to wish him or her a merry Christmas, serve meals or wash dishes in a center for the homeless in your community, etc. May His peace and joy be upon you as you share Him today!

December 26

*Jesus Christ is the same yesterday
and today and forever* (Hebrews 13:8).

It's over; another Christmas has come and gone. For many people
the day after is a time of collapse, letdown, and exhaustion. You're
probably in the throes of cleaning up the mess of crumpled wrapping
paper and Christmas dinner scraps. Perhaps you still have a house full
of relatives. The children are playing with their newly acquired toys,
and some of you are already back to work.

Here's a sobering thought: Yesterday was another of only about 70
Christmases you will experience in your lifetime. Are most of them still
ahead of you, or have you already enjoyed 40 or 50 of them? Sometimes
we are so busy with Christmas that it goes by as a blur. As you pause
to think about yesterday's experiences, discuss the following questions
together:

> 1. What do you think the day after that first Christmas
> was like for Joseph and Mary? For the shepherds? For the
> innkeeper?
>
> 2. What do you imagine non-Christians think about the
> day after Christ's birthday?
>
> 3. What traditions did you observe in your celebration
> yesterday from your original family? From your partner's orig-
> inal family? How many of these traditions are based on the
> spiritual nature of the holiday? The secular nature?
>
> 4. Some of the holiday glitter has already worn off since
> yesterday, and in a week the tree and most of the other deco-
> rations will be gone. It will be business as usual again very
> soon. How will your life during the coming year be different
> because of the celebration of Christ's birth yesterday?

Perhaps the celebration of Christmas is over, but the greatest news
of all is still with us: Jesus Christ was born and He lives today. In
that sense Christmas will remain with us for another 364 days—and
forever!

DECEMBER 27

[Abraham] was looking for the city which
has foundations, whose architect and builder
is God (Hebrews 11:10, NASB).

Television has developed a number of interesting programs in hopes
of attracting viewers. Science fiction, tales of future life, and even
programs about aliens invading our world are common. We watch programs about creatures from outer space and think, "How ridiculous!
Shows about aliens are entertaining, but they aren't realistic. Aliens
don't exist." But aliens do exist! That may come as a shock to you, but
there are aliens all around you. You may even be one yourself. Anyone
who has a relationship with God through His Son Jesus Christ is an
alien in this world.

The first alien mentioned in the Bible was Abraham: "By faith
Abraham, when he was called, obeyed by going out to a place which
he was to receive for an inheritance; and he went out, not knowing
where he was going. By faith he lived as an alien in the land of promise,
as in a foreign land, dwelling in tents...for he was looking for the city
which has foundations, whose architect and builder is God" (Hebrews
11:8-10, NASB).

Abraham recognized his temporary status. The earth was a temporary dwelling place for him. He was a stranger sojourning in the land.
He interacted with the pagan people around him and had a very fine
reputation. He was respected by others. But he never got caught up in
the lifestyle of the rich and famous of his time. He knew that he was
there for a purpose. He knew that God had called him for a task even
though he "died in faith, without receiving the promises" (Hebrews
11:13, NASB).

Where is your focus? Is your concern directed more toward the little
world around you? It's really easy to lose sight of God in this setting.
We are outnumbered by unbelievers and surrounded by a lifestyle
which certainly doesn't reflect the presence of God. Just remember—
you too are an alien. This world is not your home, you're just passing
through. How can you apply this truth to your married life today?

DECEMBER 28

Good sense makes a man restrain his anger,
and it is his glory to overlook a transgression
or an offense (Proverbs 19:11, AMP).

Today we will look into the Word of God for insight concerning anger. Reflect on these verses quoted from The Living Bible in light of your relationships with others—especially your partner.

> A short-tempered man is a fool. He hates the man who is patient (Proverbs 14:17).
>
> A quick-tempered man starts fights; a cool-tempered man tries to stop them (Proverbs 15:18).
>
> It is better to be slow-tempered than famous; it is better to have self-control than to control an army (Proverbs 16:32).
>
> A fool gets into constant fights. His mouth is his undoing! His words endanger him (Proverbs 18:6,7).
>
> A short-tempered man must bear his own penalty; you can't do much to help him. If you try once you must try a dozen times! (Proverbs 19:19).
>
> Keep away from angry, short-tempered men, lest you learn to be like them and endanger your soul (Proverbs 22:24,25).
>
> A rebel shouts in anger; a wise man holds his temper in and cools it (Proverbs 29:11).
>
> There is more hope for a fool than for a man of quick temper (Proverbs 29:20).
>
> A hot-tempered man starts fights and gets into all kinds of trouble (Proverbs 29:22).
>
> Anger doesn't make us good, as God demands that we must be (James 1:20).

Which one of these passages, lived out in your marriage, will bring about the most positive change? Talk about how you will apply the Scripture in a practical way.

December 29

Do not be afraid (Exodus 14:13).

Everyone needs a safe place in life. We all need a sanctuary where we can be who we really are with no pretense. The ideal place for relational safety is marriage. Marriage is a place for intimacy and joy to exist with the absence of fear. Did you ever think about the relationship between intimacy, joy, and fear? Let's consider some thoughts by James Olthuis. His words will probably cause you to think a bit:

> Words fail when speaking about joy. Often words come more easily when we share pain, suffering, and tragedy; somehow they seem more true to the human scene. Nevertheless, joy is an essential ingredient of intimacy. Without joy—not manufactured sensation or frantic scurrying, but the contentment that surprises—there is no time or place for the amazed lingering that is the heart and mystery of intimacy. Without joy, we remain empty and ravished, nervous lest we miss out on something, obsessed and on the run.
>
> Fear freezes; joy thaws. Sluggish hearts begin to stream with the waters of love....We can be together and it's good. It is not always (or even mainly) high-intensity baring of the soul. It may be as simple (and as difficult) as the mutual enjoyment of a cup of tea or a walk in the woods. Joy is intimacy without fear.
>
> Marital joy is intimate connection with my partner. Joy calls us to live together more fully and deeply in the Presence for the healing of ourselves, other persons, and all of God's creatures. It means taking more risks, deepening our intimacy.[18]

Share your thoughts about joy, intimacy, and fear in marriage. How do they connect and relate in your marriage?

DECEMBER 30

The Holy Spirit also testifies to us (Hebrews 10:15).

Where does a married couple find the inner strength for a godly relationship in this sinful world? In the indwelling presence of the Holy Spirit. God's Spirit is not an impersonal force; He is a living person dwelling within us to help us. Ask one another right now how much you really know about the Third Person of the Trinity.

What does Scripture say about the Holy Spirit being a person instead of a force? All the elements which make up a personality are found in the Holy Spirit. Here are several characteristics of the Holy Spirit which indicate that He is a living person:

- The Holy Spirit is endowed with understanding and wisdom (1 Corinthians 2:10);
- He has a will (1 Corinthians 12:11);
- He loves (Romans 15:30);
- People can test Him (Acts 5:9), lie to Him (Acts 5:3), and grieve Him (Ephesians 4:30);
- He speaks (1 Timothy 4:1);
- He teaches (Luke 12:12; John 14:26);
- He intercedes for us (Romans 8:26).

The Holy Spirit is also described in Scripture by personal titles. He is called the Comforter, the Witness, the Justifier, and Sanctifier.

Why is it important to your marriage to establish an understanding of the personality of God the Holy Spirit? Because the more you know about the Person you worship, follow, and receive strength from, the better prepared you will be to serve God in your marriage and minister to your spouse in a practical way. Perhaps this introduction will prompt you both to learn more about the Holy Spirit and how He can work in your life.

December 31

When the Holy Spirit controls our lives he will
produce this kind of fruit in us: love, joy, peace,
patience, kindness, goodness, faithfulness, gentleness,
and self-control (Galatians 5:22,23, TLB).

Where are you in your marital journey—the beginning, the middle, or near the end? Wherever you are in this journey, the one word which will make all the difference in the world is commitment. Commitment helps you create positive memories. It's a costly discipline which can bring tension and questions at the same time it brings peace, maturity, and stability. With change coming at us so rapidly, commitment to living by faith will guide you through this time.

As you approach the new year, commit your life to the person of Jesus Christ in a fresh way. Commit your life to the Word of God which will bring you stability. Commit yourselves as a couple to a life of prayer. It will enhance your completeness and oneness while it puts your differences and adjustments in better perspective.

Commit yourself to seeing your partner as having such worth, value, and dignity that God sent His Son to die for him or her. Commit your life to giving your marriage top priority in terms of time, energy, thought, and planning for growth. Commit yourself to a life of fidelity and faithfulness in mind and behavior regardless of your feelings or the lure of life around you.

Commit and open yourself to the working of the Holy Spirit in your life. May the fruit of the Spirit be reflected in your individual lives and in your marriage in the coming year.

NOTES

January

1. Dwight H. Small, *Christian: Celebrate Your Sexuality* (Old Tappan, NJ: Fleming H. Revell, 1974), p. 144.
2. June Hunt, *Seeing Yourself through God's Eyes* (Grand Rapids, MI: Zondervan Publishers, 1989), adapted from p. 67.
3. Lloyd John Ogilvie, *Longing to Be Free* (Eugene, OR: Harvest House Publishers, 1984), p. 23.
4. Booth Tarkington, source unknown.
5. Tim Hansel, *You Gotta Keep Dancin'* (Elgin, IL: David C. Cook Publishers, 1985), p. 55.
6. Paul Walker, *How to Keep Your Joy* (Nashville: Thomas Nelson Publishers, 1987), p. 17.
7. Quoted in Jon Johnson, *Walls or Bridges* (Grand Rapids, MI: Baker Book House, 1988), pp. 176,177. (Quoted by W.T. Purkiser, "Five Ways to Have a Nervous Breakdown," *Herald of Holiness,* October 9, 1974).
8. Larry Richards and Norman Wakefield, *Fruit of the Spirit* (Grand Rapids, MI: Zondervan Publishers, 1981), p. 108.
9. Quoted in Charles R. Swindoll, *Growing Strong in the Seasons of Life* (Portland, OR: Multnomah Press, 1983), p. 66.
10. Ibid., p. 83.
11. Source unknown.

February

1. Nancy Groom, *Married Without Masks* (Colorado Springs, CO: NavPress, 1989), pp. 98, 99.
2. Charles Haddon Spurgeon, source unknown.
3. June Hunt, *Seeing Yourself Through God's Eyes* (Grand Rapids, MI: Zondervan Publishers, 1989), adapted from p. 33.
4. Ibid., p. 61.
5. Harry Hollis, Jr., *Thank God for Sex* (Nashville: Broadman Press, 1975), pp. 11, 12, 55, 109, 110.
6. Lloyd John Ogilvie, *Longing to Be Free* (Eugene, OR: Harvest House Publishers, 1984), adapted from pp. 21-27.
7. W. Phillip Keller, *A Gardener Looks at the Fruits of the Spirit* (Waco, TX: Word Books, 1979), p. 146.
8. Jon Johnson, *Walls or Bridges* (Grand Rapids, MI: Baker Book House, 1988), adapted from pp. 194-95.
9. Charles R. Swindoll, *Growing Strong in the Seasons of Life* (Portland, OR: Multnomah Press, 1983), adapted from pp. 169, 170.
10. H. Norman Wright, *Making Peace with Your Partner* (Waco, TX: Word Books, 1988), adapted from pp. 173, 174.
11. Swindoll, *Growing Strong in the Seasons of Life,* pp. 21, 22.
12. Ibid., p. 23.

13. Johnson, *Walls or Bridges,* adapted from pp. 206-08.

14. Ogilvie, *Longing to Be Free,* p. 77.

March

1. Mike Mason, *The Mystery of Marriage* (Portland, OR: Multnomah Press, 1985), p. 85.

2. Gene Getz, *Believing God When You are Tempted to Doubt* (Ventura, CA: Regal Books, 1985), adapted from pp. 67-77.

3. Ibid., adapted from pp. 82-87.

4. Ibid., adapted from pp. 98, 99.

5. Ibid., adapted from pp. 116,117.

6. Lois Wyse, *Love Poems for the Very Married* (New York: Harper and Row, 1967), p. 41.

7. Colleen and Louis Evans, Jr., *My Lover, My Friend* (Old Tappan, NJ: Fleming H. Revell, 1976), pp. 121-23.

8. Keller, *A Gardener Looks at the Fruits of the Spirit,* pp. 126, 127.

9. Johnson, *Walls or Bridges,* adapted from pp. 185-88.

10. Gene Getz, *Living for Others When You'd Rather Live for Yourself* (Ventura, CA: Regal Books, 1985), adapted from pp. 12, 13.

11. Ibid., adapted from p. 74.

12. Ibid., adapted from pp. 78-80.

13. Lewis B. Smedes, "Forgiveness: The Power to Change the Past," *Christianity Today,* January 7, 1983, p. 26.

14. J.I. Packer, *Knowing God* (Downers Grove, IL: Inter-Varsity Press, 1973), p. 87.

15. H. Norman Wright, *Uncovering Your Hidden Fears* (Wheaton, IL: Tyndale House Publishers, 1989), adapted from pp. 71-74.

16. Joseph Cooke, *Free for the Taking* (Old Tappan, NJ: Fleming H. Revell, 1975), p. 29.

17. Lloyd John Ogilvie, *Lord of the Impossible* (Nashville: Abingdon Press, 1984), adapted from pp. 92-95.

18. Wright, *Uncovering Your Hidden Fears,* adapted from pp. 133, 134.

April

1. Chuck Swindoll, *Growing Strong in the Seasons of Life* (Portland, OR: Multnomah Press, 1983), adapted from p. 305.

2. Ibid., p. 357.

3. Ibid.

4. Ibid., adapted from pp. 357, 358.

5. Ed Wheat, *Love Life* (Grand Rapids, MI: Zondervan Publishing House, 1980), adapted from pp. 178, 179.

6. Richard Exley, *The Rhythm of Life* (Tulsa, OK: Harrison House, 1987), adapted from p. 31.

7. James C. Dobson, *Straight Talk to Men and Their Wives* (Waco, TX: Word Books, 1980), p. 148.

8. Swindoll, *Growing Strong in the Seasons of Life,* p. 111.

9. Max Lucado, *No Wonder They Call Him the Savior* (Portland, OR: Multnomah Press, 1986), pp. 105, 106.

10. Exley, *The Rhythm of Life,* p. 127.

11. Gene Getz, *Believing God When You are Tempted to Doubt* (Ventura, CA: Regal Books, 1985), adapted from pp. 28-38.

12. Ibid., adapted from pp. 42-47.

13. Ibid., adapted from pp. 48-54.

14. Margaret Davidson Campolo, "Reflecting Each Other," in Howard and Jeanne Hendricks, eds., *Husbands and Wives* (Victor Books, 1988, SP Publications Inc., Wheaton, IL), pp. 284, 285.

15. Wayne Oates, "Prayer in the Husband/Wife Relationship," in Hendricks, *Husbands and Wives,* adapted from pp. 164, 165.

16. Lloyd John Ogilvie, *God's Best for My Life* (Eugene, OR: Harvest House Publishers, 1981), from the reading for January 8.

17. David Augsburger, *Sustaining Love* (Ventura, CA: Regal Books, 1988), p. 72.

18. Daniel Levinson, *The Seasons of a Man's Life* (New York: Alfred A. Knopf, Inc., 1978), pp. 245, 246.

19. Augsburger, *Sustaining Love,* adapted from pp. 101, 102.

20. Ibid., p. 172.

21. Ibid., adapted from pp. 175, 176.

22. Harold J. Sala, *Today Can Be Different* (Ventura, CA: Regal Books, 1988), adapted from the reading for July 6.

May

1. Gene Getz, *Believing God When You are Tempted to Doubt* (Ventura, CA: Regal Books, 1985), adapted from pp. 20-26.

2. David Augsburger, *Sustaining Love* (Ventura, CA: Regal Books, 1988), p. 31.

3. Charles R. Swindoll, *The Grace Awakening* (Waco, TX: Word Books, 1990), pp. 10, 11.

4. Ibid., pp. 203-207.

5. Lloyd John Ogilvie, *God's Best for My Life* (Eugene, OR: Harvest House Publishers, 1981), from the reading for August 15.

6. Gene Getz, *When You Feel Like You Haven't Got It* (Ventura, CA: Regal Books, 1976), adapted from pp. 46-50.

7. Arthur W. Pink, *The Holy Spirit* (Grand Rapids, MI: Baker Book House, 1970), adapted from pp. 142, 143.

8. V. Gilbert Beers and Arlise Beers, "Take the Extra Honeymoon," in Howard and Jeanne Hendricks, eds., *Husbands and Wives* (Victor Books, 1988, SP Publications Inc., Wheaton, IL), pp. 388-90.

9. Ogilvie, *God's Best for My Life,* adapted from the reading for January 12.

10. Paul Tournier, *To Understand Each Other* (Richmond, VA: John Knox Press, 1967), p. 29.

11. Dwight H. Small, *After You've Said I Do* (Westwood, NJ: Fleming H. Revell, 1968), p. 119.

12. H. Norman Wright, *Communication: Key to Your Marriage* (Glendale, CA: Regal Books, 1974), p. 55.

13. David Augsburger, *Man, Am I Uptight!* (Chicago: Moody Press, 1970), p. 120.

14. Jan Congo, *Free to Be God's Woman* (Ventura, CA: Regal Books, 1985), pp. 168, 169. Used by permission.

15. William Cole, *Sex in Christianity and Psychoanalysis* (New York: Oxford University Press, 1955), p. 231.

16. Erich Fromm, *The Art of Loving* (New York: Harper and Row Publishers, 1956), p. 56.

17. Ibid.

18. Edward Ford, *Why Marriage?* (Niles, IL: Argus Communications, 1974), p. 103.

19. Joseph Simons and Jeanne Reidy, *The Risk of Loving* (New York: Herder and Herder, Inc., 1968), p. 108.

20. Penelope J. Stokes, *Grace Under Pressure* (Colorado Springs, CO: NavPress, 1990), adapted from pp. 92-102.

21. William J. Lederer and Don D. Jackson, *The Mirages of Marriage* (New York: W.W. Norton and Co., Inc., 1968), p. 108.

22. Lionel Whiston, *Are You Fun to Live With?* (Waco, TX: Word Books, 1968) p. 121.

23. Ibid., p. 123.

24. David Augsburger, *Caring Enough to Confront* (Glendale, CA: Regal Books, 1974), p. 89.

25. Augsburger, *Man, Am I Uptight!*, p. 15.

26. Ibid., p. 14.

27. Stokes, *Grace Under Pressure*, p. 14.

28. Ibid., adapted from pp. 13-18.

29. Ibid., adapted from pp. 35-39.

30. Ibid., adapted from pp. 50-58.

31. Ibid., p. 73.

32. Ibid., p. 112.

33. Ibid., adapted from pp. 103-112.

34. Ibid., adapted from pp. 62-72.

June

1. Richard Exley, *The Rhythm of Life* (Tulsa, OK: Harrison House, 1987), p. 137.

2. Lloyd John Ogilvie, *God's Best for My Life* (Eugene, OR: Harvest House Publishers, 1981), from the reading for January 16.

3. Stephen J. Carter, *My Daily Devotions* (St. Louis, MO: Concordia Publishing House, 1988), adapted from p. 317.

4. Penelope J. Stokes, *Grace Under Pressure* (Colorado Springs, CO: NavPress, 1990), adapted from pp. 124-28.

5. Gene Getz, *Believing God When You Are Tempted to Doubt* (Ventura, CA: Regal Books, 1985), adapted from pp. 142-47.

6. Gene Getz, *When You Feel Like You Haven't Got It* (Ventura, CA: Regal Books, 1976), adapted from pp. 136-38.

7. Don Wyrtzen, *A Musician Looks at the Psalms* (Grand Rapids, MI: Zondervan Publishing House, 1988), adapted from pp. 216, 217.

8. Don Wyrtzen, "Then I Remembered," (Singspiration Music).

9. David Needham, *Birthright* (Portland, OR: Multnomah Press, 1982), adapted from pp. 40-42.

10. Ibid., adapted from pp. 159, 160.

11. Lewis B. Smedes, *How Can It Be All Right When Everything Is All Wrong?* (New York: Harper and Row, 1982), pp. 54.

12. Mike Mason, *The Mystery of Marriage* (Portland, OR: Multnomah Press, 1985), p. 29.

13. Ibid., p. 34.

14. Smedes, *How Can It Be All Right When Everything Is All Wrong?* p. 61.

15. Mason, *The Mystery of Marriage,* p. 142.

16. Ibid., p. 92.

17. Ibid., p. 97.

18. Ibid., p. 91.

19. Ibid.

July

1. Tim Hansel, *When I Relax I Feel Guilty* (Elgin, IL: David C. Cook, 1979), pp. 44, 45.

2. Bill Austin, *How to Get What You Pray For* (Wheaton, IL: Tyndale House Publishers, 1984), p. 63.

3. Gene Getz, *Believing God When You Are Tempted to Doubt* (Ventura, CA: Regal Books, 1985), adapted from pp. 60-64.

4. Ibid., adapted from pp. 66-70.

5. Ibid., adapted from pp. 70-76.

6. C.A. Lufburrow, "The Echo," *Encyclopedia of 7700 Illustrations* (Rockville, MD: Assurance Publishers, 1979), p. 131.

7. Getz, *Believing God When You are Tempted to Doubt,* adapted from pp. 101-10.

8. Matthew L. Linn and D. Linn, *Healing of Memories* (Ramsey, NJ: Paulist Press, 1974), pp. 11, 12.

9. Lloyd John Ogilvie, *God's Will in Your Life* (Eugene, OR: Harvest House Publishers, 1982), p. 136.

10. Ibid., pp. 144, 145.

11. Lawrence Crabb, *Effective Biblical Counseling* (Grand Rapids, MI: Zondervan Publishing House, 1977), adapted from pp. 83, 84.

12. David and Vera Mace, *We Can Have Better Marriages If We Really Want Them* (Nashville: Abingdon Press, 1974), pp. 98, 99.

13. Dwight H. Small, *After You've Said I Do* (Westwood, NJ: Fleming H. Revell, 1968), p. 81.

14. David W. Augsburger, *Seventy Times Seven* (Chicago: Moody Press, 1970), p. 97.

15. Ibid., p. 100.

16. Roy Croft in Joan Winmill Brown and Bill Brown, *Together Each Day* (Old Tappan, NJ: Fleming H. Revell, 1980), p. 43.

August

1. Dwight Small, *Christian: Celebrate Your Sexuality* (Old Tappan, NJ: Fleming H. Revell, 1974), p. 144.

2. James Bjorge, *Forty Ways to Say I Love You* (Minneapolis: Augsburg Publishers, 1978), p. 20.

3. Linda Rich, "No One." Assigned to InterVarsity Christian Fellowship of the U.S.A., 1970. Used by permission.

4. Bill Austin, *How to Get What You Pray For* (Wheaton, IL: Tyndale House Publishers, 1984), adapted from pp. 43-45.

5. Gene Getz, *When You Feel Like You Haven't Got It* (Ventura, CA: Regal Books, 1976), adapted from pp. 138-40.

6. Stephen J. Carter, *My Daily Devotions* (St. Louis, MO: Concordia Publishing House, 1988), adapted from p. 211.

7. Jerry and Barbara Cook, *Choosing to Love* (Ventura, CA: Regal Books, 1982), pp. 18, 19.

8. Ibid., pp. 139, 140.

9. Ibid., pp. 78-80.

10. Ron Lee Davis, *Courage to Begin Again* (Eugene, OR: Harvest House Publishers, 1988), p. 41.

11. Ibid., p. 113.

12. A.W. Tozer, *The Knowledge of the Holy* (New York: Harper and Row, 1961), adapted from pp. 32-42.

13. Ibid., p. 59.

14. Ibid., adapted from pp. 55-58.

15. Ibid., adapted from pp. 71-74.

16. Ibid., adapted from pp. 88-95.

17. Fritz Ridenour, ed., *The Marriage Collection* (Grand Rapids, MI: Zondervan Publishers, 1989), p. 105, from a chapter by Dr. Ed Wheat and Gloria Okes.

18. Ibid., pp. 108, 109.

19. Ibid., pp. 396, 397.

20. Ibid., pp. 412, 413.

21. Dwight H. Small, *After You've Said I Do* (Old Tappan, NJ: Fleming H. Revell, 1968), pp. 243, 244.

22. Gene Getz, *Saying No When You'd Rather Say Yes* (Ventura, CA: Regal Books, 1983), adapted from pp. 55-58.

23. Ibid., adapted from pp. 55-58.

24. Ibid., adapted from pp. 58-60.

25. Ernie Larsen, *Stage II Relationships* (San Francisco: Harper and Row, 1987), p. 34.

September

1. Gene Getz, *Looking Up When You Feel Down* (Ventura, CA: Regal Books, 1985), adapted from pp. 75-78.

2. Richard DeHaan, *Pray, God Is Listening* (Grand Rapids, MI: Zondervan Publishers, 1980), adapted from pp. 17-21.

3. Getz, *Looking Up When You Feel Down,* adapted from pp. 78-84.

4. Bruce Narramore, *You're Someone Special* (Grand Rapids, MI: Zondervan Publisher, 1978), adapted from pp. 61, 62.

5. Ibid., adapted from pp. 142-52.

6. Tim Kimmel, *Legacy of Love* (Portland, OR: Multnomah Press, 1989), adapted from pp. 113-29.

7. David Augsburger, *Cherishable Love and Marriage* (Harrisonburg, VA: Herald Press, 1976), p. 146.

8. Paul Stevens, *Marriage Spirituality* (Downers Grove, IL: Inter-Varsity Press, 1989), adapted from pp. 50-52.

9. Charles R. Swindoll, *Living Above the Level of Mediocrity* (Waco, TX: Word Books, 1987), p. 217.

10. Ibid., adapted from pp. 217-19.

11. Russ Crossen, *Money and Your Marriage* (Waco, TX: Word Books, 1989), adapted from p. 12.

12. Ibid., adapted from pp. 5, 6.

13. Ibid., adapted from pp. 12, 13.

14. Gene Getz, *When the Pressure's On* (Ventura, CA: Regal Books, 1984), adapted from pp. 69-79.

15. Archibald Hart, *Depression: Coping and Caring* (Arcadia, CA: Cope Publications, 1978), p. 11.

16. Alan Loy McGinnis, *Bringing Out the Best in People* (Minneapolis, MN: Augsburg Press, 1985), adapted from p. 100.

17. W. Phillip Keller, *David, the Shepherd King* (Milton Keynes, England: Word Books, 1987), p. 182.

18. Ibid., adapted from pp. 182-85.

19. Gene Getz, *Joseph* (Ventura, CA: Regal Books, 1983), adapted from pp. 148-51.

20. Crossen, *Money and Your Marriage,* adapted from pp. 54-56.

October

1. William Backus, *The Hidden Rift with God* (Minneapolis: Bethany House Publishers, 1990), pp. 142, 143.

2. Ibid., pp. 143, 144.

3. Ibid., pp. 144-46.

4. William and Kristi Gaultiere, *Mistaken Identity* (Old Tappan, NJ: Fleming H. Revell, 1989), pp. 177, 178.

5. H. Norman Wright, *Uncovering Your Hidden Fears* (Wheaton, IL: Tyndale House Publishers, 1989), adapted from p. 135.

6. Charles R. Swindoll, *Living Beyond the Daily Grind* (Waco, TX: Word, 1988), adapted from pp. 170–72.

7. Ibid., p. 187.

8. Ibid., adapted from pp. 186-90.

9. William Barclay, *The Gospel of Matthew,* Volume 1 (Philadelphia: The Westminster Press, 1956), p. 93.

10. Donald R. Harvey, *The Drifting Marriage* (Old Tappan, NJ: Fleming H. Revell, 1988), p. 116, 117.

11. Swindoll, *Living Beyond the Daily Grind,* adapted from pp. 200-03.

12. Ibid., adapted from pp. 165-67.

13. Gaultiere and Gaultiere, *Mistaken Identity,* p. 99.

14. David Needham, *Birthright* (Portland, OR: Multnomah Press, 1982), adapted from pp. 224-27.

15. Ed and Carol Neuenschwander, *Two Friends in Love* (Portland, OR: Multnomah Press, 1986), p. 175.

16. David Viscott, M.D., *How to Live with Another Person* (New York: Arbor House, 1974), p. 19.

17. Dave and Jan Congo, *Free to Soar* (Old Tappan, NJ: Fleming H. Revell, 1987), p. 78.

18. Lewis B. Smedes, *How Can It Be All Right When Everything Is All Wrong?* (New York: Harper and Row, 1982), p. 56.

19. Stephen J. Carter, *My Daily Devotions* (St. Louis, MO: Concordia Publishing House, 1988), adapted from p. 288.

20. David A. Hubbard, *Is This Family Here to Stay?* (Waco, TX: Word Books, 1971), pp. 26, 27.

21. Neuenschwander and Neuenschwander, *Two Friends in Love,* adapted from pp. 28-34.

22. Lloyd John Ogilvie, *When God First Thought of You* (Waco, TX: Word Books, 1978), p. 50.

November

1. Quoted in Ogilvie, *When God First Thought of You* (Waco, TX: Word Books, 1978), p. 50.

2. Ibid., adapted from pp. 135-40.

3. Peter Lord, *Hearing God* (Grand Rapids, MI: Baker Book House, 1990), adapted from pp. 53-58.

4. Lewis B. Smedes, *How Can It Be All Right When Everything Is All Wrong?* (New York: Harper and Row, 1982), pp. 33, 34.

5. Denis Waitley, *Seeds of Greatness* (Old Tappan, NJ: Fleming H. Revell, 1983), pp. 32, 33.

6. Lord, *Hearing God,* adapted from pp. 75-80.

7. Morton Kelsey, *The Other Side of Silence* (New York: Paulist Press, 1976), p. 110.

8. Madame Jeanne Guyon, *Experiencing the Depths of Jesus Christ* (Augusta, ME: Christian Books, 1985), pp. 83, 84.

9. Lord, *Hearing God,* adapted from pp. 99-101.

10. Source unknown.

11. Lord, *Hearing God,* adapted from pp. 152-54.

12. Ogilvie, *When God First Thought of You,* adapted from pp. 193-97.

13. Judith C. Lechman, "Love as Respect," in Howard and Jeanne Hendricks, eds., *Husbands and Wives* (Victor Books, 1988, SP Publications Inc., Wheaton, IL), p. 47.

14. Ibid., adapted from pp. 46, 47.

15. Wayne Oates, "Husbands and Wives with Jesus as Lord," in Hendricks, *Husbands and Wives,* pp. 157-59.

16. Archibald Hart, *Fifteen Principles for Achieving Happiness* (Dallas, TX: Word Books, 1988), p. 47.

17. Charles R. Swindoll, *Living on the Ragged Edge* (Waco, TX: Word Books, 1985), p. 86.

18. Kenneth Boa, *Night Light* (Brentwood, TN: Wolgemuth and Hyatt, 1989), pp. 223, 224.

19. Ibid., pp. 245-47.

20. Ibid.

21. George E. Koehler and Nikki Koehler, *My Family: How Shall I Live with It?* (Chicago: Rand McNally and Co., 1968), p. 57.

22. Ibid., p. 62.

23. Ibid., p. 69.

24. Dinah Maria Mulock Craik, "Friendship," in Swindoll, *Living on the Ragged Edge.*

25. Ibid., adapted from pp. 133-41.

26. W. Phillip Keller, *Songs of My Soul* (Dallas, TX: Word Books, 1989), p. 159.

27. W. Phillip Keller, *David, the Shepherd King* (Milton Keynes, England: Word Books, 1987), adapted from p. 201.

28. Donald R. Harvey, *The Drifting Marriage* (Old Tappan, NJ: Fleming H. Revell, 1988), p. 99.

29. John Bunyan, "Of the Boy and His Butterfly," in Roger C. Palms, *Upon a Penny Loaf* (Minneapolis, MN: Bethany House Publishers, 1978), p. 33.

December

1. A.H. McNeile, *Discipleship* (London: Society for Promoting Christian Knowledge, 1923), p. 51.

2. Calvin Miller, "The Gift of Giving," *Moody Monthly* (December, 1988), pp. 23-25.

3. Lewis B. Smedes, *Forgive and Forget* (New York: Harper and Row, 1984), p. 37.

4. Gene Getz, *Living for Others When You'd Rather Live for Yourself* (Ventura, CA: Regal Books, 1985), p. 82.

5. Richard Exley, *Life's Bottom Line* (Tulsa, OK: Honor Books, 1990), adapted from pp. 27-30.

6. Paul Walker, *How to Keep Your Joy* (Nashville: Oliver-Nelson Books, 1987), p. 80.

7. Tim Kimmel, *Legacy of Love* (Portland, OR: Multnomah Press, 1989), pp. 179, 180.

8. Exley, *Life's Bottom Line,* pp. 71, 73.

9. Ibid., pp. 249, 250.

10. Smedes, *Forgive and Forget,* pp. 128, 129.

11. Getz, *Joseph,* adapted from pp. 51-53.

12. Ibid., adapted from pp. 56-59.

13. Donald R. Harvey, *The Drifting Marriage* (Old Tappan, NJ: Fleming H. Revell, 1988), pp. 143, 144.

14. Ibid., pp. 43, 44.

15. Ibid., pp. 214, 215.

16. Paul Stevens, *Marriage Spirituality* (Downers Grove, IL: InterVarsity Press, 1989), adapted from pp. 32, 33.

17. Harold J. Sala, *Today Can Be Different* (Ventura, CA: Regal Books, 1988), adapted from the entry for December 18.

18. James H. Olthuis, *Keeping Our Troth* (San Francisco: Harper and Row Publishers, 1986), p. 111.

More Great Harvest House Products
by H. Norman Wright

101 Questions to Ask Before You Get Engaged

After You Say "I Do"

After You Say "I Do" Devotional

Before You Remarry

Before You Say "I Do"®

Before You Say "I Do"® Devotional

Coping with Chronic Illness

Finding the Life You've Been Looking For

Finding the Right One for You

Helping Your Kids Deal with Anger, Fear, and Sadness

Quiet Times for Every Parent

Reflections of a Grieving Spouse

Gift Books

My Faithful Companion

Nine Lives to Love

DVD

Before You Say "I Do"™ DVD

HARVEST HOUSE
PUBLISHERS

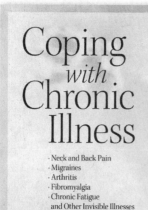

Coping
with
Chronic
Illness

· Neck and Back Pain
· Migraines
· Arthritis
· Fibromyalgia
· Chronic Fatigue
and Other Invisible Illnesses

H. Norman Wright
Lynn Ellis

YOU'RE NOT ALONE

Has chronic illness attacked you or someone you love? From fibromyalgia to arthritis, from constant back pain to frequent migraines, chronic conditions afflict more than 200 million people in the United States alone.

Respected counselor H. Norman Wright and Lynn Ellis, a researcher afflicted with chronic illness, share practical, doable steps you can take to accept and cope with an ongoing illness and the losses associated with it. You'll discover sincere encouragement, a solid foundation for hope, and proven strategies for...

- maintaining and improving relationships with family and friends
- interacting with the medical community, including finding healthcare providers who care and setting up supportive networks
- managing and even allaying the stress, fear, and depression that often accompany chronic situations
- getting the most out of life in spite of the circumstances
- helping people around you understand what's happening and how they can assist you

God is with you always. As you explore what His Word says about suffering, you'll discover many of the ways He will love you, support you, and strengthen you during this difficult time.

An informative, comprehensive resource for chronic illness sufferers, their families and friends, and medical and counseling professionals.

FROM TODDLERS TO TEENS

**Helping Your
Kids Deal with
ANGER,
FEAR, and
SADNESS**

H. NORMAN WRIGHT

*Anger...fear...sadness.
My child sometimes displays
these unsettling emotions.
What can I do?*

No parent wants to see their children struggle, especially with dark emotions such as anger, fear, and sadness. It's difficult to admit children can suffer from these suffocating feelings, but here is help! Noted Christian counselor Norm Wright addresses these emotional issues in a compassionate, family friendly way that will help you bring comfort and fresh perspectives to your children.

Conversational guidelines and learning activities to help your children work through their difficult emotions are just two of the helpful and practical offerings in this interactive manual. You'll also garner keen insights into the causes of intense moods and gain sound principles to help you deal with them effectively.

Biblically based and solution-oriented, *Helping Your Kids Deal with Anger, Fear, and Sadness* is also a great tool for grandparents, teachers, and anyone who interacts with children on a daily basis.

To learn more about Harvest House books and
to read sample chapters, log on to our website:

www.harvesthousepublishers.com

HARVEST HOUSE PUBLISHERS

EUGENE, OREGON